THE RIVER OF THE WEST

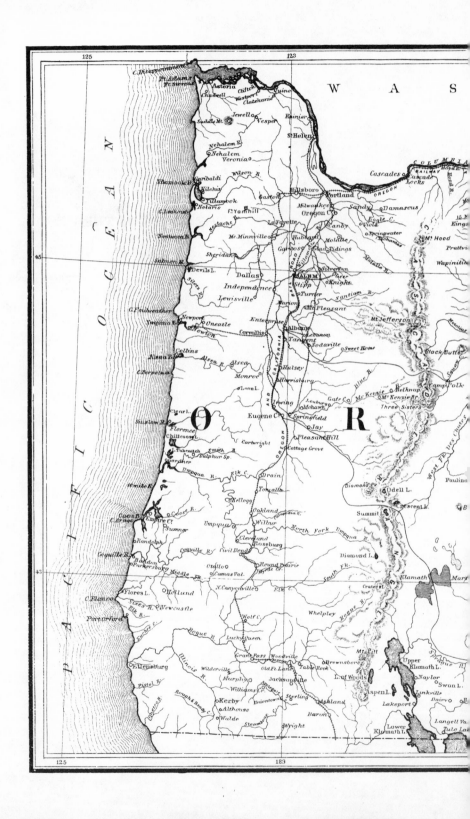

OREGON IN 1886

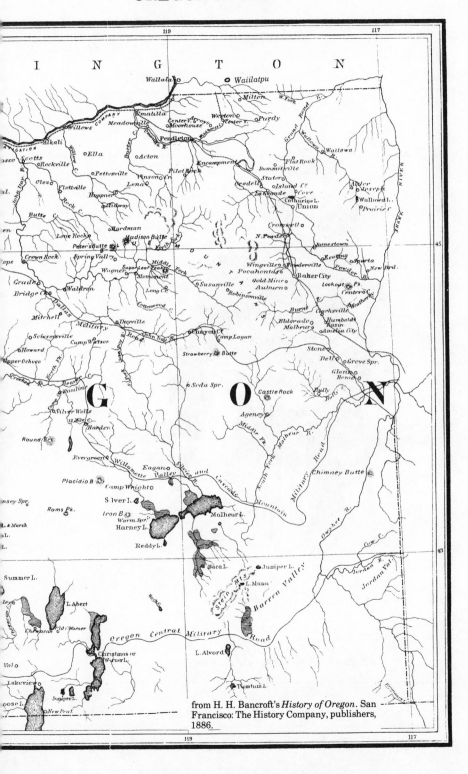

from H. H. Bancroft's *History of Oregon*. San Francisco: The History Company, publishers, 1886.

Joseph L. Meek

THE RIVER OF THE WEST
The Adventures of Joe Meek

Frances Fuller Victor

Volume Two: The Oregon Years
Edited by Lee Nash

CLASSICS OF THE FUR TRADE SERIES
Winfred Blevins, General Editor

A Copper Mountain Books, Inc., Book
Published by
MOUNTAIN PRESS PUBLISHING COMPANY
Missoula, 1985

Library of Congress Cataloging in Publication Data
(Revised for volume 2)

Victor, Frances Fuller, 1826-1902.
  The river of the West.

  (Classics of the fur trade series)
  "A Copper Mountain Books, Inc. book."
  Reprint. Originally published: Hartford, Conn.:
R. W. Bliss, 1870.
  Includes bibliographies and indexes.
  Contents: v. 1 The mountain years—v. 2 The
Oregon years / edited by Lee Nash.
  1. Meek, Joseph Lafayette, 1810-1875. 2. Northwest,
Pacific—History. 3. Northwest, Pacific—Description
and travel. 4. Indians of North America—Northwest,
Pacific—History. 5. West (U.S.)—History—1848-1950.
6. Pioneers—Northwest, Pacific—Biography. 7. Northwest,
Pacific—Biography. I. Nash, Lee. II. Title.
III. Series.
F852.M48V52 1983   979.5'03   83-11399
ISBN 0-87842-164-5 (v. 1)
ISBN 0-87842-165-3 (pbk.: v. 1)
ISBN 0-87842-178-5 (v. 2)
ISBN 0-87842-179-3 (pbk.: v. 2)

THE RIVER OF THE WEST.

LIFE AND ADVENTURE

IN THE

ROCKY MOUNTAINS AND OREGON;

EMBRACING EVENTS IN THE LIFE-TIME OF A

MOUNTAIN-MAN AND PIONEER:

WITH THE

EARLY HISTORY OF THE NORTH-WESTERN SLOPE,

INCLUDING

AN ACCOUNT OF THE FUR TRADERS, THE INDIAN TRIBES, THE OVERLAND IMMIGRA-
TION, THE OREGON MISSIONS, AND THE TRAGIC FATE OF
REV. DR. WHITMAN AND FAMILY.

ALSO, A DESCRIPTION OF THE COUNTRY,

ITS CONDITION, PROSPECTS, AND RESOURCES; ITS SOIL, CLIMATE, AND SCENERY;
ITS MOUNTAINS, RIVERS, VALLEYS, DESERTS, AND PLAINS; ITS
INLAND WATERS, AND NATURAL WONDERS.

WITH NUMEROUS ENGRAVINGS.

BY MRS. FRANCES FULLER VICTOR.

PUBLISHED BY SUBSCRIPTION ONLY.

Hartford, Conn., and Toledo, Ohio:
1870.

Introduction

by Lee Nash

Asked who was Oregon's "most reliable" historian, Editor Harvey Scott of the Portland *Oregonian* replied: "Oregon has but one historian—Mrs. F. F. Victor."[1] These decades later we could name a number of reliable Oregon historians, living and dead, but no close rival to the one who still heads the list, Frances Fuller Victor. As a busy journalist in early life she wrote much that was not history: a book of poems in her mid-twenties, followed by two others in the next half-century; a pair of dime novels to boil the pot, two long books describing her adopted Pacific Northwest for prospective migrants, many essays and varied newspaper features.

At the age of 44 she published *The River of the West* as her first book of history, and this inaugurated two greatly productive decades. In that period she wrote the two-volume *History of Oregon*, one-eighth of the two-volume *History of the Northwest Coast*, and *Washington, Idaho, and Montana*, all in the Bancroft series,[2] as well as the state-commissioned *Early Indian Wars of Oregon*. The nineteenth century featured weighty tomes. The foregoing five-plus volumes, with historical material in her two descriptive books, total over 4,000 substantial pages on the region's past, this not counting another 1,400 pages of Western history she wrote for H. H. Bancroft. And her output was not merely massive; she produced carefully-researched, analytical, brightly-written, interesting history.

With many another creative writer, Victor bridged toward history with a serious biographical project. Doing her best to flesh out the socio-economic, political setting for the life and reminiscences of Joe Meek, she found herself increasingly intrigued with the intricacies of the regional past. One sees this progress in the book itself. Volume One of *River of the West*, "The Mountain Years," was based largely on Meek the ranconteur's fantastic and fascinating yarns. Every history of the mountain men is enriched by the Victor/Meek partnership that put together that trove of tales, which are confirmed as true in outline and spirit by many mountain witnesses, if embellished some for purposes of artistic joy.[3] Yet Victor's lack of access to corroborating sources results in numerous errors in details regarding dates and geography, duly pointed out in the extensive notes to volume one of this edition.

In this second half of the book, "The Oregon Years," Victor matches Meek's move in 1840 to the more complex society of western Oregon with her broader research and more sophisticated historical analysis. Her dates and details are more reliable than before, being less dependent on Meek's selective memory. She used well the five years of Oregon residence before *River of the West* appeared in 1870, systematically harvesting the recollections, studies, and sometimes documents of such early actors as Jesse Applegate, Judge Matthew P. Deady, and J. Quinn Thornton, as well as members of John McLoughlin's family.[4]

It is this half of the book that attracted the most critical attention and controversy in the 1870s, dealing as it did with events still fresh in many Oregon memories, and with issues in which many Oregonians had vast—and varied—emotional investments. Some of that critical attention served history well, as in Jesse Applegate's extensive and detailed running commentary on *River of the West*, complete with page numbers, which he wrote for H. H. Bancroft the summer of 1878. The scholarly Applegate's repeated declarations that he could "see nothing to correct" in particular chapters constitute a significant endorsement.[5] His exceptions may be found in notes at the end of this volume.

Joe Meek was known on occasion to josh, even needle, certain of the Methodist missionaries. The Presbyterian Whitmans he treated more respectfully, even affectionately, a response to their own non-judgmental friendliness toward him. Marcus Whitman had permitted himself, for example, to rib Meek good-naturedly about the trapper's impromptu preaching to the Nez Perce that winter of 1838-39, for which phony ministry he received the gift of his wife Virginia.[6] The Methodist board, however, seemed not to realize the significance of a sense of humor in those sent to minister in difficult circumstances to an alien culture. Serious dedication there was aplenty, and sincere unselfishness, especially as modeled by leader Jason Lee. But the dedication to highly-defined duties was so single-minded that it tended to squeeze out not only humor but humane sympathies and services to non-Methodists in need, whether retired trappers or overland migrants.

By contrast, the Catholic capitalist John McLoughlin worked against the interests and wishes of his company by acting as an angel of mercy in assisting destitute Oregon Trail travelers to survive. To cap it off, certain Methodists angled to invalidate

McLoughlin's land claim at Oregon City. The ironic anomaly of it all was not lost on Meek, though he found and maintained friends among the missioners, and had his mountain marriage solemnized by one of them. But for the free-thinking Mrs. Victor, what she saw as wholesale violations of their Wesleyan ethics by the Methodists justified a full indignant exposure of unrelieved hypocrisy. While her account is supported largely by the evidence, her bias led her to select sources and slant the story somewhat. The natural result was an ill-spirited public dispute, which may best be sampled by reading J. Quinn Thornton's hostile review in the *Pacific Christian Advocate*, and Victor's vigorous reply.[7]

There is a sense in which *The River of the West* constitutes a historical apprenticeship for Victor's more intensive work in the Bancroft series later. One can go to corresponding sections of the Victor/Bancroft *History of Oregon* for interesting amplifications and modifications of her narrative and conclusions in the earlier book. Yet, more significantly, *The River of the West* holds integrity and artistic unity in its own right, as the life and times of Joseph L. Meek, a typical nineteenth-century approach toward biography. If "The Oregon Years" is not as wholly Meek's book as was the earlier volume, still the merry mountain man is never far from the narrative. A sober analysis of Provisional Government affairs is likely to be enlivened at any point by a laughing Meek with a tale of the foibles of some official or citizen, or of his own unorthodox actions as sheriff or tax collector. The stories often have a point, commonly illustrate a stage of frontier society, and keep the reader reminded that human beings inhabited early Oregon, not merely ancestors.

Joe Meek's character unfolds in this volume, if usually between the lines, and we become gradually aware that he is much more than a prankster and buffoon. He was but thirty years of age when he retired to Oregon, able one would think to switch to a new accepted and acceptable career. But the eleven adventurous years as a free trapper in the mountains disqualified or at least disinclined him from making the most obvious transition, to an industrious frontier farmer. An indifferent sort of farmer he indeed became, but it was no natural calling.

Though barely literate, Meek was equipped by personality, presence, and nerve for public leadership, and it came to him in a series of differing, appropriate ways. As sheriff, census-taker, tax collector, and legislator of the Provisional Government, as U.S. Marshal under Oregon Territory, and as Washington

County coroner after statehood, he did his duty and was honored for it. Most spectacularly, he was the "Envoy Extraordinary" chosen by his fellows to make that heroic mid-winter trek across the Rockies to Washington, D.C., and the White House in 1848, to tell the awful tidings of the Whitman tragedy and request government aid. Joe Meek, a popular leader in that time and place, was widely trusted for integrity, judgment, courage, and enormous physical competence.

This is interesting and significant history and biography, then. But there is another thing to say about it, about the special attraction of this book, and the primary justification for its reissue. More than anything else Victor wrote, or perhaps than anyone else wrote about the Oregon country until two or three novelists in the present century, *The River of the West* constitutes a kind of folk literature. It is fact, most of it, to be sure. But more than fact, too, not only in the embellishments of Meek's plots, but in the peculiar blend between what can be objectively established and what is imaginatively implied about days when there seemed to be giants in the land. The issues of life and death were often in balance, and were decided by the cool judgments of natural leaders, men and women, native and white. Those leaders come through in folk literature as heroic, but as authentically human too, to be identified with as well as admired.

It all becomes the sort of history that the great folk, the public, is able to handle, to love, and by it to be ennobled some. A present-day attempt to recapitulate this sort of folk history is the professionally-conceived and produced outdoor drama, the Champoeg Pageant, performed on site for several weeks each summer since 1982. Joe Meek is the hero-narrator, played by actor Dallas McKennon, of Daniel Boone television series fame. One cannot but think that Uncle Joe the yarn-spinner, the man of good will, the public servant, would have appreciated the folk uses of this public spectacle. Even as indeed he did appreciate and promote "his book," *The River of the West*, in the last years of his generous life.[8]

This Text

The text of this second and final volume of *The River of the West*, like that of the first volume, is a photographic reproduction of the first edition. For the convenience of the reader, the final two pages of volume one are reprinted as the first two pages of this volume. While the chapters are numbered consecutively from the first volume, the page numbers have been reset. Illustrations are original.

Footnotes

[1] Joseph Gaston, *Centennial History of Oregon* (Chicago, 1912), I, p. 621.

[2] John Walton Caughey, *Hubert Howe Bancroft: Historian of the West* (Berkeley, 1946), pp. 262-263.

[3] Don't miss Winfred Blevins' Introduction to *The River of the West*, Volume One (Missoula, 1983), p. 5-10.

[4] Hazel E. Mills, "The Emergence of Frances Fuller Victor—Historian," *Oregon Historical Quarterly*, Vol. LXII, No. 4, December, 1961, pp. 314-316, 319.

[5] Applegate to Bancroft, summer, 1878. In Bancroft Library, University of California, Berkeley.

[6] *The River of the West*, pp. 252-253, 280.

[7] *Pacific Christian Advocate* (Portland), May 21, 1870, p. 1; May 28, 1870, p. 1; June 11, 1870, p. 3.

[8] Harvey Elmer Tobie, *No Man Like Joe: The Life and Times of Joseph L. Meek* (Portland, 1949), pp. 272-280.

Acknowledgments

The editor is grateful for professional services rendered by Reference Librarian Merrill Johnson of George Fox College, and by the staff of the Oregon Historical Society. He thanks, too, Hazel Mills of Eugene, Oregon, for counsel and perspective; series editor Win Blevins for rare patience and encouragement; and especially his wife, Grayce, an indispensable working partner in this enterprise.

SUNSET AT THE MOUTH OF THE COLUMBIA.

There sinks the sun ; like cavalier of old,
    Servant of crafty Spain,
He flaunts his banner, barred with blood and gold,
    Wide o'er the western main ;
A thousand spear heads glint beyond the trees
    In columns bright and long,
While kindling fancy hears upon the breeze
    The swell of shout and song.

And yet not here Spain's gay, adventurous host
    Dipped sword or planted cross ;
The treasures guarded by this rock-bound coast
    Counted them gain nor loss.
The blue Columbia, sired by the eternal hills
    And wedded with the sea,
O'er golden sands, tithes from a thousand rills,
    Rolled in lone majesty—

Through deep ravine, through burning, barren plain,
    Through wild and rocky strait,
Through forest dark, and mountain rent in twain
    Toward the sunset gate;
While curious eyes, keen with the lust of gold,
    Caught not the informing gleam,
These mighty breakers age on age have rolled
    To meet this mighty stream.

Age after age these noble hills have kept,
    The same majestic lines ;
Age after age the horizon's edge been swept
    By fringe of pointed pines.
Summers and Winters circling came and went,
    Bringing no change of scene ;
Unresting, and unhasting, and unspent,
    Dwelt Nature here serene !

Till God's own time to plant of Freedom's seed,
  In this selected soil ;
Denied forever unto blood and greed,
  But blest to honest toil.
There sinks the sun ; Gay cavalier no more !
  His banners trail the sea,
And all his legions shining on the shore
  Fade into mystery.

The swelling tide laps on the shingly beach,
  Like any starving thing ;
And hungry breakers, white with wrath, upreach,
  In a vain clamoring.
The shadows fall ; just level with mine eye
  Sweet Hesper stands and shines,
And shines beneath an arc of golden sky,
  Pinked round with pointed pines.

A noble scene ! all breadth, deep tone, and power,
  Suggesting glorious themes ;
Shaming the idler who would fill the hour
  With unsubstantial dreams.
Be mine the dreams prophetic, shadowing forth
  The things that yet shall be,
When through this gate the treasures of the North
  Flow outward to the sea.

16

ILLUSTRATIONS

CONTENTS

18

CHAPTER XXX.

CHAPTER XXXI.

CHAPTER XXXII.

CHAPTER XXXIII.

CHAPTER XXXIV.

20

CHAPTER XL.

CHAPTER XLI.

CHAPTER XLII.

CHAPTER XLIII.

CHAPTER XLIV.

CHAPTER XLVIII.

CHAPTER XLIX.

CHAPTER XXI.

1840. When Meek arrived at Fort Hall, where Newell was awaiting him, he found that the latter had there the two wagons which Dr. Whitman had left at the points on the journey where further transportation by their means had been pronounced. impossible. The Doctor's idea of finding a passable wagon-road over the lava plains and the heavily timbered mountains lying between Fort Hall and the Columbia River, seemed to Newell not so wild a one as it was generally pronounced to be in the mountains. At all events, he was prepared to undertake the journey. The wagons were put in traveling order, and horses and mules purchased for the expedition.

"Come," said Newell to Meek, "we are done with this life in the mountains—done with wading in beaver-dams, and freezing or starving alternately—done with Indian trading and Indian fighting. The fur trade is dead in the Rocky Mountains, and it is no place for us now, if ever it was. We are young yet, and have life before us. We cannot waste it here ; we cannot or will not return to the States. Let us go down to the Wallamet and take farms. There is already quite a settlement there made by the Methodist Mission and the Hudson's Bay Company's retired servants.

"I have had some talk with the Americans who have gone down there, and the talk is that the country is going to be settled up by our people, and that the Hudson's

Bay Company are not going to rule this country much longer. What do you say, Meek? Shall we turn American settlers?"

"I'll go where you do, Newell. What suits you suits me."

"I thought you'd say so, and that's why I sent for you, Meek. In my way of thinking, a white man is a little better than a Canadian Frenchman. I'l be d——d if I'll hang 'round a post of the Hudson's Bay Company. So you'll go?"

"I reckon I will! What have you got for me to do? *I* haven't got anything to begin with but a wife and baby!"

"Well, you can drive one of the wagons, and take your family and traps along. Nicholas will drive the other, and I'll play leader, and look after the train. Craig will go also, so we shall be quite a party, with what strays we shall be sure to pick up."

Thus it was settled. Thus Oregon began to receive her first real emigrants, who were neither fur-traders nor missionaries, but true frontiersmen — border-men. The training which the mountain-men had received in the service of the fur companies admirably fitted them to be, what afterwards they became, a valuable and indispensable element in the society of that country in whose peculiar history they played an important part. But we must not anticipate their acts before we have witnessed their gradual transformation from lawless rangers of the wilderness, to law-abiding and even law-making and law-executing citizens of an isolated territory.

In order to understand the condition of things in the Wallamet Valley, or Lower Columbia country, it will be necessary to revert to the earliest history of that territory, as sketched in the first chapter of this book. A history of the fur companies is a history of Oregon up to the year 1834, so far as the occupation of the country was concerned. But its political history was begun long before—from the time (May 11th, 1792) when the captain of a New England coasting and fur-trading vessel entered the great " River of the West," which nations had been looking for for a hundred years. At the very time when the inquisitive Yankee was heading his little vessel through the white line of breakers at the mouth of the long-sought river, a British exploring expedition was scanning the shore between it and the Straits of Fuca, having wisely declared its scientific opinion that there was no such river on that coast. Vancouver, the chief of that expedition, so assured the Yankee trader, whose views did not agree with his own : and, Yankee-like, the trader turned back to satisfy himself.

A bold and lucky man was Captain Gray of the ship *Columbia.* No explorer he—only an adventurous and, withal, a prudent trader, with an eye to the main chance; emulous, too, perhaps, of a little glory! It is impossible to conceive how he could have done this thing calmly. We think his stout heart must have shivered somewhat, both with anticipation and dread, as he ran for the " opening," and plunged into the frightful tumult—straight through the proper channel, thank God! and sailed out on to the bosom of that beautiful bay, twenty-five miles by six, which the great river forms at its mouth.

We trust the morning was fine : for then Captain Gray must have beheld a sight which a discoverer should remember for a lifetime. This magnificent bay, surrounded by lofty hills, clad thick with noble forests of fir, and fretted along its margin with spurs of the highlands, forming other smaller bays and coves, into which ran streams whose valleys were hidden among the hills. From beyond

the farthest point, whose dark ridge jutted across this inland sea, flowed down the deep, broad river, whose course
and origin was still a magnificent mystery, but which indicated by its volume that it drained a mighty region of
probable great fertility and natural wealth. Perhaps Captain Gray did not fully realize the importance of his discovery. If the day was fine, with a blue sky, and the
purple shadows lying in among the hills, with smooth
water before him and the foamy breakers behind — *if* he
felt what his discovery was, in point of importance, to
the world, he was a proud and happy man, and enjoyed
the reward of his daring.

The only testimony on that head is the simple entry on
his log-book, telling us that he had named the river " *Columbia's River*," — with an apostrophe, that tiny point
intimating much. This was one ground of the American
claim, though Vancouver, after Gray had reported his
success to him, sent a lieutenant to explore the river, and
then claimed the discovery for England! The next claim
of the United States upon the Oregon territory was by
virtue of the Florida treaty and the Louisiana purchase.
These, and the general one of natural boundaries, England contested also. Hence the treaty of joint occupancy
for a term of ten years, renewable, unless one of the parties
to it gave a twelve-month's notice of intention to with-
draw. Meantime this question of territorial claims hung
over the national head like the sword suspended by a
hair, which statesmen delight in referring to. We did
not dare to say Oregon was ours, because we were afraid
England would make war on us; and England did not
dare say Oregon was hers, for the same reason. Therefore " joint-occupancy " was the polite word with which
statesmen glossed over the fact that Great Britain actually
possessed the country through the monopoly of the Hud-

son's Bay Company. That company had a good thing so long as the government of Great Britain prevented any outbreak, by simply renewing the treaty every ten years. Their manner of doing business was such as to prevent any less powerful corporation from interfering with them, while individual enterprise was sure to be crushed at the start.

Meanwhile the Yankee nation, some menfbers of which at one time had vessels trading on the northwest coast, became uneasy at this state of affairs. Since the war of 1812 and the failure of Astor's expedition, their vessels had been driven off that coast, or had been fain to content themselves with picking up cargoes of hides and tallow from the Indian missions in California. It was not in Yankee nature to stand this foreign monopoly. As if they had not land enough on the eastern side of the Rocky Mountains, they began to expatiate on the beauties and excellencies of the country which lay beyond.

As early as 1817, even before the obnoxious Convention, a Bostonian school teacher, named Hall J. Kelly, had conceived the idea of colonizing the Oregon territory. He labored to impress others with the views which he held, and formed many emigration schemes, besides memorializing Congress on the subject, as well as the legislature of his own State. Finally, in 1831, he succeeded in getting the Legislature of Massachusetts to pass an act incorporating the "*American Society for Encouraging the Settlement of the Oregon Territory*," and a large number of persons became members. But the fur companies, American as well as British, steadily discouraged all efforts which were directed towards the settlement of the coveted territory, so that nothing was accomplished by the above named society ; and at length, in 1832, Kelly sent out two young men only, for the country west of the

Rocky Mountains. On arriving at Fort Vancouver they found the same difficulties in their way which prevented Wyeth and Bonneville from succeeding. In truth, their case was worse, for there was nothing for them to do, and if there had been, they would not have been permitted to do it, except in the service of the Hudson's Bay Company. For the first winter, one of them, a Mr. Ball, was employed as teacher of the half-breed children at the Fort. The following spring, Ball and his companion, Tibbits, began farming. This, however, proving unprofitable business in a country where there was no market, Ball returned to the States, and Tibbits remained to teach the school at Fort Vancouver. In the meantime, Kelly was trying to organize an expedition to proceed by sea. This also failed to be successful, through the inaction of the general government and the antagonism of the fur companies. Persisting in his plan of colonizing Oregon and opening commerce on the west coast, Kelly went to Mexico and endeavored to open a trade between that country and Oregon. But the Mexican revenue officers remorselessly robbed him of a large share of the goods he was taking to Oregon, so that by the time he arrived at Fort Vancouver there was little or nothing left of his stock in trade, while he was broken down in health and spirits. Like Wyeth, he returned home without having been able to realize any one of his many schemes of profit.

Such was the experience of all who in that early day attempted to oppose themselves to the Hudson's Bay Company. For this reason all these adventurers execrated its influence, and denounced everything British. The truth was, however, that the case would have been just the same had it been an American company which occupied the Columbia River, so far as their fortunes

were concerned.   Any company, to succeed in that far
off wilderness country, must have done just as the English company did do.   To enter into competition among
the Indians was to ruin the trade for all concerned, to induce misunderstandings with the savages, and finally to
devastate, instead of settling up, the country.   This the
Hudson's Bay Company understood, and they would
rather lose money by trying to keep other traders out,
than to make it for a little while by competing with
them.

But "man proposes and God disposes."   In 1834, the
Methodist Episcopal Board of Missions sent out four missionaries to labor among the Indians.   These were two
preachers, the Rev. Messrs. Jason and Daniel Lee, and
two lay members, Cyrus Shepard and P. L. Edwards.
These gentlemen were liberally furnished with all the
necessaries and comforts of life by the Board, in addition
to which they received the kindest attentions and consideration from the officers of the Hudson's Bay Company at
Vancouver.   Their vessel, the *May Dacre*, Captain Lam-
bert, had arrived safely in the river with the mission
goods.   The gentlemen at Vancouver encouraged their
enterprise, and advised them to settle in the Wallamet
valley, the most fertile tract of country west of the Rocky
Mountains.   Being missionaries, nothing was to be feared
from them in the way of trade.   The Wallamet valley
was a good country for the mission—at the same time it
was south of the Columbia River.   This latter consideration was not an important one with the Hudson's Bay
Company, it being understood among those in the confidence of the British government, that in case the Oregon
territory had to be divided with the United States, the
Columbia River would probably be made the northern
boundary of the American possessions.   The missionaries

being content to settle south of the Columbia, all went well.

These three points were what the Hudson's Bay Company must insist upon, so far as, under the terms of the treaty, they could do : first, that the Americans occupying the country jointly with them, should not attempt to trade with the Indians; secondly, that they should confine themselves to agricultural pursuits and missionary labor; and thirdly, that the settlers should keep to the south side of the Columbia. Not that the servants of the Hudson's Bay Company confined themselves to the north side of this probable boundary; on the contrary, the retired servants of that company had begun to settle in the Wallamet valley in 1831.

We have said that the political history of Oregon began near the close of the last century. As early as the winter of 1820–21, the first proposition was made in Congress for the occupation and settlement of the Columbia River.

"It * was made by Dr. Floyd, a representative from Virginia, a man of ability, and strongly imbued with western feelings, from a long residence in Kentucky. It required both energy and courage to embrace a subject which seemed likely to bring more ridicule than credit to its advocate. He took up the idea from some essays of Mr. Benton's, which had been published the year previous. He had also made the acquaintance of Mr. Russell Farnham and Mr. Ramsey Crooks, who had been in the employment of Astor in founding the colony at Astoria. He resolved to bring forward the question of occupation, and did so. He moved for a select committee to consider and report upon the subject. The committee was granted by the House, more through courtesy to a respected member, than with any view to business results. It was a committee of three, himself chairman according to a parliamentary rule, and Thomas Metcalf of Kentucky, and Thomas V. Swearingen of Virginia, both, like himself, ardent men, and strong in western feeling. They reported a bill within six days after the committee was raised, " to authorize the occupation of the Columbia River, and to regulate trade and intercourse with the Indian tribes thereon." In their report they represented the advantages of the fur trade, the Asiatic trade, and the preservation of our own territory. Nothing

---

* From *Benton's Thirty Years in Congress.*

18

further was done at that session, but enough had been said to awaken public attention, and the facts set forth in the report made a lodgement in the public mind."

At a subsequent session, both Floyd and Benton pursued the subject with ardor, and the latter dwelt strongly on the danger of a contest with Great Britain, to whom had been granted joint occupancy, and who had already taken possession ; and reminded the Government "that a vigorous effort of policy, and perhaps of arms, might be necessary to break her hold." Unauthorized or individual occupation was intimated as a consequence of government neglect, and what has since taken place was foreshadowed in the following sentence : "Mere adventurers may enter upon it, as Æneus entered upon the Tiber, and as our forefathers came upon the Potomac, the Delaware, and the Hudson, and renew the phenomenon of individuals laying the foundations of future empire." He predicted the intercourse with China and Japan which has since followed, and prophesied that the overflowing population of those countries would seek our Pacific shores.

Mr. Benton said, when the subject of the joint occupation treaty was before the House in 1825 :—

"The claim of Great Britain is nothing but a naked pretension, founded on the double prospect of benefitting herself and injuring the United States. The fur-trader, Sir Alexander McKenzie, is at the bottom of this policy. Failing in his attempt to explore the Columbia River in 1793, he nevertheless urged upon the British government the advantages of taking it to herself, and of expelling the Americans from the whole region west of the Rocky Mountains. He recommended that the Hudson's Bay and Northwest companies should be united, and they have been united. He proposed to extend the fur trade to the Pacific Ocean, and it has been so extended. He proposed that a chain of trading posts should be formed through the continent, from sea to sea, and it has been formed. He recommended that no boundary line should be formed which did not give the Columbia River to the British, and the British Ministry declare that none other shall be formed. He proposed to obtain the command of the fur trade from latitude 45° North, and they have it, even to the Mandan villages and the neighborhood of Council Bluffs. He recommended the expulsion of the American traders from the whole region west of the Rocky Mountains, and they are expelled from it."

In addition to the influence of the fur companies, political considerations also governed Great Britain in acquiring possession of the Northwest coast, and the command of the Pacific Ocean.

In a Pacific Railroad speech which Mr. Benton made at Brunswick, Mo., thirty years later, there occurs this paragraph:

"I caught the idea (of a Pacific Railroad) from Mr. Jefferson, who in his message to Congress proposing the expedition of Lewis and Clarke, presented the commercial communication as the leading object, and the one which gave Congress the Constitutional jurisdiction in the case; and the extension of geographical science as the incident to the pursuit of that main object. That was before we acquired Oregon, or set up any claim to territory on the Pacific Ocean."

From these extracts it will appear that while the fur Companies were contending for the occupation of the Oregon territory, and had finally parceled it off as we have already seen,—the American companies keeping in and about the Rocky Mountains, and the Hudson's Bay Company excluding them from the country west of the Blue Mountains, while that which laid between had been contested ground,—two governments were equally active and studious in their efforts to substantiate their claims.

But it was not, after all, either the fur companies or the general government which directed the entering wedge in the settlement of the much-talked-of claims. It was the missionary settlements which effected this.

There was nothing in the character of the Christian Missionary's labor which the Hudson's Bay Company could possibly object to without a palpable violation of the

THE MISSIONARY
WEDGE.

Convention of 1818. Therefore, although the Methodist mission in the Wallamet Valley received a large accession to its numbers in 1837, they were as kindly welcomed as had been those of 1834; and also those Presbyterian missionaries of 1836, who had settled in the "upper country."

Not an immigrant entered Oregon in that day who did not proceed at once to Vancouver: nor was there one, in any way deserving, who did not meet with the most liberal and hospitable treatment. Neither was this hospitality a trifling benefit; to the weary traveler just arrived from a long and most fatiguing journey, it was extremely welcome and refreshing. At Vancouver was the only society, and the only luxurious living to be enjoyed on the whole Northwest coast.

At the head of the first was Dr. John McLaughlin, already mentioned as the Chief Factor, and Deputy Governor of the Hudson's Bay Company in Oregon, and all the Northwest. He was of Scotch origin, and Canadian birth, a gentleman bred, with a character of the highest integrity, to which were united justice and humanity. His position as head of the Hudson's Bay Company's affairs, was no enviable one during that period of Oregon history which followed the advent of Americans in the Wallamet Valley. Himself a British subject, and a representative of that powerful corporation which bent the British Government to its will, he was bound to execute its commands when they did not conflict too strongly with his consciousness of right and justice. And while he was willing and anxious to do his duty towards the company he served, circumstances arose, and occasions grew out of those circumstances which tried his loyalty, integrity, and humanity, to the utmost. One course, however, he steadily pursued, which was that of a beneficent friend toward all who deserved his friendship, and many who did not, in all private and personal matters. Hence of the many who went to Vancouver, all were kindly received; and every man of any intelligence or position among the Americans was most hospitably treated, not only by himself but by all the factors, traders, and clerks of the establishment. It often happened in the early days of Oregon that some of the most prominent Americans were not decently clad, through their inability to procure clothing suitable to their position. But the seat of honor at the Chief Factor's table was reserved with as much punctiliousness for these ragged pioneers, as if they had come clad in beautiful raiment. Nor were finger bowls and napkins withheld from the use of soiled and blackened pioneer fingers. Wine, and good cheer, and cultivated conversation, were freely offered and enjoyed. There was nothing in the line of his duty which prevented Dr. McLaughlin from exercising private hospitality and gentlemanly courtesy toward the Americans. A man of religious feeling himself, he respected the motive which was presumed to actuate the missionaries. To be sure, he had been educated in the Roman Catholic doctrines; but yet he was not unwilling that the Protestants should entertain and disseminate their own religious views. As a representative of the Hudson's Bay Company he had one duty to execute: as a Christian gentleman, another. That these separate duties sometimes conflicted will appear in the course of this narrative. So far, however, as encouraging the missionaries in their undertakings was concerned, he did not hold them to be conflicting; not, at all events, until they undeceived him, by entering upon secular enterprisés.

As has been stated, the Methodist mission settlement was reinforced in 1837, by the arrival of about twenty persons, among whom were several ladies, and a few children. These, like those preceding them, were first entertained at Fort Vancouver before proceeding to the mission, which was between fifty and sixty miles up the Wallamet, in the heart of that delightful valley. These persons came by a sailing vessel around Cape Horn, bringing with them supplies for the mission.

In the two following years there were about a dozen missionary arrivals overland, all of whom tarried a short time at the American Company's rendezvous, as before related. These were some of them designed for the upper country, but most of them soon settled in the Wallamet valley.

During these years, between 1834 and 1840, there had drifted into the valley various persons from California, the Rocky Mountains, and from the vessels which sometimes appeared in the Columbia; until at the time when Newell and Meek resolved to quit the mountains, the American settlers numbered nearly one hundred, men, women, and children. Of these, about thirty belonged to the missions; the remainder were mountain-men, sailors, and adventurers. The mountain-men, most of them, had native wives. Besides the Americans there were sixty Canadian Frenchmen, who had been retired upon farms by the Hudson's Bay Company; and who would probably have occupied these farms so long as the H. B. Company should have continued to do business in Oregon.

With the American mountain-men it was, however, different. It was the fact of the mission having been estab-

lished there, with all the means and appliances of a settlement independent of the H. B. Company, which induced
them to remain and settle also upon farms. They looked
to the Mission to become to them, what Fort Vancouver
was to the Canadians, a supply station; an expectation
which was only half fulfilled, as will be seen hereafter.

The Missionaries themselves had been compelled to depend upon Fort Vancouver for many things, and among
others for cattle, and milch cows. It was a matter of serious complaint among the American settlers that the H. B.
Company would sell none of their stock. Lend it they
would; *sell* it they would not. This effort on the part of
the company to retain a monopoly in so important an element of civilized comfort as oxen, beef-cattle, and milch
cows, created much ill feeling for a time, as it cramped
the means of productive labor excessively.

But in 1837 there appeared in the Columbia river the
U. S. Brig *Loriot*, Captain Slocum, on an errand of
observation. Upon learning from the settlers that no
cattle could be procured in Oregon, Captain Slocum
encouraged a plan which was then on foot, of sending to California for a supply of Spanish stock. To
further this enterprise he contributed fifteen dollars, and
offered a free passage to such persons as wished to go to
California on this errand. The way being thus opened, a
meeting of the settlers was held, and shares taken in what
was called the "California Cattle Company." Whatever
may have been the feelings of the H. B. Company, they
offered no direct opposition: on the contrary, Dr. Mc
Laughlin took several shares in the Cattle Company, on
his own account. The expedition was headed by Mr. P. L.
Edwards of the Methodist mission, and Mr. Ewing Young
of the American settlement. Young was of the same
class as the mountain-men, and had in fact been a trader

at Taos in New Mexico; after which he had led a hunting and trapping party through California; and had accompanied Kelly in his journey to Oregon in 1835. He was just the man to conduct an expedition such as this one; though the Mission thought it necessary to send Mr. Edwards along to look out for the funds of the company. The expedition set sail in January, and returned by land in the autumn, with several hundred head of cattle; having met with some loss of stock, by an attack from the Rogue River Indians, or Shastas,—the same tribe who attacked Smith's party in 1829. The cattle were then divided up among the settlers according to the shares previously taken; those who went to California receiving pay for their services out of the herd. This importation of cattle placed the American colony, for such it now really was, on a more independent footing, besides furnishing a means for the rapid acquisition of wealth.

The distribution of settlers was as follows: the mission proper, about fifty-two miles above the mouth of the Wallamet; the Canadian settlement ten or twelve miles below the mission, and Wallamet Falls, or as it afterwards was called, Oregon City. At this latter place Dr. McLaughlin, as early as 1829, had begun the erection of a mill, and had continued to make improvements from time to time, up to 1840, when some members of the Mission applied to him for permission to erect a building for mission purposes upon the land claimed and improved by the Doctor. This request was granted, together with another for the use of some timbers already squared for building, which had been intended for the mill. At the same time that Dr. McLaughlin made these generous concessions to the mission gentlemen, he notified them that he intended to claim the land already improved by him, so soon as the boundary line was drawn by a proper survey.

CHAPTER XXII.

WHEN it was settled that Newell and Meek were to go to the Wallamet, they lost no time in dallying, but packed the wagons with whatever they possessed in the way of worldly goods, topped them with their Nez Perce wives and half-breed children, and started for Walla-Walla, accompanied by Craig, another mountain-man, and either followed or accompanied by several others. Meek drove a five-in-hand team of four horses and one mule. Nicholas drove the other team of four horses, and Newell, who owned the train, was mounted as leader.

The journey was no easy one, extending as it did over immense plains of lava, round impassable canyons, over rapid unbridged rivers, and over mountains hitherto believed to be only passable for pack trains. The honor which has heretofore been accorded to the Presbyterian missionaries solely, of opening a wagon road from the Rocky Mountains to the Columbia River, should in justice be divided with these two mountaineers, who accomplished the most difficult part of this difficult journey.

Arrived at Fort Boise, a post of the Hudson's Bay Company, the little caravan stopped for a few days to rest and recruit their animals. With the usual courtesy of that Company, Mr. Payette, the trader in charge, offered Newell quarters in the fort, as leader of his party. To Meek and Craig who were encamped outside, he sent a piece of sturgeon with his compliments, which our incipient Oregonians sent back again with *their* compliments. No Hudson's Bay distinctions of rank for them! No, indeed! The moment that an American commenced to think of himself as a settler on the most remote corner of American soil, that moment, as if by instinct, he began to defend and support his republicanism.

After a few days' rest, the party went on, encountering, as might be expected, much difficulty and toil, but arriving safely after a reasonable time at the Columbia River, at the junction of the Umatilla. Here the wagons and stock were crossed over, and the party proceeded directly to Dr. Whitman's mission at Waiilatpu. Dr. Whitman gave them a friendly reception; killing for them, if not the fatted calf, the fattest hog he had; telling Meek at the same time that "fat pork was good for preachers," referring to Meek's missionary labors among the Nez Perces.

During the three years since the commencement of the mission at Waiilatpu considerable advancement had been made in the progress of civilization among the Cayuses. Quite a number of Indian children were domesticated with Mrs. Whitman, who were rapidly acquiring a knowledge of housekeeping, sewing, reading, and writing, and farm labor. With Mrs. Whitman, for whom Meek still entertained great admiration and respect, he resolved to leave his little girl, Helen Mar; the fruit of his connexion with the Nez Perce woman who persisted in abandoning him in the mountains, as already related. Having thus made provision for the proper instruction of his daughter, and conferred with the Doctor on the condition of the American settlers in Oregon — the Doctor being an ardent American—Meek and his associates started once more for the Wallamet.

At Walla-Walla Newell decided to leave the wagons, the weather having become so rainy and disagreeable as

to make it doubtful about getting them over the Cascade
Mountains that fall.   Accordingly the goods were trans-
ferred to pack-horses for the remainder of the journey.
In the following year, however, one of the wagons was
brought down by Newell, and taken to the plains on the
Tualatin River, being the first vehicle of the kind in the
Wallamet Valley.

On arriving at the Dalles of the Columbia, our mountain men found that a mission had been established at that
place for the conversion of those inconscionable thieves,
the Wish-ram Indians, renowned in Indian history for their
acquisitiveness.   This mission was under the charge of
Daniel Lee and a Mr. Perkins, and was an offshoot of the
Methodist Mission in the Wallamet Valley.   These gentlemen having found the benighted condition of the Indians
to exceed their powers of enlightment in any ordinary
way, were having recourse to extraordinary efforts, and
were carrying on what is commonly termed a *revival;*
though what piety there was in the hearts of these savages
to be revived, it would be difficult to determine.   However, they doubtless hoped so to wrestle with God themselves, as to compel a blessing upon their labors.

The Indians indeed were not averse to prayer.   They
could pray willingly and sincerely enough when they could
hope for a speedy and actual material answer to their
prayers.   And it was for that, and that only, that they
importuned the Christian's God.   Finding that their
prayers were not answered according to their desire, it at
length became difficult to persuade them to pray at all.
Sometimes, it is true, they succeeded in deluding the missionaries with the belief that they were really converted,
for a time.   One of these most hopeful converts at the
Dalles mission, being in want of a shirt and capote, volun-
teered to "pray for a whole year," if Mr. Lee would furnish him with these truly desirable articles.

It is no wonder that with such hopeless material to work upon the Dalles missionaries withdrew from them a portion of their zeal, and bestowed it, where it was quite as much needed, upon any "stray mountain-man" who chanced to be entertained "within their gates." Newell's party, among others, received the well-meant, but not always well-received or appreciated attentions of these gentlemen. The American mountaineer was not likely to be suddenly surprised into praying in earnest; and he generally had too much real reverence to be found making a jest in the form of a mocking prayer.

Not so scrupulous, however, was Jandreau, a lively French Canadian, who was traveling in company with the Americans. On being repeatedly importuned to pray, with that tireless zeal which distinguishes the Methodist preacher above all others, Jandreau appeared suddenly to be smitten with a consciousness of his guilt, and kneeling in the midst of the 'meeting,' began with clasped hands and upturned eyes to pour forth a perfect torrent of words. With wonderful dramatic power he appeared to confess, to supplicate, to agonize, in idiomatic French. His tears and ejaculations touched the hearts of the missionaries, and filled them with gladness. They too ejaculated and wept, with frequently uttered "Amens" and "hallelujahs," until the scene became highly dramatic and exciting. In the midst of this grand tableau, when the enthusiasm was at its height, Jandreau suddenly ceased and rose to his feet, while an irrepressible outburst of laughter from his associates aroused the astonished missionaries to a partial comprehension of the fact that they had been made the subjects of a practical joke, though they never knew to exactly how great an extent.

The mischievous Frenchman had only recited with truly artistic power, and with such variations as the situation suggested, one of the most wonderful and effective tales from the *Arabian Nights Entertainment*, with which he was wont to delight and amuse his comrades beside the winter camp-fire!

But Jandreau was called to account when he arrived at Vancouver. Dr. McLaughlin had heard the story from some of the party, and resolved to punish the man's irreverence, at the same time that he gave himself a bit of amusement. Sending for the Rev. Father Blanchet, who was then resident at Vancouver, he informed him of the circumstance, and together they arranged Jandreau's punishment. He was ordered to appear in their united presence, and make a true statement of the affair. Jandreau confessed that he had done what he was accused of doing—made a mock of prayer, and told a tale instead of offering a supplication. He was then ordered by the Rev. Father to rehearse the scene exactly as it occurred, in order that he might judge of the amount of his guilt, and apportion him his punishment.

Trembling and abashed, poor Jandreau fell upon his knees and began the recital with much trepidation. But as he proceeded he warmed with the subject, his dramatic instinct asserted itself, tears streamed, and voice and eyes supplicated, until this second representation threatened to outdo the first. With outward gravity and inward mirth his two solemn judges listened to the close, and when Jandreau rose quite exhausted from his knees, Father Blanchet hastily dismissed him with an admonition and a light penance. As the door of Dr. McLaughlin's office closed behind him, not only the Doctor, but Father Blanchet indulged in a burst of long restrained laughter at the comical absurdities of this impious Frenchman.

To return to our immigrants. On leaving the Dalles they proceeded on down the south side of the river as far as practicable, or opposite to the Wind Mountain. At this point the Indians assisted to cross them over to the north side, when they again made their way along the river as far as *Tea Prairie* above Vancouver. The weather was execrable, with a pouring rain, and sky of dismal gray; December being already far advanced. Our travelers were not in the best of humors: indeed a saint-like amiability is seldom found in conjunction with rain, mud, fatigue, and an empty stomach. Some ill-natured suspicions were uttered to the effect that the Indians who were assisting to cross the party at this point, had stolen some ropes that were missing.

Upon this dishonorable insinuation the Indian heart was fired, and a fight became imminent. This undesirable climax to emigrant woes was however averted by an attack upon the indignant natives with firebrands, when they prudently retired, leaving the travelers to pursue their way in peace. It was on Sunday that the weary, dirty, hungry little procession arrived at a place on the Wallamet River where the present town of Milwaukie is situated, and found here two missionaries, the Rev. Messrs. Waller and Beers, who were preaching to the Indians.

Meek immediately applied to Mr. Waller for some provisions, and received for answer that it was "Sunday." Mr. Waller, however, on being assured that it was no more agreeable starving on Sunday than a week-day, finally allowed the immigrants to have a peck of small potatoes. But as a party of several persons could not long subsist on so short allowance, and as there did not seem to be any encouragement to expect more from the missionaries, there was no course left to be pursued but to make an appeal to Fort Vancouver.

To Fort Vancouver then, Newell went the next day, and returned on the following one with some dried salmon, tea, sugar, and sea-bread. It was not quite what the mountain-men could have wished, this dependence on the Hudson's Bay Company for food, and did not quite agree with what they had said when their hearts were big in the mountains. Being patriotic on a full stomach is easy compared to being the same thing on an empty one; a truth which became more and more apparent as the winter progressed, and the new settlers found that if they would eat they must ask food of some person or persons outside of the Methodist Mission. And outside of that there was in all the country only the Hudson's Bay Company, and a few mountain-men like themselves, who had brought nothing into the country, and could get nothing out of it at present.

There was but short time in which to consider what was to be done. Newell and Meek went to Wallamet Falls, the day after Newell's return from Vancouver, and there met an old comrade, Doughty, who was looking for a place to locate. The three made their camp together on the west side of the river, on a hill overlooking the Falls. While in camp they were joined by two other Rocky Mountain men, Wilkins and Ebbarts, who were also looking for a place to settle in. There were now six of the Rocky Mountain men together; and they resolved to push out into the plains to the west of them, and see what could be done in the matter of selecting homes.

As for our hero, we fear we cannot say much of him here which would serve to render him heroic in criticising Yankee eyes. He was a mountain-man, and *that only*. He had neither book learning, nor a trade, nor any knowledge of the simplest affairs appertaining to the ordinary ways of getting a living. He had only his strong hands, and a heart naturally stout and light.

His friend Newell had the advantage of him in several

particulars. He had rather more book-knowledge, more business experience, and also more means. With these advantages he became a sort of "Booshway" among his old comrades, who consented to follow his lead in the important movement about to be made, and settle in the Tualatin Plains should he decide to do so.

Accordingly camp was raised, and the party proceeded to the Plains, where they arrived on Christmas, and went into camp again. The hardships of mountain life were light compared to the hardships of this winter. For in the mountains, when the individual's resources were exhausted, there was always the Company to go to, which was practically inexhaustible. Should it be necessary, the Company was always willing to become the creditor of a good mountain-man. And the debtor gave himself no uneasiness, because he knew that if he lived he could discharge his indebtedness. But everything was different now. There was no way of paying debts, even if there had been a company willing to give them credit, which there was not, at least among Americans. Hard times they had seen in the mountains; harder times they were likely to see in the valley; indeed were already experiencing.

Instead of fat buffalo meat, antelope, and mountain mutton, which made the plenty of a camp on Powder River, our carniverous hunters were reduced to eating daily a little boiled wheat. In this extremity, Meek went on an expedition of discovery across the highlands that border the Lower Wallamet, and found on Wappatoo (now Sauvis) Island, a Mr. and Mrs. Baldra living, who were in the service of the Hudson's Bay Company, and drew rations from them. With great kindness they divided the provisions on hand, furnishing him with dried salmon and sea-bread, to which he added ducks and swans procured from the Indians. Poor and scanty as was the supply thus obtained, it was, after boiled wheat, comparative luxury while it lasted.

1841. The winter proved a very disagreeable one. Considerable snow fell early, and went off with heavy rains, flooding the whole country. The little camp on the Tualatin Plains had no defence from the weather better than Indian lodges, and one small cabin built by Doughty on a former visit to the Plains; for Doughty had been one of the first of the mountain-men to come to the Wallamet on the breaking up of the fur companies. Indian lodges, or no lodges at all, were what the men were used to; but in the dryer climate of the Rocky Mountains it had not seemed such a miserable life, as it now did, where, for months together, the ground was saturated with rain, while the air was constantly charged with vapor.

As for going anywhere, or doing anything, either were equally impossible. No roads, the streams all swollen and out of banks, the rains incessant, there was nothing for them but to remain in camp and wait for the return of spring. When at last the rainy season was over, and the sun shining once more, most of the mountain-men in the Tualatin Plains camp took land-claims and set to work improving them. Of those who began farming that spring, were Newell, Doughty, Wilkins, and Walker. These obtained seed-wheat from the Hudson's Bay Company, also such farming implements as they must have, and even oxen to draw the plow through the strong prairie sod. The wheat was to be returned to the company—the cattle also; and the farming implements paid for whenever the debtor became able. This was certainly liberal conduct on the part of a company generally understood to be opposed to American settlement.

19

CHAPTER XXIII.

WE find, according to their own account, that about 1838–9, "Jason Lee was lecturing in New England, on the Oregon Missions, and creating considerable zeal for the cause. As the result of his labors before the Board and elsewhere, $40,000 were collected for missionary purposes, and thirty-six additional assistants, viz: five missionaries, one physician, six mechanics, four farmers, one steward, four female teachers, with millers and others, were sent out to strengthen the mission, besides a saw mill, grist mill, agricultural and mechanical tools. This last reinforcement arrived in 1840, some months earlier than the mountain-men. A new mission was projected about ten miles above the old one, on the present site of Salem, the capital of Oregon.

Here the mills were to be erected, a new school building put up, and other substantial improvements carried on. There was no poverty among the members of the mission; on the contrary, according to Commodore Wilkes, there was wastefulness and reprehensible neglect of the agricultural and mechanical tools so generously furnished by the Board at home, who believed the mission to be doing a good work. So far, however, from benefitting the Indians, they were an actual injury to them. The sudden and absolute change of habits which the Indian students were compelled to make did not agree with them. The first breaking up of the ground for making

farms caused malaria, and induced much sickness among
them.   Many had died, and many others had gone back
to their former habits.   Much vice and disease also prevailed among the natives, which had been introduced by
deserting sailors and other profligate adventurers.   The
Indians could not be made to comprehend the spiritual
meaning of religion, and seeing among the whites themselves so frequent violations of what was represented to
be their belief, they ceased to regard their teachings,
until their moral condition became worse in their half-
civilized condition than it had been in their savage state.
The mission school had degenerated to such a mere pre-
tense of a school that in 1841, when Wilkes visited the
mission, he was not permitted to see it.

Hence, at the time when other settlers began to gather
into Oregon, the Methodist Mission was such by courtesy
only, and not in fact ; and of this the Hudson's Bay Company and the mountain-men were perfectly aware.   This
was a colony, an American colony, stolen in under the
very nose of the Hudson's Bay Company, claiming their
friendship and their services on account of their holy calling.   And if the home. Board was deceived, what mat-
tered it? " they builded better than they knew :" they
furnished the means by which an American colony established itself on Oregon soil, and being once established,
it could not be dislodged.

It is no part of the writer's design to say that the event
which happened was foreseen.   It was the logical result
of unforeseen circumstances.   A few religious enthusiasts
had undertaken what they could not perform—the Chris-
tianizing of a low order of savages.   They found themselves in a distant and beautiful country, where it was
easier to remain than to return.   Homes were growing
up around them ; children were born here ; it was a mild

and salubrious climate : why should they desire to quit it ? As for the mission property, had it not been intended to benefit them ? why should they relinquish it ? Let the future take care of itself.

All this is not so very difficult to understand. What was ill-looking and hard to be comprehended was the reluctance with which they ever assisted any other American settlers. It would seem natural that, in their isolated situation, surrounded by Indians, and subject most completely to the will of the anti-American Hudson's Bay Company, they should ardently desire an influx of their own countrymen, even at a considerable expense to themselves ; for they were exceeding jealous of the British influence, and of the designs of the British government. Already had they memorialized Congress that they had "settled themselves in said Territory, under the belief that it was a part of the public domain of said States, (United States,) and that they might rely upon the government thereof for the blessings of free institutions and the protection of its arms."

They had also intimated that they had reason not only to fear the Indians, but "also others that would do them harm," meaning the Hudson's Bay Company. In this early memorial they set forth, in glowing colors, the natural advantages and abundant resources of the Territory, and warned the Government of the intention of the English to claim that portion of it, at least, which laid north of the Columbia River, and closed by respectfully asking for the "civil institutions of the American Republic."

In the main the memorial was correct enough, as the Government was aware. It was, however, ungenerous and *ungrateful* toward the Hudson's Bay Company, or its representative, Dr. McLaughlin, who certainly had done nothing but good to themselves and their country-

men. Unless, indeed, they considered it evil for him to
be faithful to the interests of the Company, and the British Government, as they meant to be to the interests of
their own.

It was truly an unenviable position which Dr. McLaughlin held during those years of waiting for the settlement
of the boundary question. Even in his own particular
place and private domain he was not left at peace. For
at Vancouver there were two parties, the Patriots or
British, and the Philosophers or Liberals.* Of the latter
was Dr. McLaughlin, "who held that American principles
of legislation, in commercial and civil matters, were, generally speaking, just and humane ; and from which even
British legislation derived some useful hints." It required,
what 'Dr. McLaughlin was, a man of unusual force of
character and goodness of heart, to preserve the peace in
Oregon as he did do.

Had he been what he was continually suspected and
accused of being, the enemy of American settlement and
settlers, it would have been an easy matter enough to have
got rid of them altogether. Instead of entertaining, helping, and succoring them on all occasions, if he had simply
let them quite alone they must have perished. No small
community like the Methodist Mission could have sustained
itself in Oregon without a government, without arms,
without a market, and surrounded as they were by twenty
thousand savages. It was Fort Vancouver which kept the
Indians quiet. It was the Hudson's Bay Company who
settled all difficulties with the savages, and who furnished
means of communication, transportation, and protection
at the same time. With unblushing selfishness the missionaries never ceased to accept and even solicit every benefit

---

* *Oregon Territory, By John Dunn* of the H. B. C.

the Company could bestow, at the same time they continually uttered their suspicions and charges against the Company's principal agent, who continued with wonderful magnanimity to load them with his favors.

It was not altogether because Dr. McLaughlin was a representative of the British influence in the country, that the missionaries persisted in misconstruing his every action. Quite as strong a reason was his sectarian belief. A Roman Catholic was, in those days of religious prejudice, something totally abhorrent in Protestant estimation. The Oregon missionaries, neither Methodist nor Presbyterian, could ever quite rid themselves of the notion that Dr. McLaughlin was in some secret and mysterious manner implicated in a design to overthrow Protestantism in Oregon, and by a sort of second St. Bartholomew's Eve, to exterminate every man, woman, and child who professed it. What especially confirmed their suspicions was the fact that after the Protestant missionaries had been sometime settled in the country, the Doctor invited some priests of his own church to do the same; having one stationed at Vancouver, and another over the Canadian settlement at Champoeg. Then, as might be expected, others followed, and settled among the Indians in the Upper country. That the multitude of doctrines afterwards created distrust in the minds of the savages, there can be no doubt; but then, could they not see that the Protestants differed among themselves, and that the Catholics did not?

Besides the mission party, which was inimical to the British influence, and even to the name of anything British, there was also the American party, which was made up of everybody American outside of the Mission. The mountain-men were antagonistic from long habit, from the custom of making war upon the Hudson's Bay Company, which the leaders of the American Fur Companies inculcated during years of rivalry in the mountains. As for the few other adventurers then in Oregon, most of them had some personal quarrel with the H. B. Company's agents, or simply joined the American party from a sentiment of patriotism.

In the case of Ewing Young, for example : When he first came into the country from California, he was accompanied by Mr. Kelly, whose history has already been given. Besides Kelly, there were a number of sailors, deserters from vessels, and not having a very reputable appearance. This party traveled in company with the Hudson's Bay trading party through the most dangerous part of the country, accompanying them to Vancouver.

It so happened that the trader from California brought a letter to Dr. McLaughlin from the Spanish governor of California, warning him against Kelly and Young, saying that they had stolen horses. On this information, Dr. McLaughlin refused to have anything to do with Young and his associates, except Kelly, who being ill, was placed in a house at the fort, and nursed and fed through the winter, and finally sent to the Sandwich Islands in one of the Company's vessels.

In revenge for the slight put upon him by Dr. McLaughlin, Young and one of his associates, in the following year, started the erection of a distillery, with the intention of selling liquor to the Indians. But upon this movement the missionaries took alarm, and offered to pay Young the full value of his outlay if he would give up the business and undertake something else. To this Young and his partner consented on being properly petitioned by nearly all the white settlers in the country outside of the Hudson's Bay Company.

Shortly after this the Cattle Company was formed, and the mission gave Young something to do, by sending him

to California for cattle, and as he received cattle for payment, and stock was immensely high in Oregon, he soon
became a man of wealth and standing. The mission made
much of him, because he was as it were, a brand snatched
from the burning, and a good hater of the Hudson's Bay
Company besides. In truth Mr. Young became a historical character by dying in the summer of 1841, and thereby
causing to be held the first Primary Meeting of the People
of Oregon. Having died possessed of considerable wealth,
and no heirs appearing to claim it on the spot, his friends,
after first prudently burying him, adjourned from the grave
to the shade of a tree, and took prompt measures to "call
a public meeting for the purpose of appointing officers for
the government of the community, and *particularly to
provide for the proper disposition of the estate of Ewing
Young.*" The legend runs, that the state, that is to say
the Mission, divided the property affectionately among
themselves, and that afterwards there appeared a claimant
who succeeded in regaining a portion ; but that is neither
here nor there in this narrative.

It is the writer's opinion that earthly perfection is far to
seek and hard to find; and that it does not reside in Fur
Companies' forts, nor mission establishments.   One thing,
however, the mind persists in asking itself: Would there
not have been more unity among all the American settlers,
more respect for religion, and more universal benevolence
in Oregon, had the prominent men of the mission party
shown themselves less selfish and grasping?   No wonder
that when the superior benevolence of the Hudson's Bay
Company put to shame their avarice, many accounted for
the superior kindness of Dr. McLaughlin by calling it *Jesuitical.*   A little more of the same Jesuitical spirit would
have softened and brightened the character of those missionaries to the future historian of Oregon.

Yet be it not said that they did no good in their day and generation. If they were not all consistent Christian teachers, a few were. If as a class or party they proved themselves selfish and illiberal, they were yet as a class advocates of good morals, and good order, of industry, education, and free institutions.

It will be readily understood that there could be little sympathy between the missionaries and the mountain-men, for while one party prayed a great deal and very conspicuously, the other never prayed at all, but on the contrary rather inclined to make a jest of sacred matters, and pious observances. Then too, the mission party were well-to-do, and continually increasing their worldly goods by sharp bargains and general acquisitiveness, while the mountain-men were poor, prodigal, and not always industrious. In short, the aristocracy of American Oregon was the Methodist mission, an aristocracy second only to that of the Hudson's Bay Company, while the mountain-men, with big, rebellious hearts, were compelled, at the same time that they refused, to accept the position thrust upon them.

CHAPTER XXIV.

1841. WHEN spring opened, Meek assisted Newell in breaking the ground for wheat. This done, it became necessary to look out for some immediately paying employment. But paying occupations were hard to find in that new country. At last, like everybody else, Meek found himself, if not "hanging about," at least frequently visiting Vancouver. Poor as he was, and unpromising as looked the future, he was the same light-hearted, reckless, and fearless Joe Meek that he had been in the mountains: as jaunty and jolly a ragged mountaineer as ever was seen at the Fort. Especially he delighted in recounting his Indian fights, because the Company, and Dr. McLaughlin in particular, disapproved the American Company's conduct with the Indians.

When the Doctor chanced to overhear Meek's stories, as he sometimes did, he would say. "Mr. Joe, Mr. Joe,—(a habit the Doctor had of speaking rapidly, and repeating his words,)—Mr. Joe, Mr. Joe, you must leave off killing Indians, and go to work."

"I can't work," Meek would answer in his impressively slow and smooth utterance, at the same time giving his shoulders a slight shrug, and looking the Doctor pleasantly in the face.

During the summer, however, the United States Exploring Squadron, under Commodore Wilkes, entered the Columbia River, and proceeded to explore the country in several directions; and it was now that Meek found an employment suited to him; being engaged by Wilkes as pilot and servant while on his several tours through the country.

On the arrival of three vessels of the squadron at Vancouver, and the first ceremonious visit of Dr. McLaughlin and his associates to Commodore Wilkes on board, there was considerable display, the men in the yards, saluting, and all the honors due to the representative of a friendly foreign power. After dinner, while the guests were walking on deck engaged in conversation, the talk turned upon the loss of the *Peacock*, one of the vessels belonging to the U. S. squadron, which was wrecked on the bar at the mouth of the Columbia. The English gentlemen were polite enough to be expressing their regrets at the loss to the United States, when Meek, who had picked up a little history in spite of his life spent in the mountains, laughingly interrupted with:

"No loss at all, gentlemen. Uncle Sam can get another Peacock the way he got that one."

Wilkes, who probably regretted the allusion, as not being consonant with the spirit of hospitality, passed over the interruption in silence. But when the gentlemen from Vancouver had taken leave he turned to Meek with a meaning twinkle in his eyes:

"Meek," said he, "go down to my cabin and you'll find there something good to eat, and some first-rate brandy." Of course Meek went.

While Wilkes was exploring in the Cowelitz Valley, with Meek and a Hudson's Bay man named Forrest, as guides, he one day laid down in his tent to sleep, leaving his chronometer watch lying on the camp-table beside him. Forrest, happening to observe that it did not agree with his own, which he believed to be correct, very kindly, as he supposed, regulated it to agree with his. On awakening and taking up his watch, a puzzled expression came over Wilkes' face for a moment, as he discovered the change in the time; then one of anger and disappointment, as what had occurred flashed over his mind; followed by some rather strong expressions of indignation. Forrest was penitent when he perceived the mischief done by his meddling, but that would not restore the chronometer to the true time: and this accident proved a serious annoyance and hindrance during the remainder of the expedition.

After exploring the Cowelitz Valley, Wilkes dispatched a party under Lieutenant Emmons, to proceed up the Wallamet Valley, thence south along the old trail of the Hudson's Bay Company, to California. Meek was employed to pilot this party, which had reached the head of the valley, when it became necessary to send for some papers in the possession of the Commodore; and he returned to Astoria upon this duty. On joining Emmons again he found that some of his men had become disaffected toward him; especially Jandreau, the same Frenchman who prayed so dramatically at the Dalles.

Jandreau confided to Meek that he hated Emmons, and intended to kill him. The next morning when Lieut. E. was examining the arms of the party, he fired off Jandreau's gun, which being purposely overcharged, flew back and inflicted some injuries upon the Lieutenant.

"What do you mean by loading a gun like that?" inquired Emmons, in a rage.

"I meant it to kill two Injuns;—one before, and one behind;" answered Jandreau.

As might be conjectured Jandreau was made to fire his own gun after that.

The expedition had not proceeded much farther when it again became necessary to send an express to Vancou-

ver, and Meek was ordered upon this duty. Here he
found that Wilkes had purchased a small vessel which he
named the *Oregon*, with which he was about to leave the
country. As there was no further use for his services our
quondam trapper was again thrown out of employment.
In this exigency, finding it necessary to make some provision for the winter, he became a gleaner of wheat in the
fields of his more provident neighbors, by which means a
sufficient supply was secured to keep himself and his small
family in food until another spring.

When winter set in, Meek paid a visit to the new mission. He had been there once before, in the spring, to
buy an axe. Think, O reader, of traveling fifty or more
miles, on horseback, or in a small boat, to procure so simple and necessary an article of civilized life as an axe!
But none of the every-day conveniencies of living grow
spontaneously in the wilderness—more's the pity:—else
life in the wilderness would be thought more delightful
far than life in the most luxurious of cities; inasmuch as
Nature is more satisfying than art.

Meek's errand to the mission on this occasion was to
find whether he could get a cow, and credit at the same
time: for the prospect of living for another winter on
boiled wheat was not a cheerful one. He had not succeeded, and was returning, when at Champoeg he met
a Mr. Whitcom, superintendent of the mission farm. A
conversation took place wherein Meek's desire for a cow
became known. The missionaries never lost an opportunity of proposing prayers, and Mr. Whitcom thought this
a good one. After showing much interest in the condition of Meek's soul, it was proposed that he should pray.

"*I* can't pray: that's your business, not mine," said
Meek pleasantly.

"It is every man's business to pray for himself," answered Whitcom.

"Very well; some other time will do for that. What I want now is a cow."

"How can you expect to get what you want, if you wont ask for it?" inquired Whitcom.

"I reckon I have asked you; and I don't see nary cow yet."

"You must ask God, my friend: but in the first place you must pray to be forgiven for your sins."

"I'll tell you what I'll do. If you will furnish the cow, I'll agree to pray for half an hour, right here on the spot."

"Down on your knees then."

"You'll furnish the cow?"

"Yes," said Whitcom, fairly cornered.

Down on his knees dropped the merry reprobate, and prayed out his half hour, with how much earnestness only himself and God knew.

But the result was what he had come for, a cow; for Whitcom was as good as his word, and sent him home rejoicing. And thus, with what he had earned from Wilkes, his gleaned wheat, and his cow, he contrived to get through another winter.

The summer had not been altogether wasted either, in other respects. He had seen nearly the whole of Western Oregon; had acquired not only an understanding of its geography, but had learned to appreciate it, and its consequence in a national point of view. He had found it lovely, genial, and productive above any country he had ever seen, excepting that portion of California which he had once visited;—in some respects superior even to that. He had begun to comprehend the political position of Oregon more thoroughly than before; he thought he knew what was good and what was bad about the Hudson's Bay Company's influence, and the mission influence;—in short he had been learning to be an American citizen, instead of a mountain ranger—an individual instead of a fraction of a company.

The events which he had been a witness to, and the associations he had enjoyed, had been doing much to educate in him unbiased views of Oregon affairs. The great event of that summer, in Oregon, had been the presence of the American Squadron in Oregon waters. It was understood by the Americans to be significant on the part of the Government, of some action which it was about to take in regard to the treaty of joint occupancy. So also it was understood by the Hudson's Bay Company. The Americans were naturally anxious to find Commodore Wilkes favorably impressed with the country and its natural wealth. They were also very desirous that he should sympathize with their desire to have the United States extend its government over them.

As has been elsewhere stated, the death of Ewing Young, which occurred early in this year, furnished the pretext for the first primary meeting in Oregon. Following up the idea of a form of laws, the mission party consulted with the United States officers on the propriety of establishing a civil code for the government of the colony, and were disappointed, and not a little hurt, at finding that they did not see the necessity for it.

" A committee of five," says Wilkes, " principally lay-members of the mission, waited upon me to consult and ask advice relative to the establishment of laws, etc. After hearing attentively all their arguments and reasons for this change, I could see none sufficiently strong to induce this step. No crime appears yet to have been committed, and the persons and property of settlers are secure. Their principal reasons appear to me to be, that it would give them more importance in the eyes of others at a distance, and induce settlers to flock in, thereby raising the value of their farms and stock. I could not view the subject in such a light, and differed with them entirely as to the necessity or policy of adopting the change."

Commodore Wilkes knew, and everybody knew, that the British interest already felt itself threatened by the presence of the exploring expedition. So sensitive was Wilkes on this subject, that he preferred camping outside the Fort to accepting its hospitalities. He felt that for the Americans to follow it up immediately with any attempt at an independent government, would, or might be, to precipitate upon the Government the necessity of action for which it was not yet prepared, or to provoke an enmity by no means desirable in their present weak condition.

Another difficulty was also submitted to Commodore Wilkes. A party of eight young men from the States, who had, like other adventurers, drifted into Oregon from the mountains and California, had determined to return to their homes, because, as they said, there were no young white women in that country to marry, and they were unwilling to remain without female society, or to take native wives. Not being able to recross the continent, they had determined to build a vessel and to go by sea, at least so far as the Bay of San Francisco, where they might fall in with a trading vessel going home. Not one of them knew anything about navigation, though one of them was a ship-carpenter, but they trusted they should be able to sail their little craft, which they had named the *Star of Oregon*, safely to some port where assistance could reach them. What they wanted of the Commodore was a sea-letter, and that he should intercede with Dr. McLaughlin, who, through some misunderstanding, had refused them any further supplies. On receiving advice from Wilkes that they should explain to Dr. McLaughlin whatever seemed wrong to him, they did so, and obtained the necessary ropes, sails, provisions, etc., for their vessel, and finally made a safe voyage to San Francisco, where they sold their vessel for a good price, and took passage home by some larger one. Such were some of the examples of successful daring which the early history of Oregon furnished.

During this summer, also, a trading vessel—the *Thomas Perkins*, from Boston, *Varney*, master,—entered the Columbia with a cargo of Indian goods and liquor. To prevent the liquor being sold to the Indians, Dr. McLaughlin bought up the whole cargo, storing the liquor at Vancouver, where it remained for several years untasted. Had that liquor got among the Indians, it is most probable that the American colony would have been destroyed, or driven into Fort Vancouver for protection.

Perhaps the most important personal event which distinguished this year in Meek's history, was the celebration, according to the rites of the Christian church, of his marriage with the Nez Perce woman who had already borne him two children, and who still lives, the mother of a family of seven.

CHAPTER XXV.

1842. By the opening of another spring, Meek had so far overcome his distaste for farm labor as to put in a field of wheat for himself, with Doughty, and to make some arrangements about his future subsistence. This done, he was ready, as usual, for anything in the way of adventure which might turn up. This was, however, a very quiet summer in the little colony. Important events were brooding, but as yet results were not perceptible, except to the mind of a prophet. The Hudson's Bay Company, conformably to British policy, were at work to turn the balance of power in Oregon in favor of British occupation, and, unknown even to the colonists, the United States Government was taking what measures it could to shift the balance in its own favor. Very little was said about the subject of government claims among the colonists, but a feeling of suspense oppressed all parties.

The work of putting in wheat and improving of farms had just begun to slacken a little, when there was an arrival in the Columbia River of a vessel from Boston—the *Chenamus*, Captain Couch. The *Chenamus* brought a cargo of goods, which were placed in store at Wallamet Falls, to be sold to the settlers, being the first successful attempt at trade ever made in Oregon, outside of the Hudson's Bay and Methodist Mission stores.

When the Fourth of July came, the *Chenamus* was

lying in the Wallamet, below the Falls, near where the present city of Portland stands. Meek, who was always first to be at any spot where noise, bustle, or excitement might be anticipated, and whose fine humor and fund of anecdote made him always welcome, had borrowed a boat from Capt. Couch's clerk, at the Falls, and gone down to the vessel early in the morning, before the salute for the Glorious Fourth was fired. There he remained all day, enjoying a patriotic swagger, and an occasional glass of something good to drink. Other visitors came aboard during the day, which was duly celebrated to the satisfaction of all.

Towards evening, a party from the Mission, wishing to return to the Falls, took possession of Meek's borrowed boat to go off with. Now was a good opportunity to show the value of free institutions. Meek, like other mountain-men, felt the distance which the missionaries placed between him and themselves, on the score of their moral and social superiority, and resented the freedom with which they appropriated what he had with some trouble secured to himself. Intercepting the party when more than half of them were seated in the boat, he informed them that they were trespassing upon a piece of property which for the present belonged to him, and for which he had a very urgent need. Vexed by the delay, and by having to relinquish the boat to a man who, according to their view of the case, could not "read his title clear," to anything either on earth or in heaven, the missionaries expostulated somewhat warmly, but Meek insisted, and so compelled them to wait for some better opportunity of leaving the ship. Then loading the boat with what was much more to the purpose—a good supply of provisions, Meek proceeded to drink the Captain's health in a very ostentatious manner, and take his leave.

This slight encounter is related only to illustrate the sort of feeling which made the missionaries and those Americans usually denominated as "settlers," two parties instead of one.

The summer passed away, the harvest was gathered, and in September there was a fresh excitement in the Valley. Dr. White, a member of the mission, who came out in 1840, quarreled with the superintendent of the mission, Mr. Lee, and returned to the States in 1841, now re-appeared in Oregon as the bearer of glad tidings. It appeared that Dr. White, after settling his affairs with the Board at home, had given such information to the Government concerning Oregon affairs, as had induced the Executive to commission him Indian Agent, with certain not very clearly defined powers. What these powers were, did not at first so much interest the community, as that he had any at all; for the fact of his holding any commission from the United States indicated to them that the Government was about to take a step in their behalf, which their eager imaginations willingly construed into a settlement of the boundary question, the erection of a territorial government in Oregon, and the complete discomfiture of the Hudson's Bay Company.

In addition to the pleasure which Dr. White's commission gave, he was able to furnish another and equally good promise for the future, in the shape of a printed copy of a bill, then before the Senate, proposing to donate 640 acres of land to every white male inhabitant, half that quantity to a wife, and one-fourth to every child under eighteen years of age. That these liberal offers were contained in Mr. Linn's bill was well understood to be a bid for settlers, nor did the colonists doubt that it would induce emigration.

To crown their satisfaction, over a hundred immigrants

had accompanied Dr. White on his return, each with a copy of Mr. Linn's bill in their hands, as it were to show their title to the country.   These immigrants had left their wagons at Fort Hall, having been overtaken by heavy storms, and concluded their journey on horseback, traveling from the Dalles of the Columbia to the Wallamet Falls, by a trail over the Cascade mountains and around the base of Mt. Hood, thus avoiding Fort Vancouver entirely.

To receive the new comers properly, required some considerable exertion on the part of the colony, which was hardly prepared in matter of tenements and provisions for such an influx of population.   However, being the first invoice, they were made very welcome, and the more so, that there were among them a number of intelligent professional gentlemen, with their families, and that, for the most part, all were in independent circumstances.

The only thing that dampened the ardor of the colonists was, that Dr. White affirmed that his authority among them amounted to that of governor of the colony.   Now, in the first place, they had not any government, therefore could not have any governor.   True, there had been certain persons elected to fill certain offices, on the occasion before referred to, of the death of Young.   But there had been no occasion for the exercise of their various functions, and the whole matter was of doubtful substantiality.   Besides, if they were to have a governor, which they persisted they did not need, they would have desired to signify their preference.   After considerable controversy, Dr. White was finally obliged to be satisfied with his Indian agency, and Oregon got on as before, without a governor.

As might be anticipated, the Hudson's Bay Company were not well pleased with the turn affairs seemed taking.

They, on their own part, were watching the action of their own and the United States government, and had their colonization schemes beside, as well as the Americans. Sir George Simpson, governor·of the Hudson's Bay Company, had induced about one hundred and fifty of the French Canadian and Scotch settlers of the Red River settlement to come down into Oregon and locate on the North side of the Columbia. Their arrival happened rather later than that of the American immigrants, and was in no way satisfactory, since most of them disliked the portion of country assigned to them, that being the gravelly region around Puget Sound, and finally settled in the Wallamet Valley.

In the meantime, however, Dr. Whitman, of the Waiilatpu Mission, in the upper country, was so fearful of the intentions of the British government that he set out for Washington late in the autumn of 1842, to put the Secretary of State on his guard concerning the boundary question, and to pray that it might be settled conformably with the wishes of the Americans in Oregon. On his arrival he found that the treaty known as the "Ashburton Treaty" had been confirmed in the preceding summer, and that it avoided all reference to the Oregon boundary, by simply fixing upon a line for our frontier, extending from the Atlantic coast to the Lake of the Woods, or less than half-way across the continent. He, however, conferred with Mr. Webster on the subject, representing to him the folly of being persuaded to "swap off the Oregon territory for a cod-fishery," and probably was able to enlighten him on the value of said territory.

It was in March, 1843, that Dr. Whitman arrived at Washington. On reaching the Missouri frontier he had found that a large number of persons held themselves in readiness to emigrate, on the strength of Mr. Linn's bill, should it pass. To these he spoke encouragingly, advising them to go without delay, as such a bill would certainly be passed. Hastening over his business at Washington, he returned to the frontier early, joining the emigration, to whom he proved a most useful friend, and indefatigable guide and assistant. Such was the struggle for the possession of the Oregon Territory.

There was one feature, however, of this otherwise rather entertaining race for possession, which was becoming quite alarming. In all this strife about claiming the country, the Indian claim had not been considered. It has been already mentioned that the attempt to civilize or Christianize the Indians of western Oregon was practically an entire failure. But they were not naturally of a warlike disposition, and had been so long under the control of the Hudson's Bay Company that there was comparatively little to apprehend from them, even though they felt some discontent at the incoming immigration.

But with the Indians of the upper Columbia it was different; especially so with the tribes among whom the Presbyterian missionaries were settled—the Walla-Wallas, Cayuses, and Nez Perces, three brave and powerful nations, much united by intermarriages. The impression which these people had first made on the missionaries was very favorable, their evident intelligence, inquisitiveness, and desire for religious teachings seeming to promise a good reward of missionary labor. Dr. Whitman and his associates had been diligent in their efforts to civilize and Christianize them—to induce the men to leave off their migratory habits and learn agriculture, and the women to learn spinning, sewing, cooking, and all the most essential arts of domestic life. At the first, the novelty of these new pursuits engaged their interest, as it also excited their hope of gain. But the task of keeping them to their work with sufficient steadiness, was very great. They required, like children, to be bribed with promises of more or less immediate reward of their exertions, nor would they relinquish the fulfilment of a promise, even though they had failed to perform the conditions on which the promise became binding.

By-and-by they made the discovery that neither the missionaries could, nor the white man's God did, confer upon them what they desired—the enjoyment of all the blessings of the white men—and that if they wished to enjoy these blessings, they must labor to obtain them. This discovery was very discouraging, inasmuch as the Indian nature is decidedly averse to steady labor, and they could perceive that very little was to be expected from any progress which could be achieved in one generation. As for the Christian faith, they understood about as much of its true spirit as savages, with the law of blood written in their hearts, could be expected to understand. They looked for nothing more nor less than the literal fulfilment of the Bible promises—nothing less would content them; and as to the forms of their new religion, they liked them well enough—liked singing and praying, and certain orderly observances, the chiefs leading in these as in other matters. So much interest did they discover at first, that their teachers were deceived as to the actual extent of the good they were doing.

As time went on, however, there began to be cause for mutual dissatisfaction. The Indians became aware that no matter how many concessions their teachers made to them, they were still the inferiors of the whites, and that they must ever remain so. But the thought which produced the deepest chagrin was, that they had got these white people settled amongst them by their own invitation and aid, and that now it was evident they were not to be benefited as had been hoped, as the whites were turning their attention to benefiting themselves.

As early as 1839, Mr. Smith, an associate of Mr. Spalding in the country of the Nez Perces, was forbidden by the high chief of the Nez Perces to cultivate the ground. He had been permitted to build, but was assured that if he broke the soil for the purpose of farming it, the ground so broken should serve to bury him in. Still Smith went on in the spring to prepare for ploughing, and the chief seeing him ready to begin, inquired if he recollected that he had been forbidden. Yet persisting in his undertaking, several of the Indians came to him and taking him by the shoulder asked him again "if he did not know that the hole he should make in the earth would be made to serve for his grave." Upon which third warning Smith left off, and quitted the country. Other missionaries also left for the Wallamet Valley.

In 1842 there were three mission stations in the upper country; that of Dr. Whitman at Waiilatpu on the Walla-Walla River, that of Mr. Spalding on the Clearwater River, called Lapwai, and another on the Spokane River, called Cimakain. These missions were from one hundred and twenty to three hundred miles distant from each other, and numbered altogether only about one dozen whites of both sexes. At each of these stations there was a small body of land under cultivation, a few cattle and hogs, a flouring and saw mill, and blacksmith shop, and such improvements as the needs of the mission demanded. The Indians also cultivated, under the direction of their teachers, some little patches of ground, generally but a small garden spot, and the fact that they did even so much was very creditable to those who labored to instruct them. There was no want of ardor or industry in the Presbyterian mission; on the contrary they applied themselves conscientiously to the work they had undertaken.

But this conscientious discharge of duty did not give them immunity from outrage. Both Mr. Spalding and Dr. Whitman had been rudely handled by the Indians, had been struck and spat upon, and had nose and ears pulled. Even the delicate and devoted Mrs. Spalding had been grossly insulted. Later the Cayuses had assailed Dr. Whitman in his house with war-clubs, and broken down doors of communication between the private apartments and the public sitting room. Explanations and promises generally followed these acts of outrage, yet it would seem that the missionaries should have been warned.

The station at Waiilatpu being near fort Walla-Walla was much resorted to by visitors and travelers. Dr. Whitman, who looked upon the country as belonging to the United States, and who was actively opposed to British influence from patriotic motives, had frequent and long conversations with his visitors not only on the subject of the American claim, but upon the natural advantages of the country, the fertility of its soil, and kindred topics, much of which the Indians, who were always about the mission, were able to understand, and from which they gathered that the Americans intended to possess the country which they considered as their own. They had seen that year by year, for a long time, some Americans had passed through their country and gone down to settle in the Walla-met Valley. They had had a fresh alarm in the recent emigration which had accompanied Dr. White from the States. But most conclusive of all was the fact of Dr. Whitman's visit to Washington, and his avowed intention of bringing back with him a large party of settlers to hold the country against the English.

Taking advantage of Dr. Whitman's absence, the Cayuses had frightened Mrs. Whitman from her home to the Methodist mission at the Dalles, by breaking into her bed-chamber at night, with an infamous design from which she barely escaped, and by subsequently burning down the mill and destroying a considerable quantity of grain. About the same time the Nez Perces at the Lapwai mission were very insolent, and had threatened Mr. Spalding's life; all of which, one would say, was but a poor return for the care and instruction bestowed upon them during six years of patient effort on the part of their teachers.   Poor as it was, the Indians did not see it in that light, but only thought of the danger which threatened them, in the possible loss of their country.

The uneasiness among the Indians had so much increased since Dr. Whitman's departure, that it became necessary, in November, for the newly arrived Indian agent to make a journey to the upper country to inquire into the cause of the disturbances, and if possible to adjust the difficulties.   In order the better to succeed in this, Dr. White obtained the services of Thomas McKay of the Hudson's Bay Company—a son of that ill-fated McKay who perished on board the *Tonquin* in 1811, and whose mother, a half-breed woman, was afterwards married to Dr. McLaughlin.

Both by his Indian blood, his long service in the Hudson's Bay Company, and the natural urbanity of his disposition, Mr. McKay was a man of note among the Indians; understanding their peculiarities better, and having more influence over them than almost any trader in the whole country.   Half a dozen well armed men, and two interpreters, were the only escort which, according to McKay, was thought necessary.   With this small party the agent proceeded to the mission station at Waiilatpu, where some gentlemen of the mission were staying, Mrs. Whitman being absent at the Dalles. After taking note of the injury done to the mission property here, the party continued on to the Lapwai mission, where they had sent word for the chiefs of the disaffected tribes to meet them.

Then took place the customary exchange of "talks" which always characterize the Indian council. The Indians were grave and dignified; they heard the addresses of the agent and his friends, and received the compliments paid to their advancement in the arts and in letters, with the utmost decorum. They professed themselves desirous of peace, and appeared satisfied with the promises made by the agent concerning what the Great Father of the United States intended doing for them.

As has been stated in another place, the Hudson's Bay Company had done all it could to destroy chieftainships among the tribes, in order to prevent coalitions among them. Dr. White restored it among the Nez Perces, by counseling them to elect one high chief, and to have besides a chief to every village, in all about a dozen, to assist him in the administration of the laws. A code of laws for their government was then proposed and agreed to, which made hanging the punishment for murder or for burning a dwelling house. Theft was punishable by double payment, and by whipping. Misdemeanors generally were left to the discretion of the chiefs, the penalties being in most cases fines, and in some cases whipping.

The naturally good character of the Nez Perces, and the presence and sanction of two of the Hudson's Bay Company, McKay, and McKinley of Walla-Walla, made it comparatively easy for Dr. White to arrange a peace with the Indians at Lapwai. On returning to

Waiilatpu, however, few of the chiefs were found to be assembled, while many of them held aloof, and nothing satisfactory was concluded. Under these circumstances Dr. White left an appointment to meet them in April, of the next year, for the purpose of holding a council. He then returned to the Wallamet, to watch the course of events in the colony.

CHAPTER XXVI.

1842–3. The plot thickened that winter, in the little drama being enacted west of the Rocky Mountains. As much as Dr. McLaughlin had felt it to be his duty towards his country and the company he served, to do what he could to secure their interests, he had also always acknowledged the claims of humanity, hospitality, and social good feeling. So much, in fact, did his nature lean towards the social virtue of brotherly love, that he became sometimes the object of criticism bordering on censure, to his associates, who on their side were as patriotic as the Americans on theirs.

But so rapidly portentous events seemed hurrying on at this particular juncture, that the good Doctor was led to doubt almost that he had done the best thing in extending the hand of fellowship so freely to the political enemies of Great Britain. His critics might with·some justice accuse him of encouraging American settlement in Oregon, and of giving just that touch required, to shift the balance of power into the hands of the United States. Such a suspicion against him would be bad enough in the eyes of his superiors; but the pain it would occasion him could hardly be exceeded by that occasioned by the denial to such a suspicion given by the settlers themselves.

In a memorial to the Congress of the United States they had petitioned for the protection of Government upon the express ground that they apprehended harm, not only from the Indians, but from the Hudson's Bay Company; which apprehension was a direct insinuation or accusation against Dr. McLaughlin. Naturally of a temper as irritable as his heart was warm and generous, these attacks upon his honor and humanity by the very individuals whom he had ever shown himself willing to serve, annoyed him excessively, and occasioned him to say that to those individuals who had signed the obnoxious memorial he would never more show favor. As might be expected, this pardonable show of indignation was made to stand for a threat against the welfare of the whole colony.

To add to the confusion, the subject of a form of government continued to be agitated in the colony. So far as legal forms were necessary to the welfare of the Hudson's Bay Company, they had in their charter certain privileges of arrest and punishment sufficient for the preservation of good order among their employés; hence had no need for any thing further in the way of laws. Why then should they be desirous of joining any foreign organization, or of subscribing to the laws made by a people who owed allegiance to a rival government, and thereby strengthening their hands against their own government? Such was the logical reasoning of the Canadian settlers on the Wallamet, who at that time rather out-numbered the Americans.

On the other hand, it was equally logical for the Americans to fear that a code of laws intended only to apply to a portion of the population, would prove of little service, and might be provocative of frequent difficulties; inasmuch as any criminal might take refuge under the flag of the Hudson's Bay Company, and escape by that Company's denial of jurisdiction.

In this interval of doubt, the colony managed to get along very well without any laws. But the subject was not allowed to rest. Some truly long-headed politicians had hit upon an expedient to unite the population, Canadian and American, upon one common ground of interest.

The forests which clad the mountains and foot-hills in perpetual verdure, and the thickets which skirted the numerous streams flowing into the Wallamet, all abounded in wild animals, whose depredations upon the domestic cattle, lately introduced into the country, were a serious drawback to their natural increase. Not a settler, owning cattle or hogs, but had been robbed more or less frequently by the wolves, bears, and panthers, which prowled unhindered in the vicinity of their herds.

This was a ground of common interest to all settlers of whatever allegiance. Accordingly, a notice was issued that a meeting would be held at a certain time and place, to consider the best means of preventing the destruction of stock in the country, and all persons interested were invited to attend. This meeting was held on the 2d of February, 1843, and was well attended by both classes of colonists. It served, however, only as a preliminary step to the regular "Wolf Association" meeting which took place a month later. At the meeting, on the 4th of March, there was a full attendance, and the utmost harmony prevailed, notwithstanding there was a well-defined suspicion in the minds of the Canadians, that they were going to be called upon to furnish protection to something more than the cattle and hogs of the settlers.

After the proper parliamentary forms, and the choosing of the necessary officers for the Association, the meeting proceeded to fix the rate of bounty for each animal killed by any one out of the Association, viz: $3.00 for a large wolf; $1.50 for a lynx; $2.00 for a bear; and $5.00 for a panther. The money to pay these bounties was to be raised by subscription, and handed over to the treasurer

for disbursement; the currency being drafts on Fort Vancouver, the Mission, and the Milling Company; besides
wheat and other commodities.

This business being arranged, the real object of the
meeting was announced in this wise:

"*Resolved*,—That a committee be appointed to take into
consideration the propriety of taking measures for the
civil and military protection of this colony."

A committee of twelve were then selected, and the
meeting adjourned. But in that committee there was a
most subtle mingling of all the elements—missionaries,
mountain-men, and Canadians—an attempt by an offer of
the honors, to fuse into one all the several divisions of political sentiment in Oregon.

That the Canadians were prepared for something of this
kind was probable from several circumstances. In the
first place, the subject of government, in several forms,
had been openly discussed that winter. The immigration,
of the previous autumn had added much to the social resources of the colony, both in numbers, and in variety of
ideas. The colony was not so much a missionary institution as formerly, simply because there had been an influx
of other than missionary brains; and there were people
now in Oregon, who, after studying the position of affairs,
were able to see the merits and demerits of the various
propositions brought up. Even in the Debating Society,
which was maintained by the most able men of the colony
and of the Hudson's Bay Company, at the Wallamet Falls,
the subject of a provisional form of government was freely
and fully discussed;—some parties favoring the adoption
of a simple code of such laws as were needful to regulate
society in that isolated country, temporarily, until the
United States should recognize and adopt them into the
Union. Others wished for an independent form of gov-

ernment, acknowledging no allegiance to any other, either then or later. A few still argued for no change in the then existing state of things, feeling that no necessity had yet arisen for manufacturing governments.

Of the independent government party Dr. McLaughlin was believed to be. Even some of the mission party favored a separate government, if, after waiting a term of four years, the United States had set up no claim to their allegiance. But the greater number of the people, not Canadians, and the mountain-men especially, were for a provisional government to last as long as in the course of events it was needed, after which its powers were to revert to the United States.

In view of all this talk, the Canadians were prepared with an address which was to express their view of the case, and would have presented it at the meeting of the Wolf Association, had not that meeting been so thoroughly "wolfish" in its action as almost to disarm suspicion, and quite prevent any reference to the main topic of thought in all minds. The address was therefore reserved for a more appropriate occasion, which was not long in coming.

On the 2d day of May, 1843, the committee appointed March 4th to "take into consideration the propriety of taking measures for the civil and military protection of the colony," met at Champoeg, the Canadian settlement, and presented to the people their ultimatum in favor of organizing a provisional government.

On a motion being made that the report of the committee should be accepted, it was put to vote, and lost. All was now confusion, various expressions of disappointment or gratification being mingled in one tempest of sound.

When the confusion had somewhat subsided, Mr. G. W. LeBreton made a motion that the meeting should divide; those who were in favor of an organization taking their positions on the right hand; and those opposed to it on the left, marching into file. The proposition carried; and Joe Meek, who, in all this historical reminiscence we have almost lost sight of—though he had not lost sight of events—stepped to the front, with a characteristic air of the free-born American in his gait and gestures:—

"Who's for a divide! All in favor of the Report, and an Organization, follow me!"—then marched at the head of his column, which speedily fell into line, as did also the opposite party.

On counting, fifty-two were found to be on the right hand side, and fifty on the left,—so evenly were the two parties balanced at that time. When the result was made known, once more Meek's voice rang out—

"Three cheers for our side!"

It did not need a second invitation; but loud and long the shout went up for FREEDOM; and loudest and longest were heard the voices of the American "mountain-men." Thus the die was cast which made Oregon ultimately a member of the Federal Union.

The Canadians were somewhat alarmed at the demonstrations they had witnessed, and withdrew from the meeting soon after the last vote was taken, not, however, without presenting the address, which had been previously prepared; and which is given here, both as a curiosity of literature, and a comprehensive bit of Oregon history.

ADDRESS
OF THE CANADIAN CITIZENS OF OREGON TO THE MEETING AT CHAMPOEG.

MARCH 4th, 1843.

We, the Canadian citizens of the Willamette, considering, with interest and reflection, the subject which unites the people at the present meeting, present to the American citizens, and particularly to the gentlemen who called said meeting, the unanimous expression of our sentiments of cordiality, desire of union and inexhaustible peace between all the people, in view of our duty and the interest of the new colony, and declare :—

1st. That we wish for laws, or regulations, for the welfare of our persons, and the security of our property and labors.

2d. That we do not intend to rebel against the measures of that kind taken last year, by a party of the people;—although we do not approve of certain regulations, nor certain modes of laws;—let those magistrates finish their time.

3d. That we will not address a new petition to the Government of the United States, because we have our reasons, till the line be decided, and the frontiers of the states are fixed.

4th. That we are opposed to the regulations anticipated, and exposed to consequences for the quantity, direction, &c., of lands, and whatsoever expense for the same lands, because we have no direct guarantee from the government to come, and, perhaps, to-morrow, all those measures may be broken.

5th. That we do not wish a provisional mode of government, too self-interested, and full of degrees, useless to our power, and overloading the colony instead of improving it; besides, men of laws and science are too scarce, and have too much to do in such a new country.

6th. That we wish either the mode of senate or council, to judge the difficulties, punish the crimes, (except capital penalties,) and make the regulations suitable to the people.

7th. That the same council be elected, and composed of members from all parts of the country, and should act in body, on the plan of civilized countries in parliament, or as a jury, and to be represented, for example, by the president of said council, and another member, as judge of peace, in each county, allowing the principle of recalling to the whole senate.

8th. That the members should be influenced to interest themselves to their own welfare, and that of the public, by the love of doing good, rather than by the hope of gain, in order to take off from the esteem of the people all suspicions of interest in the persons of their representatives.

9th. That they must avoid every law loading, and inexpedient to the people, especially to the new arrivals. Unnecessary taxes, and whatever records are of that kind, we do not want them.

10th. That the militia is useless at present, and rather a danger of bad suspicion to the Indians, and a delay for the necessary labors, in the same time it is a load; we do not want it, either, at present.

11th. That we consider the country free, at present to all nations, till government shall have decided; open to every individual wishing to settle, without any distinction of origin, and without asking him anything, either to become an English, Spanish, or American citizen.

12th. So we, English subjects, proclaim to be free, as well as those who came from France, California, United States, or even natives of this country; and we desire unison with all the respectable citizens who wish to settle in this country; or, we ask to be recognized as free amongst ourselves, to make such regulations as appear suitable to our wants, save the general interest of having justice from all strangers who might injure us, and that our reasonable customs and pretensions be respected.

13th.   That we are willing to submit to any lawful government, when it comes.

14th.   That we do not forget that we must make laws only for necessary circumstances.   The more laws there are, the more opportunities for roguery, for those who make a practice of it, and, perhaps, the more alterations there will be some day.

15th.   That we do not forget in a trial, that before all fraud on fulfilling of some points of law, the ordinary proofs of the certainty of the fact ought to be duly weighed, so that justice may be done, and no shame given for fraud.

16th.   In a new country, the more men employed and paid by the public, the less remains for industry.

17th.   That no one can be more desirous than we are for the prosperity, ameliorations, and general peace of the country, and especially for the guarantee of our rights and liberties; and such is the wish we make for all those who are, or may become, our fellow-countrymen, &c., for long years of peace.

[Then follow our names and persons.]

The business of the meeting was concluded by the election of a Supreme Judge, with probate powers, a clerk of the court, a sheriff, four magistrates, four constables, a treasurer, a mayor, and a captain,—the two latter officers being instructed to form companies of mounted riflemen.   In addition to these officers, a legislative committee was chosen, consisting of nine members, who were to report to the people at a public meeting to be held at Champoeg on the 5th of July following.   Of the legislative committee, two were mountain-men, with whose names the reader is familiar—Newell and Doughty.   Among the other appointments, was Meek, to the office of sheriff; a position for which his personal qualities of courage and good humor admirably fitted him in the then existing state of society.

And thus was formed the Provisional Government of Oregon—a country without a governor, or any magisterial head; and without a treasury, or means to pay its legislative committee, except by subscription, and at the rate of $1.25 per day in orders on some of the few business firms west of the Rocky Mountains.   On the 4th of

July the people met at Champoeg to celebrate the day, and camped on the ground, to be in readiness for the meeting of the 5th. At this meeting the reports of the various committees of the legislature were approved by the people, Dr. McLaughlin voting with the others.

At this meeting the Judiciary Committee recommended that the executive power should be vested in a *committee of three persons*, elected by qualified voters at the annual election, who should have power to grant pardons and reprieve for offences against the laws of the territory; to call out the military force of the territory to repel invasion or suppress insurrection, to take care that the laws were faithfully executed, and to recommend such laws as they may consider necessary, to the representatives of the people, for their action: two members of this committee to constitute a quorum to transact business.

Among the most notable of the acts of the first Oregon legislature, was one which regarded a militia law, ordering the territorial militia to be formed into one battalion consisting of three companies of mounted riflemen; and another regarding marriage, which permitted "All male persons, of the age of sixteen and upwards, and all females of the age of fourteen and upwards" to engage in marriage, provided the sanction of the parents could be obtained. Unfortunately for the good of Oregon there were too many parents, who, looking forward to the passage of the Donation Act, and being desirous of gaining possession through their children of large bodies of land, were only too eager to see their children married and assuming the responsibilities of parentage, before their own childhood was fairly passed.

As for the laws generally adopted, they were those of Iowa and New York mixed, and made suitable to the condition of the colony.

The result of success in the matter of effecting an organization was not altogether unalloyed happiness. The Indians in the upper country were again in a tumult, and freely expressed their dread of the coming immigration, then on its way, under the leadership of Dr. Whitman. They were not ignorant of what had taken place in the Wallamet Valley; neither, upon reflection, did they look upon the visit of the Indian agent in the previous autumn as a promise of good, but regarded it rather as a token of the encroachments of the whites. So far as the Nez Perces were concerned, they had kept the laws given them at that time, partly through the natural prudence of their dispositions, and partly through the wise counsels of their head chief, Ellis, who, having been educated at the Red River settlement of the Hudson's Bay Company, was prepared to use a reasonable discretion in controling the bad passions of his people.

But the Cayuses and Walla-Wallas, the allies and relatives of the Nez Perces, were in a different frame of mind, having more immediate cause for alarm, from the fact that their own teacher, Dr. Whitman, was bringing upon them the curse they dreaded. In a state of mind totally unsettled and rebellious, they waited for the promised visit of Dr. White in the spring.

Such were the reports which had reached the Wallamet from the upper country of the turbulence of the Indians, that it was regarded as a dangerous movement for the agent to go among them. However, he resolved to undertake it, and accompanied by only one gentleman from the mission, Mr. Hines, and their servants, set out for the infected district. Before reaching Vancouver they were met by a letter from Dr. McLaughlin, advising them not to proceed, and informing them that, from intelligence lately received, there was really much to apprehend. He also informed them that the Indians had expressed their determination not to make war upon the Hudson's Bay Company, but only upon the Americans; and gave it as his opinion that the best way to end the disturbance was to remain quietly at home.

Not agreeing with Dr. McLaughlin in respect to the best manner of soothing the Indians, Dr. White and Mr. Hines proceeded to the fort, where they wished to obtain supplies of goods, provisions, powder, and balls for the expedition. This visit to the fort, under the circumstances, was one of those frequent acts, half cringing and half audacious, which the sensitive historian rather flinches from recording, as reflecting upon the honor and dignity of Americans. In explanation we shall quote Mr. Hines' own words:

" Called on Dr. McLaughlin for goods, provisions, powder, balls, &c., for our accommodation on our voyage up the Columbia; and although he was greatly suprised that, under the circumstances, we should think of going among those excited Indians, yet he ordered his clerks to let us have whatever we wanted. However, we found it rather squally at the fort, not so much on account of our going among the Indians of the interior, as in consequence of a certain memorial having been sent to the United States Congress, *implicating the conduct of Dr. McLaughlin and the Hudson's Bay Company*, and bearing the signatures of seventy Americans. I inquired of the Doctor if he had refused to grant supplies to those Americans who had signed that document; he replied that he had not, but that the authors of the memorial need expect no more favors from him. *Not being one of the authors, but merely a signer of the petition, I did not come under the ban of the company, consequently I obtained my outfit for the expedition, though at first there were strong indications that I would be refused.*"

To the honor of Dr. McLaughlin be it said, that however great the provocation, he never avenged his injuries upon the American settlers, by refusing to aid them in their times of want or peril.

Arrived at the Dalles, the Indian agent tarried only long enough to inquire into the working of the system of laws which he had persuaded them to accept on his previous visit.   The report which the Indians had to give was both melancholy and amusing.   According to Mr. Hines' Journal of the expedition:

"The chiefs had found much difficulty in enforcing the laws; in punishing delinquents, some of the Indians resisting even to the point of the knife.   The chiefs who were appointed through the influence of Dr. White, were desirous that these regulations should continue, evidently because they placed the people under their absolute control, and gave them the power to regulate all their intercourse with the whites, and with the other Indian tribes.   But the other influential men, who were not in office, desired to know of Dr. White, of what benefit this whipping system was going to be to them.   They said they were willing it should continue, provided they were to receive blankets, shirts, and pants, as a reward for being whipped.   They had been whipped a good many times, and they had got nothing for it, and it had done them no good.   If this state of things was to continue it was all good for nothing, and they would throw it all away.   In reply they were told by the Doctor that we could not be detained to settle any of their difficulties now, that we were going farther into the interior, and were in a very great hurry, and that when we returned he would endeavor to make all straight.   But he wished them to understand that they need not expect pay for being flogged, when they deserved it.   They laughed heartily at the idea, and dispersed, giving us an opportunity to make arrangements for the continuance of our journey."

On leaving the Dalles, Dr. White proceeded as rapidly as possible, now with horses instead of boats, to the station at Waiilatpu, where Mrs. Whitman and a Mr. Giger of the mission were awaiting them with anxious expectation.   Dr. White found quite as much uneasiness as he had anticipated, and learned incidentally why he had been counseled at Fort Vancouver not to attempt going among the Indians.   It appeared on investigation that a mischievous half-breed, named Dorio, son of the same Madame Dorio who figures as a heroine in Irving's *Astoria*, being well informed in Indian sentiments, and influential as an interpreter among them, had wickedly inflamed the passions of the Indians by representing to them that it was useless making farms and building houses, as in a short time the whites would overrun their land, and destroy everything, besides killing them.

This evil counsel so well agreed with what they had seen and heard, and had reason to apprehend, that much excitement was the result. The warriors among the Cayuses were eager to go to war at once, and exterminate all the white settlements on the Wallamet and elsewhere. But the old men counseled patience and caution, advising a consultation with the Hudson's Bay Company, who had always been their friends. They remembered the answer they had received, when on the first breaking out of their fear of the Americans they had gone to Fort Walla-Walla, to ask McKinley's opinion of the expediency of driving the missionaries away from their lands. "You are braves," said McKinley, "and there are many of you. It would be easy to kill two men and two women, and a few little children. Go quickly and do it, if you wish; but remember if you do so, that I will have you punished." For that time the subject was dropped.

But now that their fears were thoroughly aroused, the Cayuses resolved to send a messenger to Dr. McLaughlin at Vancouver to inquire what had better be done in view of their difficulties, and to take observations in the lower country, for the Indians were well aware that the whites had not been at peace among themselves, and that Fort Vancouver had been strengthened in its defences, and had had a government vessel lying before it the previous winter. Seeing that there seemed more unity between the Hudson's Bay Company and the Americans, a new fear entered into their minds lest they might combine against them.

Full of such feelings, a Walla-Walla chief, called Yellow-Serpent, made a journey to Vancouver and opened his heart to Dr. McLaughlin. In answer to his inquiries the Doctor assured him that there was nothing to apprehend from any class of whites; that he could not believe the

Americans had any warlike designs toward them, and that if they should make war on them, they would not be joined by the Hudson's Bay men. Comforted by the assurances of the great white chief, Yellow-Serpent returned, and reported to his people, and for a time they were quiet, and worked at their little plantations, as taught them by Dr. Whitman.

As we have seen it was but a brief lull in the rising tempest. The wicked Dorio still continued to poison their minds, and to stir up all the native suspiciousness and jealousy of the Indian character. Thus it happened that on Dr. White's arrival they were full of mutiny, as difficult of approach as in the preceding autumn. However, Dr. White, with Mr. Hines, Mrs. Whitman and Mr. Giger, made many friendly advances, and a meeting was finally appointed to take place after the agent had first made a visit to the Nez Perces.

The Nez Perces were found to have remembered their promises, and to have continued to profit by the instructions of their teachers. They received the agent in a cordial manner, entertaining him and his friends with a rehearsal of a late battle with the Blackfeet in which they had been victorious. Arrangements were then made for Mr. Spalding, Ellis, and several hundreds of men, women and children to visit Waiilatpu in company with the Doctor, as the Cayuses would agree to nothing without first consulting with the chief of the Nez Perces.

Nor were they all inclined to receive the agent hospitably, even in company with Ellis. The reception was conducted in the usual style of Indian welcome, by first exhibiting their warlike accomplishments in a sham battle, so well fought and life-like in its representation that even Ellis was almost persuaded some real fighting would follow. The excitement was finally allayed by Mr. Spalding proposing to adjourn to the house of worship for evening prayers, after which the people scattered to their lodges to await the meeting of the next day.

On the following morning the chiefs came together at Dr. Whitman's, and Dr. White addressed them. He assured them that if they feared war on the part of the whites, they were quite mistaken; that the Great Father of the whites had not sent him among them for that purpose, but to come to some understanding about their future intercourse. He promised them that if they would lay aside their former practices, as they had been instructed by the missionaries to do, leave off feuds among themselves, and cultivate the land, they might become a great and happy people. He counseled unity between the chiefs, and consideration and kindness towards the people, and also counseled the people to obey the chiefs, and love and pray for them.

The subject of the laws was then brought forward, and the young men were exhorted to accept and keep them, that when they became chiefs their people might obey them. The laws were then read both in English and Nez Perce, when the Walla-Walla chief, Yellow-Serpent, arose and said:

"I have a message to you. Where are these laws from? Are they from God, or from the earth? I would you might say they were from God. But I think they are from the earth, because, what I know of white men, they do not honor these laws." A short speech, and to the point.

When it was explained to him that in all civilized countries men were bound to honor the laws, he replied that he was "glad to learn that it was so, because many of his people had been angry with him when he had whipped them for crime, and had told him that God would send him to hell for it, and he was glad to know that it was not displeasing to God."

Other chiefs then spoke in turn, one favoring the adoption of the laws, another rejecting, and giving as a reason that the chief in favor was a Catholic; to which Doctor White replied that religious belief had nothing to do with the making or keeping of laws. And after this an old chief, who had seen Lewis and Clarke when they were in the country, spoke of the treaty made with them ; adding that " ever since that time people had been coming along and promising to do them good; but that they had all passed by and left no blessing behind them. That the Hudson's Bay Company had persuaded them to keep good friends with them, and to let the Americans alone. But if the Americans designed to do good to them, why did they not bring goods with them to leave with their people. They were fools to listen to the promises of the Americans; they only would talk, while the Hudson's Bay Company gave presents." In reply to which begging speech the Doctor reminded them that his business with them was that neither of missionary or trader.

After a day spent in listening to and answering speeches. the meeting adjourned. In the evening the Nez Perce chief, Ellis, and his associate Sawyer, held a talk with Dr. White in which they demanded a salary, as chiefs ; and thought that they were already entitled to enough to make them wealthy. So avaricious is the Indian in all his feelings and pursuits.

On the day following the speeches were resumed, the laws finally accepted, and the Catholic chief Tan-i-tan was elected to the office of head chief, but resigned it the next day in favor of his brother Five-Crows, because, as he said, his religion differed from that of most of his nation, and Five-Crows would be more agreeable to them.

His decision proved his wisdom as well as his generosity; for the people declared themselves delighted with the change, though they had nothing against Tan-i-tan.

At the conclusion of each day the Indians had been feasted with fat beef and pork, obtained from the mission; and on the last day a grand feast was spread, to which Dr. White's party were invited, and at which, contrary to Indian custom, the women were permitted to appear and partake; Dr. White having made this a special request, and furnished them with new dresses for the occasion. After this happy conclusion of business in the Indian country, Dr. White appointed his leave-taking for the next morning. Mrs. Whitman, who had been an anxious and interested spectator of events, notwithstanding the amicable termination of the agent's efforts, thought it prudent to return with his party to the lower country until the time approached for her husband's return. Better for both had they never returned to Waiilatpu. Many were the warnings which those missionaries had, and disregarded. Many times had the Indians said to them " we do not wish to go to war, but if the Americans come to take away our lands, and reduce us to a state of vassalage, we will fight so long as we have a drop of blood." Yet no one more than Dr. Whitman, did everything in his power to encourage the settlement of the country. He was an enthusiast in the cause of the American occupation of Oregon; and like many another, in all the great questions of time, his enthusiasm won for him only the crown of a martyr.

Dr. White remained some time at the Dalles, on his return, endeavoring to bring the Indians into a cheerful subjection to the laws that had been given them. The success of the Doctor's labors may be pretty correctly estimated from events which will hereafter be related.

CHAPTER XXVII.

THE immigration into Oregon of the year 1843, was the first since Newell and Meek, who had brought wagons through to the Columbia River; and in all numbered nearly nine hundred men, women, and children. These immigrants were mostly from Missouri and other border States. They had been assisted on their long and perilous journey by Dr. Whitman, whose knowledge of the route, and the requirements of the undertaking, made him an invaluable counselor, as he was an untiring friend of the immigrants.

At the Dalles of the Columbia the wagons were abandoned; it being too late in the season, and the wants of the immigrants too pressing, to admit of an effort being made to cut out a wagon road through the heavy timber of the Cascade mountains. Already a trail had been made over them and around the base of Mount Hood, by which cattle could be driven from the Dalles to the settlements on the Wallamet; and by this route the cattle belonging to the train, amounting to thirteen hundred, were passed over into the valley.

But for the people, especially the women and children, active and efficient help was demanded. There was something truly touching and pitiable in the appearance of these hundreds of worn-out, ragged, sun-burnt, dusty, emaciated, yet indomitable pioneers, who, after a journey of nearly two thousand miles, and of several months duration, over fertile plains, barren deserts, and rugged mountains, stood at last beside the grand and beautiful river of their hopes, exhausted by the toils of their pilgrimage, dejected and yet rejoicing.

Much they would have liked to rest, even here; but their poverty admitted of no delay. The friends to whom they were going, and from whom they must exact and receive a temporary hospitality, were still separated from them a weary and dangerous way. They delayed as little as possible, yet the fall rains came upon them, and snow fell in the mountains, so as seriously to impede the labor of driving the cattle, and hunger and sickness began to affright them.

In this unhappy situation they might have remained a long time, had there been no better dependence than the American settlers already in the valley, with the Methodist Mission at their head; for from them it does not appear that aid came, nor that any provision had been made by them to assist the expected immigrants. As usual in these crises, it was the Hudson's Bay Company who came to the rescue, and, by the offer of boats, made it possible for those families to reach the Wallamet. Not only were the Hudson's Bay Company's boats all required, but canoes and rafts were called into requisition to transport passengers and goods. No one, never having made the voyage of the Columbia from above the Dalles to Vancouver, could have an adequate idea of the perils of the passage, as it was performed in those days, by small boats and the flat-bottomed "Mackinaw" boats of the Hudson's Bay Company. The Canadian "voyageurs," who handled a boat as a good rider governs a horse, were not always able to make the passage without accident: how, then, could the clumsy landsmen, who were more used to the feel of a plow handle than an oar, be expected to do so?

Numerous have been the victims suddenly clutched from life by the grasp of the whirlpools, or dashed to death among the fearful rapids of the beautiful, but wild and pitiless, Columbia.

The immigration of 1843 did not escape without loss and bereavement. Three brothers from Missouri, by the name of Applegate, with their families, were descending the river together, when, by the striking of a boat on a rock in the rapids, a number of passengers, mostly children of these gentlemen, were precipitated into the frightful current. The brothers each had a son in this boat, one of whom was lost, another injured for life, and the third escaped as by a miracle. This last boy was only ten years of age, yet such was the presence of mind and courage displayed in saving his own and a companion's life, that the miracle of his escape might be said to be his own. Being a good swimmer, he kept himself valiantly above the surface, while being tossed about for nearly two miles. Succeeding at last in grasping a feather bed which was floating near him, he might have passed the remaining rapids without serious danger, had he not been seized, as it were, by the feet, and drawn down, down, into a seething, turning, roaring abyss of water, where he was held, whirling about, and dancing up and down, striking now and then upon the rocks, until death seemed not only imminent but certain. After enduring this violent whirling and dashing for what seemed a hopelessly long period of time, he was suddenly vomited forth by the whirlpool once more upon the surface of the rapids, and, notwithstanding the bruises he had received, was able, by great exertion, to throw himself near, and seize upon a ledge of rocks. To this he clung with desperation, until, by dint of much effort, he finally drew himself out of the water, and stretched himself on the narrow shelf, where,

22

for a moment, he swooned away. But on opening his eyes, he beheld, struggling in the foaming flood, a young man who had been a passenger in the wrecked boat with himself, and who, though older, was not so good a swimmer. Calling to him with all his might, to make his voice heard above the roar of the rapids, he at last gained his attention, and encouraged him to try to reach the ledge of rocks, where he would assist him to climb up ; and the almost impossible feat was really accomplished by their united efforts. This done, young Applegate sank again into momentary unconsciousness, while poor exhausted Nature recruited her forces.

But, although they were saved from immediate destruction, death still stared them in the face. That side of the river on which they had found lodgment, was bounded by precipitous mountains, coming directly down to the water. They could neither ascend nor skirt along them, for foot-hold there was none. On the other side was level ground, but to reach it they must pass through the rapids —an alternative that looked like an assurance of destruction.

In this extremity, it was the boy who resolved to risk his life to save it. Seeing that a broken ledge of rock extended nearly across the river from a point within his reach, but only coming to the surface here and there, and of course very slippery, he nevertheless determined to attempt to cross on foot, amidst the roaring rapids. Starting alone to make the experiment, he actually made the crossing in safety, amid the thundering roar and dizzying rush of waters—not only made it once, but returned to assure his companion of its practicability. The young man, however, had not the courage to undertake it, until he had repeatedly been urged to do so, and at last only by being pursuaded to go before, while his younger comrade fol-

WRECKED IN THE RAPIDS.

lowed after, not to lose sight of him, (for it was impossible to turn around,) and directed him where to place his steps. In this manner that which appears incredible was accomplished, and the two arrived in safety on the opposite side, where they were ultimately discovered by their distressed relatives, who had believed them to be lost. Such was the battle which young Applegate had with the rocks, that the flesh was torn from the palms of his hands, and his whole body bruised and lacerated.

So it was with sorrow, after all, that the immigrants arrived in the valley. Nor were their trials over when they had arrived. The worst feature about this long and exhausting journey was, that it could not be accomplished so as to allow time for recruiting the strength of the travelers, and providing them with shelter before the rainy season set in. Either the new arrivals must camp out in the weather until a log house was thrown up, or they must, if they were invited, crowd into the small cabins of the settlers until there was scarce standing room, and thus live for months in an atmosphere which would have bred pestilence in any other less healthful climate.

Not only was the question of domiciles a trying one, but that of food still more so. Some, who had families of boys to help in the rough labor of building, soon became settled in houses of their own, more or less comfortable ; nor was anything very commodious required for the frontiers-men from Missouri ; but in the matter of something to eat, the more boys there were in the family, the more hopeless the situation. They had scarcely managed to bring with them provisions for their summer's journey — it was not possible to bring more. In the colony was food, but they had no money—few of them had much, at least ; they had not goods to exchange ; labor was not in demand : in short, the first winter in

Oregon was, to nearly all the new colonists, a time of
trial, if not of actual suffering. Many families now occupying positions of eminence on the Pacific coast, knew
what it was, in those early days, to feel the pangs of
hunger, and to want for a sufficient covering for their
nakedness.

Two anecdotes of this kind come to the writer's memory, as related by the parties themselves: the Indians,
who are everywhere a begging race, were in the habit of
visiting the houses of the settlers and demanding food.
On one occasion, one of them came to the house of a now
prominent citizen of Oregon, as usual petitioning for something to eat. The lady of the house, and mother of several young children, replied that she had nothing to give.
Not liking to believe her, the Indian persisted in his demand, when the lady pointed to her little children and
said, "Go away; I have nothing—not even for those."
The savage turned on his heel and strode quickly away,
as the lady thought, offended. In a short time he reap-
peared with a sack of dried venison, which he laid at her
feet. "Take that," he said, "and give the *tenas tillicum*
(little children) something to eat." From that day, as
long as he lived, that humane savage was a "friend of the
family."

The other anecdote concerns a gentleman who was
chief justice of Oregon under the provisional government, afterwards governor of California, and at present a
banker in San Francisco. He lived, at the time spoken
of, on the Tualatin Plains, and was a neighbor of Joe
Meek. Not having a house to go into at first, he was permitted to settle his family in the district school-house,
with the understanding that on certain days of the month
he was to allow religious services to be held in the building. In this he assented. Meeting day came, and the

family put on their best apparel to make themselves tidy in the eyes of their neighbors. Only one difficulty was hard to get over : Mr. ——— had only one shoe, the other foot was bare. But he considered the matter for some time, and then resolved that he might take a sheltered position behind the teacher's desk, where his deficiency would be hidden, and when the house filled up, as it would do very rapidly, he could not be expected to stir for want of space. However, that happened to the ambitious young lawyer which often does happen to the "best laid schemes of mice and men"—his went "all aglee." In the midst of the services, the speaker needed a cup of water, and requested Mr. ——— to furnish it. There was no refusing so reasonable a request. Out before all the congregation, walked the abashed and blushing pioneer, with his ill-matched feet exposed to view. This mortifying exposure was not without an agreeable result; for next day he received a present of a pair of moccasins, and was enabled thereafter to appear with feet that bore a brotherly resemblance to each other.

About this time, the same gentleman, who was, as has been said, a neighbor of Meek's, was going to Wallamet Falls with a wagon, and Meek was going along. "Take something to eat," said he to Meek, "for I have nothing;" and Meek promised that he would.

Accordingly when it came time to camp for the night, Meek was requested to produce his lunch basket. Going to the wagon, Meek unfolded an immense pumpkin, and brought it to the fire.

"What!" exclaimed Mr. ———, "is that all we have for supper?"

"Roast pumpkin is not so bad," said Meek, laughing back at him; "I've had worse fare in the mountains. It's buffalo tongue compared to ants or moccasin soles."

And so with much merriment they proceeded to cut up their pumpkin and roast it, finding it as Meek had said— "not so bad" when there was no better.

These anecdotes illustrate what a volume could only describe—the perils and privations endured by the colonists in Oregon. If we add that there were only two flouring mills in the Wallamet Valley, and these two not convenient for most of the settlers, both belonging to the mission, and that to get a few bushels of wheat ground involved the taking of a journey of from four to six days, for many, and that, too, over half-broken roads, destitute of bridges, it will be seen how difficult it was to obtain the commonest comforts of life. As for such luxuries as groceries and clothing, they had to wait for better times. Lucky was the man who, "by hook or by crook," got hold of an order on the Hudson's Bay Company, the Methodist Mission, or the Milling Company at the Falls. Were he thus fortunate, he had much ado to decide how to make it go farthest, and obtain the most. Not far would it go, at the best, for fifty per cent. profit on all sales was what was demanded and obtained. Perhaps the holder of a ten dollar draft made out his list of necessaries, and presented himself at the store, expecting to get them. He wanted some unbleached cotton, to be dyed to make dresses for the children; he would buy a pair of calf-skin shoes if he could afford them; and—yes—he would indulge in the luxury of a little—a very little— sugar, just for that once!

Arrived at the store after a long, jolting journey, in the farm wagon which had crossed the continent the year before, he makes his inquiries: "Cotton goods?" "No; just out." "Shoes?" "Got one pair, rather small— wouldn't fit you." "What have you got in the way of goods?" "Got a lot of silk handkerchiefs and twelve dozen straw hats." "Any pins?" "No; a few knitting needles." "Any yarn?" "Yes, there's a pretty good lot of yarn, but don't you want some sugar? the last ship that was in left a quantity of sugar." So the holder of the draft exchanges it for some yarn and a few nails, and takes the balance in sugar: fairly compelled to be luxurious in one article, for the reason that others were not to be had till some other ship came in.

No mails reached the colony, and no letters left it, except such as were carried by private hand, or were sent once a year in the Hudson's Bay Company's express to Canada, and thence to the States. Newspapers arrived in the same manner, or by vessel from the Sandwich Islands. Notwithstanding all these drawbacks, education was encouraged even from the very beginning; a library was started, and literary societies formed, and this all the more, perhaps, that the colony was so isolated and dependent on itself for intellectual pleasures. Such was the state of the colony when the Indian Agent returned from the upper country, when the Provisional Government was formed, and when the emigration arrived at the close of 1843.

The spring of 1844 saw the colony in a state of some excitement on account of an attempt to introduce the manufacture of ardent spirits. This dangerous article had always been carefully excluded from the country, first by the Hudson's Bay Company, and secondly by the Methodist Mission; and since the time when Ewing Young had been induced to relinquish its manufacture, no serious effort had been made to introduce it.

It does not appear from the Oregon archives, that any law against its manufacture existed at that time: it had probably been overlooked in the proceedings of the legislative committee of the previous summer; neither was there yet any executive head to the Provisional Government, the election not having taken place. In this dilemma the people found themselves in the month of February, when one James Conner had been discovered to be erecting a distillery at the Falls of the Wallamet.

Now when Dr. White had so speedily returned from the States, whither he had as speedily gone, after a few months residence in Oregon, and a quarrel with the mission to which he was surgeon—with a commission from the United States which he wished to construe as conferring on him the authority of governor of the colony, his pretentions were regarded as insufferable, and he was given to understand that he would do well to confine himself to his duties as Indian agent. There was a great deal that was absurd about the whole matter, and the United States had as little right to appoint an Indian agent as a governor—neither being consistent with the terms of the treaty of joint occupation. But it was not that question which the settlers regarded; they were willing enough to acknowledge the authority of the United States to do anything; and were constantly petitioning the government to do those things which threatened to involve the country in war; in which case they would doubtless have been immediately exterminated; for it only required a hint to the Indians that the " King George men " and the "Bostons" were at war, to bring them down upon the settlers in one fell swoop.

What the colonists, and especially the mission, did not like about the matter, was Dr. White himself. They would have been glad enough to have had a governor appointed; but there were other men in and out of the mission, more pleasing to them than the Doctor for governor; and perhaps the most pleasing man of all to each one, was himself. But as they could not all be governors, it was decided at the meeting in the previous July that a trinity of governors would answer their purpose, and divide the honors.

It happened, however, that an occasion for the exercise of executive power had occurred before the election of the executive committee, and now what was to be done? It was a case too, which required absolute power, for there was no law on the subject of distilleries. After some deliberation it was decided to allow the Indian agent temporary power, and several letters were addressed to him, informing him of the calamity which threatened the community at the Falls. "Now, we believe that if there is anything which calls your attention in your official capacity, or anything in which you would be most cordially supported by the good sense and prompt action of the better part of community, it is the present case. We do not wish to dictate, but we hope for the best, begging pardon for intrusions." So read the closing paragraph of one of the letters.

Perhaps this humble petition touched the Doctor's heart; perhaps he saw in the circumstance a possible means of acquiring influence; at all events he hastened to the Falls, a distance of fifty miles, and entered at once upon the discharge of the executive duties thus thrust upon him in the hour of danger. Calling upon Meek, who had entered upon his duties as sheriff the previous summer, he gave him his orders. Writ in hand, Meek proceeded to the distillery, frightened the poor sinner into quiet submission with a display of his mountain manners; made a bugle of the worm, and blew it, to announce to the Doctor his complete success; after which he tumbled the distillery apparatus into the river, and retired. Connor was put under three hundred dollar bonds, and so the case ended.

But there were other occasions on which the Doctor's

authority was put in requisition. It happened that a vessel from Australia had been in the river, and left one Madam Cooper, who was said to have brought with her a barrel of whisky. Her cabin stood on the east bank of the Wallamet, opposite the present city of Portland. Not thinking it necessary to send the sheriff to deal with a woman, the Doctor went in person, accompanied by a couple of men. Entering the cabin the Doctor remarked blandly, " you have a barrel of whisky, I believe."

Not knowing but her visitor's intention was to purchase, and not having previously resided in a strictly temperance community, Madam Cooper replied frankly that she had, and pointed to the barrel in question.

The Doctor then stepped forward, and placing his foot on it, said "In the name of the United States, I levy execution on it!"

At this unexpected declaration, the English woman stared wildly one moment, then recovering herself quickly, seized the poker from the chimney corner, and raising it over the Doctor's head, exclaimed—" In the name of Great Britain, Ireland, and Scotland, I levy execution on you!"

But when the stick descended, the Doctor was not there. He had backed out at the cabin door; nor did he afterwards attempt to interfere with a subject of the crown of Great Britain.

On the following day, however, the story having got afloat at the Falls, Meek and a young man highly esteemed at the mission, by the name of Le Breton, set out to pay their respects to Madam Cooper. Upon entering the cabin, the two callers cast their eyes about until they rested on the whisky barrel.

"Have *you* come to levy on my whisky?" inquired the now suspicious Madam.

"Yes," said Meek, "I have come to levy on it; but as
I am not quite so high in authority as Doctor White, I
don't intend to levy on the whole of it at once. I think
about a quart of it will do me."

Comprehending by the twinkle in Meek's eye that she
had now a customer more to her mind, Madam Cooper
made haste to set before her visitors a bottle and tin cup,
upon which invitation they proceded to levy frequently
upon the contents of the bottle; and we fear that the
length of time spent there, and the amount of whisky
drank must have strongly reminded Meek of past rendezvous times in the mountains; nor can we doubt that he
entertained Le Breton and Madam Cooper with many reminiscences of those times. However that may be, this
was not the last visit of Meek to Madam Cooper's, nor his
last levy on her whisky.

The sheriff, despite his natural antagonism to what is
usually denominated the better portion of the community,"
or putting it more correctly, despite their antagonism to
him, on account of his mountain ways and Indian wife,
was becoming a man of note amongst them. They might
denominate him amongst themselves as "old Joe Meek"
at thirty-four years of age, because he cared nothing whatever for their pious prejudices, and broke through their
solemn prohibitions as if they had been ropes of sand;
yet when courage and firmness were required to get them
out of a difficulty, they appealed deferentially enough to
"Mr. Meek."

Shortly after his election as sheriff he had been called
upon to serve a writ upon a desperate character, for an
attempt to kill. Many persons, however, fearing the result of trying to enforce the law upon desperadoes, in the
then defenceless condition of the colony, advised him to
wait for the immigration to come in before attempting the

arrest. But Meek preferred to do his duty then, and went with the writ to arrest him. The man resisted, making an attack on the sheriff with a carpenter's axe; but Meek coolly presented a pistol, assuring the culprit of the uselessness of such demonstrations, and soon brought him to terms of compliance. Such coolness, united with a fine physique, and a mountain-man's reputation for reckless courage, made it very desirable that Meek should continue to hold the office of sheriff during that stage of the colony's development.

CHAPTER XXVIII.

1844. As has before been mentioned, the Indians of the Wallamet valley were by no means so formidable as those of the upper country: yet considering their numbers and the condition of the settlers, they were quite formidable enough to occasion considerable alarm when any one of them, or any number of them betrayed the savage passions by which they were temporarily overcome. Considerable excitement had prevailed among the more scattered settlers, ever since the reports of the disaffection among the up-country tribes had reached them; and Dr. White had been importuned to throw up a strong fortification in the most central part of the colony, and to procure arms for their defence, at the expense of the United States.

This excitement had somewhat subsided when an event occurred which for a time renewed it: a house was plundered and some horses stolen from the neighborhood of the Falls. An Indian from the Dalles, named Cockstock, was at the bottom of the mischief, and had been committing or instigating others to commit depredations upon the settlers, for a year previous, because he had been, as he fancied, badly treated in a matter between himself and a negro in the colony, in which the latter had taken an unfair advantage of him in a bargain.

To crown his injuries Dr. White had caused a relative of his to be flogged by the Dalles chief, for entering the house of the Methodist missionary at that place, and tying him, with the purpose of flogging him. (It was a poor law, he thought, that would not work both ways.)

In revenge for this insult Cockstock came to the Doctor's house in the Wallamet, threatening to shoot him at sight, but not finding him at home, contented himself for that time, by smashing all the windows in the dwelling and office of the Doctor, and nearly frightening to death a young man on the premises.

When on the Doctor's return in the evening, the extent of the outrage became known, a party set out in pursuit of Cockstock and his band, but failed to overtake them, and the settlers remained in ignorance concerning the identity of the marauders. About a month later, however, a party of Klamath and Molalla Indians from the south of Oregon, numbering fifteen, came riding into the settlement, armed and painted in true Indian war-style. They made their way to the lodge of a Calapooya chief in the neighborhood—the Calapooyas being the Indians native to the valley. Dr. White fearing these mischievous visitors might infect the mind of the Calapooya chief, sent a message to him, to bring his friends to call upon him in the morning, as he had something good to say to them.

This they did, when Dr. White explained the laws of the Nez Perces to them, and told them how much it would be to their advantage to adopt such laws. He gave the Calapooya chief a fine fat ox to feast his friends with, well knowing that an Indian's humor depends much on the state of his stomach, whether shrunken or distended. After the feast there was some more talk about the laws, in the midst of which the Indian Cockstock made his appearance, armed, and sullen in his demeanor. But as Dr. White did not know him for the perpetrator of the outrage on his premises, he took no notice of him more than of the others. The Molallas and Klamaths finally agreed to receive the laws; departing in high good humor, singing and shouting. So little may one know of the savage heart from the savage professions! Some of these Indians were boiling over with secret wrath at the weakness of their brethren in consenting to laws of the Agent's dictation; and while they were crossing a stream, fell upon and massacred them without mercy, Cockstock taking an active part in the murder.

The whites were naturally much excited by the villianous and horrible affray, and were for taking and hanging the murderers. The Agent, however, was more cautious, and learning that there had been feuds among these Indians long unsettled, decided not to interfere.

In February, 1844, fresh outrages on settlers having been committed so that some were leaving their claims and coming to stop at the Falls through fear, Dr. White was petitioned to take the case in hand. He accordingly raised a party of ten men, who had nearly all suffered some loss or outrage at Cockstock's hands, and set out in search of him, but did not succeed in finding him. His next step was to offer a reward of a hundred dollars for his arrest, meaning to send him to the upper country to be tried and punished by the Cayuses and Nez Perces, the Doctor prudently desiring to have them bear the odium, and suffer the punishment, should any follow, of executing justice on the Indian desperado. Not so had the fates ordained.

About a week after the reward was offered, Cockstock came riding into the settlement at the Falls, at mid-day, accompanied by five other Indians, all well armed, and frightfully painted. Going from house to house on their horses, they exhibited their pistols, and by look and gesture seemed to defy the settlers, who, however, kept quiet through prudential motives. Not succeeding in provoking the whites to commence the fray, Cockstock finally retired to an Indian village on the other side of the river, where he labored to get up an insurrection, and procure the burning of the settlement houses.

Meantime the people at the Falls were thoroughly alarmed, and bent upon the capture of this desperate savage. When, after an absence of a few hours, they saw him recrossing the river with his party, a crowd of persons ran down to the landing, some with offers of large reward to any person who would attempt to take him, while others, more courageous, were determined upon earning it. No definite plan of capture or concert of action was decided on, but all was confusion and doubt. In this frame of mind a collision was sure to take place; both the whites and Indians firing at the moment of landing. Mr. LeBreton, the young man mentioned in the previous chapter, after firing ineffectually, rushed unarmed upon Cockstock, whose pistol was also empty, but who still had his knife. In the struggle both fell to the ground, when a mulatto man, who had wrongs of his own to avenge, ran up and struck Cockstock a blow on the head with the butt of his gun which dispatched him at once.

Thus the colony was rid of a scourge, yet not without loss which counterbalanced the gain. Young LeBreton besides having his arm shattered by a ball, was wounded by a poisoned arrow, which occasioned his death; and Mr. Rogers, another esteemed citizen, died from the same cause; while a third was seriously injured by a slight wound from a poisoned arrow. As for the five friends of Cockstock, they escaped to the bluffs overlooking the settlement, and commenced firing down upon the people. But fire-arms were mustered sufficient to dislodge them, and thus the affair ended; except that the Agent had some trouble to settle it with the Dalles Indians, who came down in a body to demand payment for the loss of their brother. After much talk and explanation, a present to the widow of the dead Indian was made to smooth over the difficulty.

Meek, who at the time of the collision was rafting timber for Dr. McLaughlin's mill at the Falls, as might have been expected was appealed to in the melee by citizens who knew less about Indian fighting.

A prominent citizen and merchant, who probably seldom spoke *of* him as Mr. Meek, came running to him in great affright:—"Mr. Meek! Mr. Meek! Mr. Meek!—I want to send my wife down to Vancouver. Can you assist me? Do you think the Indians will take the town?"

" It 'pears like half-a-dozen Injuns might do it," retorted Meek, going on with his work.

"What do you think we had better do, Mr. Meek?—What do you advise?"

"I think *you'd* better RUN."

In all difficulties between the Indians and settlers, Meek usually refrained from taking sides—especially from taking sides against the Indians. For Indian slayer as he had once been when a ranger of the mountains, he had too much compassion for the poor wretches in the Wallamet Valley, as well as too much knowledge of the savage nature, to like to make unnecessary war upon them. Had he been sent to take Cockstock, very probably he would have done it with little uproar; for he had sufficient influence among the Calapooyas to have enlisted them in the undertaking. But this was the Agent's business and he let him manage it; for Meek and the Doctor were not in love with one another; one was solemnly audacious, the other mischievously so. Of the latter sort of audacity,

23

here is an example. Meek wanted a horse to ride out to the Plains where his family were, and not knowing how else to obtain it, helped himself to one belonging to Dr. White; which presumption greatly incensed the Doctor, and caused him to threaten various punishments, hanging among the rest. But the Indians overhearing him replied,

" *Wake nika cumtux*—You dare not.—You no put rope round Meek's neck. He *tyee* (chief)—no hang him."

Upon which the Doctor thought better of it, and having vented his solemn audacity, received smiling audacity with apparent good humor when he came to restore the borrowed horse.

While Indian affairs occupied so much of the attention of the colony, other topics of interest were not overlooked, and colonial politics were as jealously guarded as ever by the American party. The unique form of government hit upon by the genius of the American people, which consisted of a legislative committe who might frame laws for the people to vote upon at the ensuing election, and an executive committee, equally under the control of the people, promised to prove a success. However, that passion by which " the angels fell," did not sleep in Oregon more than in other portions of the globe, and there were those in the legislative committee for 1844, and in the executive committee also, who were revolving in their minds the question of an independent government; that is, a government owning no allegiance either to the United States or Great Britain, but which should lay the foundations of empire on the Pacific coast.

The first message of the executive committee recommended the vesting of the executive power in a single individual, the appointment of several judges, and a general amendment of the organization with a view to increasing its strength. It was also decided this year to increase the legislative committee, so that it should number no less than thirteen, nor more than sixty members. An assessor was appointed as a preliminary measure to imposing taxes: an act passed to exclude slavery from Oregon, and also an act to prevent the manufacture or sale of intoxicating drinks. On the two latter acts the people were generally very well agreed, seeing that temperance was necessary to the preservation of the colony; and the majority favoring the exclusion of negroes from Oregon. That there should have been so general a sentiment against the introduction of blacks seems rather remarkable, when it is remembered that a large proportion of the settlers were from the border slave states. Perhaps, having experienced the disadvantages of being "poor whites" in a slave-holding community, and being without the means of procuring slaves, they resolved to prevent any future influx of slave-holders, who should reduce them to the condition of "poor whites" in the country of their adoption. So fearful were they that the negro element might be introduced into their social and political affairs that it was made an offence even for a free negro to be found in the territory, for which offence he was ordered to be sold to the lowest bidder, who was obligated to send the unfortunate black out of the territory, as soon as he had paid himself for the expense of doing so, out of his services.

But on the matter of taxes the people were not so well agreed, the general determination being, however, to pay the expenses of the government only by subscription, as agreed to by a vote of the people the previous year.

The American settlers were averse to being taxed for the support of a government which might become a burden to them in this way; and the most politic of the politicians in the American party feared that by taxing the people they should alarm the Canadians, whom they had again invited to join the organization. As there were dissenters among the voters, there were also two parties in the legislature on this subject.

However, an issue was started this year in the legislature, which governed the election of the next year's legislature. Its purpose was pretty clearly shadowed forth in the following paragraph from the message of the executive committee:

"And we sincerely hope that Oregon, by the special aid of Divine Providence, may set an unprecedented example to the world, of industry, morality, and virtue. And, although we may now be unknown as a state *or power*, yet we have the advantages by united efforts of our increasing population, in a diligent attention to agriculture, arts, and literature, of attaining, at no distant day, to as conspicuous an elevation as any state *or power* on the continent of America."

This feeler put forth by the executive committee, one of whom was the candidate for Governor, of the Independent party, while it struck a responsive chord in the hearts of a portion of the legislative committee, had the effect to alarm the patriotism of the loyal American; an alarm which spread, and which expressed itself in the choice of the legislature of 1845, as well as in the choice of a governor, defeating entirely the hopes and designs of the would-be founders of an Independent Government.

CHAPTER XXIX.

1842–4. In all the movements which had been made by either party in Oregon the Hudson's Bay Company had not been lost sight of. Each one had something to gain or lose by the approval or disapproval of that company. A few individuals, however, belonging to the mission, under the pretence of taking care of the rights of American citizens, made continual war on Dr. McLaughlin as the representative of the Company, and scrupled not to set his rights at defiance.

The Rev. Father Waller, who had in 1840 obtained the Doctor's permission to build a mission school and storehouse on the land claimed by him since 1830, found so many points of merit in the situation of the land that he resolved to set up a counter claim, and hold it by possession. The first intimation that the Doctor had of such an intention was in 1842, when a rumor of that kind was afloat. On inquiring of the superintendent of the mission concerning the truth of the matter, he was told that Mr. Waller denied setting up any claim to the land. Yet when the Doctor, a few days later wished to give a lot to a settler, Mr. Waller would not allow it to be given away, saying he was "very much obliged to Dr. McLaughlin for disposing of *his* property." Then commenced a tedious and irritating struggle with the Reverend claim-jumper. On appealing to the superintendent a second time the Doctor was informed that Mr. Lee had "understood Mr.

Waller to say that he had set up no claim in opposition to the Doctor's, but that if the Doctor's claim failed, *and the mission did not put in a claim*, he (Waller) considered that he had a better right than any other man, and should secure the title if· he could." It was evident from this admission that Mr. Waller expected that the mission would put in a claim, failing to do which he should do so for himself.

Again, Mr. Lee informed the Doctor that "a citizen of the United States, by becoming a missionary. did not renounce any civil or political rights," therefore he could not control his associates in such matters. Upon which information, Dr. McLaughlin called upon Mr. Waller in order to seek an adjustment of the difficulty. In the interview which followed, Mr. Waller again by implication denied his intention to wrong the Doctor, and agreed that if he were allowed to retain possession of that portion of the Doctor's land which he had cleared and improved, he would give in exchange for it an equal amount of land out of his claim which adjoined the Doctor's. To this Dr. McLaughlin consented, and sent a man to survey and measure the lots which Mr. Waller had improved, or given away to his friends, in order to mark out an equal portion for himself on that portion of Waller's claim adjoining his. But no sooner had he done this than Mr. Waller declared that he would not consent to the arrangement, saying, "keep you yours, I will keep mine;" a mode of settlement most agreeable to the Doctor, only that while Mr. Waller kept his own, he kept the Doctor's also.

A few months later there came to the Falls a lawyer, who was on his way to the Sandwich Islands, a Mr. Ricord. This gentleman, in a conversation with Mr. McLaughlin, gave it as his opinion that the Doctor could not hold his claim at the Falls, because he was a British subject. Here then, was another and an unexpected bar to his rights, and the Doctor was fain to offer Mr. Ricord a fee if he could show him any way by which he *could* hold his claim. This proposition after some deliberation, and consultation with the mission gentlemen, was entertained on the following terms: That the Doctor was to relinquish his claim to an island in the river whereon the mission had erected a gristmill, that Mr. Waller was to retain two lots on the town site of Oregon City, already occupied by him, and other lots besides, to the amount of five acres, to be chosen by himself: that Rev. Jason Lee should be in like manner secured in regard to certain town lots, in behalf of the Methodist mission, and that for his services in bringing about this exceedingly just and equitable arrangement, and giving his advice, Mr. Ricord was to receive the sum of three hundred pounds sterling. To such a proposition the Doctor declined to give his assent, and the matter rested for a time.

However, before Mr. Ricord left the colony, which he did on one of the Company's vessels, another conversation was had with him, and also with Mr. Lee, in which the Doctor submitted another proposition, in which he offered the mission two lots for a church, two lots for the clergyman, two lots 'for the school-house, and two lots for the school-master; said lots to be taken out of a specified portion of the town site. He also offered to pay for the building occupied by Mr. Abernethy, a member of the mission, and subsequently Governor of the colony, but not for that portion of Mr. Waller's house which had been built out of his own squared timbers, lent for that purpose and never returned or paid for, but for all other improvements which had been made on those lots which he wanted for business purposes.

He further offered to let the milling company go on as they

were doing, until the boundary line was settled, when, if his claim was admitted, he would pay them for the work done and the fair value of the mill as decided by arbitrators. To this proposition Mr. Lee and Mr. Ricord gave their approval, expressing their sense of the Doctor's fairness and generosity. As Mr. Lee was about to set out for Washington, he requested the Doctor to leave the mission in possession until his return, which was agreed to without suspicion.

Nearly four months subsequently, Mr McLaughlin was presented with a copy of a caveat, made out against him three days previous to the last mentioned conversation, the original of which was in the pocket of one of these gentlemen at the very moment they were expressing their sense of his generosity, and asking for a little time before disturbing the mission, and which ran as follows:

" You will please to take notice that my client, Mr. A. F. Waller, has taken formal measures at Washington to substantiate his claim as a preëmptor and actual settler upon the tract of land, sometimes called the Wallamet Falls settlement and sometimes Oregon City, comprising six hundred and forty acres ; and being aware that, although a foreigner, you claim to exercise acts of ownership over said land, this notice is given to apprise you that all sales you may make of lots or other subdivisions of said farm, after the receipt hereof, will be regarded by my client, and by the government, as absolutely fraudulent, and will be made at your peril.   Then followed the grounds upon which the Doctor's claim was denied. *First*, that he was an alien ; *Secondly*, that he was the chief of a foreign corporate monopoly ; *Thirdly*, that he had not resided upon the land in question for a year previous ; *Fourthly*, that he did not hold the land for himself but the company ; *Fifthly*, that his claim, if he had any, arose two years subsequent to Mr. Waller's settlement thereon.   This flattering document closed with Mr. Ricord's regrets that he had " failed to make an amicable compromise " of the matter between the Doctor and his client, and also that his " client had been driven to the vexatious proceedings of the law, in order to establish his rights as an American citizen."

Poor old long-suffering Dr. McLaughlin ! it would hardly have been strange had he hated the name of an "American citizen," so often was it assumed only to give countenance to the greatest abuses. At the time, too, that it was so frequently used and abused, there was only a suppositious right to the soil on the side of the Americans, and a British citizen had quite as many rights really as an American. Besides, Mr. Linn's bill, which was the foundation of the colony's assumptions, made no distinction between people of any nationality but provided that every white male citizen might claim six hundred and forty acres of land. Nor had the colonists ever thought of interfering with the Canadians who were settled upon farms in the Wallamet. It was only Dr. McLaughlin, and the gentlemen of the Hudson's Bay Company who were so obnoxious to a portion of the Americans.

We think it was about this time that Meek once surprised the Doctor at his devotions, in his office, where he was probably praying for patience. However that was, Meek was coming in at the door, but seeing the Doctor on his knees, praying and crossing himself—for he was a good Catholic—he paused to await the conclusion. On rising, the Doctor glanced round, and met the mirthful look of the irreverent Joe.

"Oh, Mr. Jo! Mr. Jo! the devil, the devil!" cried the Doctor, greatly surprised at the intrusion, and giving vent to those rapid ejaculations which always escaped him when annoyed. Then immediately repenting of his haste in giving way to his irritability, he exclaimed in the next breath "God forgive me, God forgive me!" rubbing his stomach with a little rapid movement peculiar to him; his fine honest Scotch face flushing in contrast to the long white hair which imparted such distinction to his appearance.

But to finish the story of the Oregon City claim. In April of 1844, Doctor McLaughlin consented that Doctor White should speak to Mr. Waller about the matter, and find whether or not it could be adjusted, because all this discussion was producing delays ruinous to the business of Dr. McLaughlin. It was at last determined to leave the settlement to arbitrators, and Mr. James Douglas, a Chief Factor and associate of the Doctor's, Mr. Gilpin, and Dr. White, were chosen to act for Dr. McLaughlin. The terms exacted by Mr. Waller were five acres and five hundred dollars to himself, and fourteen lots to the Methodist mission. To the credit of the two Americans chosen, be it said, that they opposed this exorbitant demand; and were only persuaded to accede to it by Mr. Douglas.

When the terms were made known to the Doctor, he exclaimed to his arbitrators all, "Gentlemen, you have bound me;" but Mr. Gilpin instantly disavowed having a hand in the arrangement. Then said the Doctor to Mr. Douglas, "This is your doings!"

"Yes," answered Douglas, who felt how much the constant jarring had annoyed his chief, "I thought it best for your sake to give you one good fever, and have done with it. I have acceded to the terms and signed the papers."

Unfortunately for Mr. Douglas' intentions, this was not the last 'good fever' into which the Methodist mission was to throw the Doctor. Not two months after the settlement was made, it was resolved to dissolve the mission; and in July Mr. Gary, the new superintendent, began to sell the mission property. Knowing that the lots they held were particularly desirable to Dr. McLaughlin for his own use, Mr. Gary called on him in company with Mr. Hines and one other gentleman of the mission, and offered to sell them back to him for the sum of six thousand dollars, with the improvements; reserving, however, two lots for the church, all the fruit trees, and garden vegetables then growing, and the use of the warehouse for one year.

In vain the Doctor remonstrated against the valuation put upon the property, and against being made to pay one hundred dollars for Mr. Waller's old house built with timber borrowed from himself; no other terms would the mission consent to. At last, wearied out with contention, and needing them for his own business, Dr. McLaughlin agreed to give them their price for his lots, as he had just before given them the lots.

Thus, with much cost and annoyance, the question of ownership in Oregon City was settled; and after some solicitation the legislative committee passed an incorporation act recognizing its right to be called a town. The island on which the milling company had their grist mill, which had once formed a part of the Doctor's claim, still remained in the hands of the company, more than three-fourths of whom were members of the mission.

But the end was not yet, and we do not choose to anticipate. It is enough to say here, that from this time on, for a period of four years, Dr. McLaughlin was permitted to pursue his business at Oregon City, or Wallamet Falls as it has heretofore been called, without any serious interruption.

The mission party were still opposed to anything which the Hudson's Bay Company might do, thus compelling them to form a party by themselves, between whom and the mission party stood the American party, made up of the more liberal-minded settlers, the late immigrants, and the greater number of the mountain-men. In each of the colonial parties, mission and American, were a few independent individuals, who were friendly to, or at enmity with the Hudson's Bay Company, without consulting party feeling at all. So strong was the prejudice, however, which the mission party, and a few individuals of the American party, indulged towards the Hudson's Bay Company, and

Dr. McLaughlin in particular, that there had always been much uneasiness felt at Vancouver concerning the safety of the fort.

There had been, from the first of the American settlement, some lawless and desperate characters in the country, coming either from California, the mountains, or from trading vessels visiting the Columbia. These persons belonged to no party, nor had any association with the actual settlers. They were frowned down by all good citizens alike. Yet this class of persons invariably took the tone of extravagant Americanism, and refused to be snubbed by the Hudson's Bay Company, whatever slights they were compelled to bear from any other quarter. Many were the threats which had been made against the Hudson's Bay Company's property at Vancouver; and serious, at times, were Dr. McLaughlin's apprehensions lest he should not be able to protect it. While the colonists, in 1843, were memorializing Congress that they were in fear and danger from the Indians and the Hudson's Bay Company, Dr. McLaughlin was writing to the Directors of that Company, that he was in fear of the colonists.

He explained the position of affairs in this wise : there were large numbers of immigrants coming into the territory from that portion of the United States most hostile in feeling to British interests, which hostility was greatly excited by the perusal of Irving's Astoria, and the published letters of Kelly and Spaulding, which represented the Company's conduct in the falsest colors. These immigrants had received such an impression, that they really feared the Company might set the Indians on them, and although they now knew better, it was hard overcoming such prejudices ; besides, there were always some who were ready to avail themselves of the prejudices of others to get up an issue. Threats had been uttered against Vancouver, and really the people were encouraged to make an attack, by the public prints in the United States stating that British subjects ought not to be allowed to remain in Oregon. There was no dependence in the common men about the fort to do sentry duty beyond a few nights, nor were there officers enough to be put upon guard without deranging the whole business of the department. To burn the fort would be an easy matter enough in the dry season, everything about it being of combustible material. And so the Doctor asked that a government vessel be sent to protect Fort Vancouver. No answer, however, had come to this demand up to the month of June, 1845.

We have seen how, with affairs in this condition at Vancouver, and with the settled hostility of the Mission party against Dr. McLaughlin, the peace was yet maintained by the constant and unremitting kindness of the Doctor towards the American settlers. He had for some time, in his own mind, yielded the question of the future sovereignty of the country. That the Americans would hold all of Oregon south of the Columbia was beyond a peradventure; how much more, it remained for the heads of government to decide. The only question was, how to keep at peace with them until the boundary should be agreed upon; and how to maintain his own rights in Oregon, as a citizen, until the charter of the Company should expire, leaving him free to choose whether he would be an American or a British subject.

CHAPTER XXX.

1845. The pressure of all these circumstances induced Dr. McLaughlin to consider whether it were not best to unite with the American Organization. It was true the Hudson's Bay Company's charter provided for the government of its employes. But it had no authority over Americans, and if a desperado calling himself an American citizen chose to destroy the Company's property, as was continually threatened, he could do so with impunity, so far as the Company's power to punish was concerned.

There were a few men in the Wallamet colony with whom Dr. McLaughlin was somewhat confidential, and to whom he had spoken of his difficulties. Some of these were members of the legislature, and determined to use their influence to remove the chief obstacle to the Doctor's co-operation with the Provisional Government. Accordingly when the legislature convened in the summer of 1845, the form of the oath of membership was so altered as to bind the person taking it to support the Organic Laws only "so far as they were consistent with their duties as citizens of the United States, *or subjects of Great Britain.*"

The Doctor understood this alteration in the form of the oath as an invitation to him to join the organization in behalf of the Hudson's Bay Company, and a letter to him from the gentlemen in the legislature confirmed him in this belief. Convinced that it was the best thing to do, for the peace and security of all concerned, the Doctor, after consulting with his associate, Mr., now Sir James Douglas, became a member of the colonial organization. Now, certainly, it would seem, he might set his mind at rest, since all the people in the country were acting together under one government, which interfered with the allegiance of no one. The Canadians had already united with the Americans, leaving no outsiders except the Indians; the organization itself had been re-modeled and strengthened, the colony had a regular legislature with the full powers usual to such bodies, and had a governor, also clothed with the gubernatorial authority common to that office in the United States.

But just when Dr. McLaughlin was settling down to a somewhat composed state of mind, in view of all the amendments above mentioned, there suddenly appeared at Fort Vancouver two visitors—gentlemen of position—government officers on leave, which perhaps meant in this instance on a secret service. These two gentlemen were Lieut. Peel and Captain Park, and they brought a letter to Dr. McLaughlin from Captain Gordon, of Her Majesty's ship *America*, then in Puget Sound, and this letter was to inform him that the *America* had been sent by Admiral Seymour "to assure Her Majesty's subjects in the country of firm protection."

After the struggle seemed almost over, and light began to dawn on the vexed question of conflicting duties, too late to be of any real service, but seeming rather to be in danger of exciting fresh suspicion, the long-waited-for help had come at last. Dr. McLaughlin had plenty of reason to wish his visitors had staid away, both then and afterwards; so evident was it that their business in Oregon was that of spies—spies upon himself, as well as upon the Americans. What their report was, can only be guessed at. Certain it is, however, that the Doctor was called upon

for explanations with regard to his acts encouraging
American settlement, and his reasons for joining the American colonial organization, and that he fell under the Company's censure for the same—the misunderstanding ending
in his resignation.

Lieut. Peel and Captain Park made their visit to Vancouver agreeable to themselves, as well as serviceable to
their Government. They partook not only of the hospitality of the fort, but visited also among the American settlers, taking "pot-luck," and sleeping in a cabin loft, with
great good humor. If they sometimes displayed a little
native snobbishness toward the frontiersmen, it is not to be
wondered at.

As our friend Meek was sure to be found wherever there
was anything novel or exciting transpiring, so he was sure
to fall in with visitors so distinguished as these, and as
ready to answer their questions as they were to ask them.
The conversation chanced one day to run upon the changes
that had taken place in the country since the earliest settlement by the Americans, and Meek, who felt an honest
pride in them, was expatiating at some length, to the ill-
concealed amusement of the young officers, who probably
saw nothing to admire in the rude improvements of the
Oregon pioneers.

"Mr. Meek," said one of them, "if you have been so
long in the country and have witnessed such wonderful
transformations, doubtless you may have observed equally
great ones in nature; in the rivers and mountains, for instance?"

Meek gave a lightning glance at the speaker who had so
mistaken his respondent:

"I reckon I have," said he slowly. Then waving his
hand gracefully toward the majestic Mt. Hood, towering
thousands of feet above the summit of the Cascade range,

and white with everlasting snows: "When *I* came to this country, Mount Hood was *a hole in the ground!*"

It is hardly necessary to say that the conversation terminated abruptly, amid the universal cachinations of the bystanders.

Notwithstanding the slighting views of Her British Majesty's naval officers, the young colony was making rapid strides. The population had been increased nearly eight hundred by the immigration of 1844, so that now it numbered nearly two thousand. Grain had been raised in considerable quantities, cattle and hogs had multiplied, and the farmers were in the best of spirits. Even our hero, who hated farm labor, began to entertain faith in the resources of his land claim to make him rich.

Such was the promising condition of the colony in the summer of 1845. Much of the real prosperity of the settlers was due to the determination of the majority to exclude ardent spirits and all intoxicating drinks from the country. So well had they succeeded that a gentleman writing of the colony at that time, says: "I attended the last term of the circuit courts in most of the counties, and I found great respect shown to judicial authority everywhere; nor did I see a single *drunken juryman, nor witness, nor spectator.* So much industry, good order, and sobriety I have never seen in any community."

While this was the rule, there were exceptions to it. During the spring term of the Circuit Court, Judge Nesmith being on the bench, a prisoner was arraigned before him for "assault with intent to kill." The witness for the prosecution was called, and was proceeding to give evidence, when, at some statement of his, the prisoner vociferated that he was a "d——d liar," and quickly stripping off his coat demanded a chance to fight it out with the witness.

24

Judge Nesmith called for the interference of Meek, who had been made marshal, but just at that moment he was not to be found. Coming into the room a moment later, Meek saw the Judge down from his bench, holding the prisoner by the collar.

"You can imagine," says Meek, " the bustle in court. But the Judge had the best of it. He fined the rascal, and made him pay it on the spot ; while I just stood back to see his honor handle him. That was fun for me."

Such, however, was the good order of the colony at this time, that it was thought important to memorialize Congress on the condition and prospects of Oregon—to remind the Government of the precarious situation of its expectant children, should either the Indians or the Hudson's Bay Company make war on them ; but most important of all, to beseech the United States to put an end to the treaty of joint occupation before the expiration of the ten years now nearly concluded.

The memorial being prepared, together with a copy of the Organic Laws, and explanations and assurances to the Government that they were only adopted through necessity, these documents were signed by the members of the House of Representatives and delivered to Dr. White, who was about to leave for the States, to settle up his accounts at Washington.

Connected with this very proper and dignified proceeding, was another not strictly dignified, but on the contrary partaking largely of the ridiculous. It appeared that, although the Speaker of the House opposed the Organic Law, as recently adopted, under the impression it was his duty, he had appended his name to the copy to be transmitted to the Government, and also the resolutions of the House accompanying them. Dr. White was already on his way to Vancouver with the dispatches, when the discovery of this great misdemeanor was made known to the assembly. Immediately thereupon the Speaker was granted leave of absence, to follow and overtake Dr. White, and to erase his name from said documents. Other resolutions were passed, ordering a messenger to be des: patched to bring back the documents, and also others not by any means complimentary to Dr. White.

A day or two later, the following note was received from Dr. White:

"August 17, 1845.

To the Honorable, &c.;

GENTLEMEN:—Being on my way, and having but a moment to reflect, I have been at a loss which of your resolutions most to respect or to obey; but at length have become satisfied that the first was taken most soberly, and, as it answers my purpose best, I pledge myself to adhere strictly to that. Sincerely wishing you good luck in legislating,

I am, my dear sirs, very respectfully yours,

E. WHITE.

Not to be outwitted so handsomely by the aspiring Indian Agent, it was subsequently

"*Resolved*, That the Secretary be requested to forward to the United States Government, through the American Consul at the Sandwich Islands, a copy of the articles of compact, as adopted by the people of Oregon Territory, on the last Saturday of July, A. D. 1845 ; and that the same be signed by the Governor and attested by the Secretary ; also, all resolutions adopted by this House, relative to sending said documents by E. White, late Indian Agent of this Territory ; also a copy of the letter of E. White to this House."

Whether or not these documents were ever transmitted does not appear ; but certain it is, that Dr. White returned not again with either a gubernatorial commission or Indian agency. That he probably hoped to do so may be gathered from an extract taken from the St. Louis *New Era* of that period, which runs as follows:

"OREGON.—Mr. Elijah White is on his way to Washington, *as a delegate from the self-constituted government of Oregon, and goes to ask for a seat in Con-*

gress, to represent that distant territory.   He carries with him his credentials from the provisional government of Oregon, and a large petition from the inhabitants of that region, asking that the jurisdiction of the United States may extend over that territory.   *   *   *   *   This delegation to Congress is to induce that body to take the actual occupancy of Oregon, and on his report and success will depend the decision of the question, whether or not the people will establish a separate and independent republic on the shores of the Pacific."

But solemn audacity, like virtue, is sometimes compelled to be its own reward.

The autumn of 1845 was marked less by striking events than by the energy which the people exhibited in improving the colony by laying out roads and town-sites.   Already quite a number of towns were located, in which the various branches of business were beginning to develop themselves.   Oregon City was the most populous and important, but Salem, Champoeg, and Portland were known as towns, and other settlements were growing up on the Tualatin Plains and to the south of them, in the fertile valleys of the numerous tributaries to the Wallamet.

Portland was settled in this year, and received its name from the game of " heads you lose, tails I win," by which its joint owners agreed to determine it.   One of them being a Maine man, was for giving it the name which it now bears ; the other partner being in favor of Boston, because he was a Massachusetts man.   It was, therefore, agreed between them that a copper cent should be tossed to decide the question of the christening, which being done, heads and Portland won.

The early days of that city were not always safe and pleasant any more than those of its older rivals ; and the few inhabitants frequently were much annoyed by the raids they were subject to from the now thoroughly vagabondized Indians.   On one occasion, while yet the population was small, they were very much annoyed by the

visit of eight or ten lodges of Indians, who had somewhere obtained liquor enough to get drunk on, and were
enjoying a debauch in that spirit of total abandon which
distinguishes the Indian carousal.

Their performances at length alarmed the people, yet
no one could be found who could put an end to them.
In this dilemma the Marshal came riding into town, splen-
didly mounted on a horse that would turn at the least
touch of the rein.   The countenances of the anxious
Portlanders brightened.   One of the town proprietors
eagerly besought him to "settle those Indians."   "Very
well," answered Meek ; " I reckon it won't take me long."
Mounting his horse, after first securing a rawhide rope, he
"charged" the Indian lodges, rope in hand, laying it on
with force, the bare shoulders of the Indians offering
good *back-grounds* for the pictures which he was rapidly
executing.

Not one made any resistance, for they had a wholesome
fear of *tyee* Meek.   In twenty minutes not an Indian, man
or woman, was left in Portland.   Some jumped into the
river and swam to the opposite side, and some fled to the
thick woods and hid themselves.   The next morning,
early, the women cautiously returned and carried away
their property, but the men avoided being seen again by
the marshal who punished drunkenness so severely.

Reader's query. Was it Meek or the Marshal who so
strongly disapproved of spreeing?

Ans. It was the Marshal.

The immigration to Oregon this year much exceeded
that of any previous year ; and there was the usual
amount of poverty, sickness, and suffering of every sort,
among the fresh arrivals.   Indeed the larger the trains
the greater the amount of suffering generally ; since the
grass was more likely to be exhausted, and more hin-

drances of every kind were likely to occur. In any case, a march of several months through an unsettled country was sure to leave the traveler in a most forlorn and exhausted condition every way.

This was the situation of thousands of people who reached the Dalles in the autumn of 1845. Food was very scarce among them, and the difficulties to encounter before reaching the Wallamet just as great as those of the two previous years. As usual the Hudson's Bay Company came to the assistance of the immigrants, furnishing a passage down the river in their boats; the sick, and the women and children being taken first.

Among the crowd of people encamped at the Dalles, was a Mr. Rector, since well known in Oregon and California. Like many others he was destitute of provisions; his supplies having given out. Neither had he any money. In this extremity he did that which was very disagreeable to him, as one of the "prejudiced" American citizens who were instructed beforehand to hate and suspect the Hudson's Bay Company—he applied to the company's agent at the Dalles for some potatoes and flour, confessing his present inability to pay, with much shame and reluctance.

"Do not apologize, sir," said the agent kindly; "take what you need. There is no occasion to starve while our supplies hold out."

Mr. R. found his prejudices in danger of melting away under such treatment; and not liking to receive bounty a second time, he resolved to undertake the crossing of the Cascade mountains while the more feeble of the immigrants were being boated down the Columbia. A few others who were in good health decided to accompany him. They succeeded in getting their wagons forty miles beyond the Dalles; but there they could move no further.

In this dilemma, after consultation, Mr. Rector and Mr. Barlow agreed to go ahead and look out a wagon road. Taking with them two days' provisions, they started on in the direction of Oregon City. But they found road hunting in the Cascade mountains an experience unlike any they had ever had. Not only had they to contend with the usual obstacles of precipices, ravines, mountain torrents, and weary stretches of ascent and descent; but they found the forests standing so thickly that it would have been impossible to have passed between the trees with their wagons had the ground been clear of fallen timber and undergrowth. On the contrary these latter obstacles were the greatest of all. So thickly were the trunks of fallen trees crossed and recrossed everywhere, and so dense the growth of bushes in amongst them, that it was with difficulty they could force their way on foot.

It soon became apparent to the road hunters, that two days' rations would not suffice for what work they had before them. At the first camp it was agreed to live upon half rations the next day ; and to divide and subdivide their food each day, only eating half of what was left from the day before, so that there would always still remain a morsel in case of dire extremity.

But the toil of getting through the woods and over the mountains proved excessive ; and that, together with insufficient food, had in the course of two or three days reduced the strength of Mr. Barlow so that it was with great effort only that he could keep up with his younger and more robust companion, stumbling and falling at every few steps, and frequently hurting himself considerably.

So wolfish and cruel is the nature of men, under trying circumstances, that instead of feeling pity for his weaker and less fortunate companion, Mr. Rector became impatient, blaming him for causing delays, and often requiring assistance.

To render their situation still more trying, rain began to fall heavily, which with the cold air of the mountains, soon benumbed their exhausted frames. Fearing that should they go to sleep so cold and famished, they might never be able to rise again, on the fourth or fifth evening they resolved to kindle a fire, if by any means they could do so. Dry and broken wood had been plenty enough, but for the rain, which was drenching everything. Neither matches nor flint had they, however, in any case. The night was setting in black with darkness; the wind swayed the giant firs over head, and then they heard the thunder of a falling monarch of the forest unpleasantly near. Search-

THE ROAD-HUNTERS.

ing among the bush-es, and under fallen timber for some dry leaves and sticks, Mr. Rector took a bundle of them to the most sheltered spot he could find, and set himself to work to coax a spark of fire out of two pieces of dry wood which he had split for that purpose. It was a long and weary while before success was attained, by vigorous rubbing together of the dry wood, but it was attained at last; and the stiffening limbs of the road-hunters were warmed by a blazing camp-fire.

The following day, the food being now reduced to a crumb for each, the explorers, weak and dejected, toiled on in silence, Mr. Rector always in advance. On chancing to look back at his companion he observed him to be brushing away a tear. " What now, old man?" asked Mr. R. with most unchristian harshness.

" What would you do with me, Rector, should I fall and break a leg, or become in any way disabled?" inquired Mr. Barlow, nervously.

"Do with you? *I would eat you!*" growled Mr. Rector, stalking on again.

As no more was said for some time, Mr. R.'s conscience rather misgave him that he treated his friend unfeelingly; then he stole a look back at him, and beheld the wan face bathed in tears.

"Come, come, Barlow," said he more kindly, "don't take affairs so much to heart. You will not break a leg, and I should not eat you if you did, for you have'nt any flesh on you to eat."

" Nevertheless, Rector, I want you to promise me that in case I should fall and disable myself, so that I cannot get on, you will not leave me here to die alone, but will kill me with your axe instead."

" Nonsense, Barlow; you are weak and nervous, but you are not going to be disabled, nor eaten, nor killed. Keep up man; we shall reach Oregon City yet."

So, onward, but ever more slowly and painfully, toiled again the pioneers, the wonder being that Mr. Barlow's fears were not realized, for the clambering and descending gave him many a tumble, the tumbles becoming more frequent as his strength declined.

Towards evening of this day as they came to the precipitous bank of a mountain stream which was flowing in
the direction they wished to go, suddenly there came to
their ears a sound of more than celestial melody; the
tinkling of bells, lowing of cattle, the voice of men hal-
looing to the herds. They had struck the cattle trail,
which they had first diverged from in the hope of finding
a road passable to wagons. In the overwhelming revul-
sion of feeling which seized them, neither were able for
some moments to command their voices to call for assistance. That night they camped with the herdsmen, and
supped in such plenty as an immigrant camp afforded.

Such were the sufferings of two individuals, out of a
great crowd of sufferers; some afflicted in one way and
some in another. That people who endured so much to
reach their El Dorado should be the most locally patriotic
people in the world, is not singular. Mr. Barlow lived to
construct a wagon road over the Cascades for the use of
subsequent immigrations.

CHAPTER XXXI.

EARLY in 1846, Meek resigned his office of marshal of the colony, owing to the difficulty of collecting taxes; for in a thinly inhabited country, where wheat was a legal tender, at sixty cents per bushel, it was rather a burdensome occupation to collect, in so ponderous a currency; and one in which the collector required a granary more than a pocket-book. Besides, Meek had out-grown the marshalship, and aspired to become a legislator at the next June election.

He had always discharged his duty with promptitude and rectitude while sheriff; and to his known courage might be attributed, in many instances, the ready compliance with law which was remarkable in so new and peculiar an organization as that of the Oregon colony. The people had desired not to be taxed, at first; and for a year or more the goverment was sustained by a fund raised by subscription. When at last it was deemed best to make collections by law, the Canadians objected to taxation to support an American government, while they were still subjects of Great Britain; but ultimately yielded the point, by the advice of Dr. McLaughlin.

But it was not always the Canadians who objected to being taxed, as the following anecdote will show. Dr. McLaughlin was one day seated in his office, in conversation with some of his American friends, when the tall form of the sheriff darkened the doorway.

"I have come to tax you, Doctor," said Meek with his

blandest manner, and with a merry twinkle, half sup-
pressed, in his black eyes.

"To tax me, Mr. Jo. I was not aware—I really was
not aware—I believed I had paid my tax, Mr. Jo,"
stammered the Doctor, somewhat annoyed at the prospect
of some fresh demand.

"Thar is an old ox out in my neighborhood, Doctor,
and he is said to belong to you. Thar is a tax of twenty-
five cents on him."

"I do not understand you, Mr. Jo. I have no cattle out
in your neighborhood."

"I couldn't say how that may be, Doctor. All I do
know about it, is just this. I went to old G—'s to collect
the tax on his stock—and he's got a powerful lot of cattle,—and while we war a countin 'em over, he left out
that old ox and said it belonged to you."

"Oh, oh, I see, Mr. Jo: yes, yes, I see! So it was
Mr. G—," cried the Doctor, getting very red in the face.
"I do remember now, since you bring it to my mind, that
I lent Mr. G— that steer six years ago! Here are the
twenty-five cents, Mr. Jo."

The sheriff took his money, and went away laughing;
while the Doctor's American friends looked quite as much
annoyed as the Doctor himself, over the meanness of some
of their countrymen.

The year of 1846 was one of the most exciting in the
political history of Oregon. President Polk had at last
given the notice required by the Joint occupation treaty,
that the Oregon boundary question must be settled. For
years the Oregon question had been before Congress, and
the people had taken an extraordinary interest in the manner in which it should be arranged. Ever since the emigration to Oregon had set in, the frequent memorials from
the far-off colony, and the letters which private individu-

als were continually writing to friends in the states, concerning the beauty, fertility, and healthfulness of the new territory, kept alive the interest of the people. As the time drew nigh when a notice might be given, thousands were anxiously waiting to learn what course the President would take with regard to it. And when at length the notice appeared, there was equally great anxiety to have the government demand every inch of territory that could be claimed under the most strict construction of the Florida treaty; i. e., as far north as latitude 54° 40.

So much had the subject been discussed, and so greatly had the feeling against the Hudson's Bay Company's monopoly been strengthened since the colonization of Oregon by the Americans, that the people did not take into consideration the Mexican War, nor the designs of the British government on California, but adopted for their watchword "fifty-four forty or fight," with the greatest enthusiasm; as if the "universal Yankee nation" need not fear the combined attacks of England, Mexico, and California, with twenty or thirty thousand Indians thrown in.

That government was more cautious, was perhaps a gain to our territorial possessions, of California, although by it we lost some degrees of less desirable soil. However that may be, both the British lion and the American eagle kept watch and guard over Oregon in that summer of suspense, 1846. About the close of that year there were fifteen English vessels of war in the Pacific, and eight American war vessels;—there had been nine. The total number of guns in the English squadron was 335; in the American, 310.

Agreeably to the promise which Dr. McLaughlin had received from the British Admiral, H. B. M. Sloop of war *Modeste* had arrived in the Columbia River in the month of October, 1845, and had wintered there. Much as the

Doctor had wished for protection from possible outbreaks, he yet felt that the presence of a British man-of-war in the Columbia, and another one in Puget Sound, was offensive to the colonists. He set himself to cover up as carefully as possible the disagreeable features of the British lion, by endeavoring to establish social intercourse between the officers of the *Modeste* and the ladies and gentlemen of the colony, and his endeavors were productive of a partial success.

During the summer, however, the United States Schooner *Shark* appeared in the Columbia, thus restoring the balance of power, for the relief of national jealousy. After remaining for some weeks, the *Shark* took her departure, but was wrecked on the bar at the mouth of the river, according to a prophecy of Meek's, who had a grudge against her commander, Lieut. Howison, for spoiling the sport he was having in company with one of her officers, while Howison was absent at the Cascades.

It appears that Lieut. Schenck was hospitably inclined, and that on receiving a visit from the hero of many bear-fights, who proved to be congenial on the subject of good liquors, he treated both Meek and himself so freely as to render discretion a foreign power to either of them. Varied and brilliant were the exploits performed by these jolly companions during the continuance of the spree; and still more brilliant were those they talked of performing, even the taking of the *Modeste*, which was lying a little way off, in front of Vancouver. Fortunately for the good of all concerned, Schenck contented himself with firing a salute as Meek was going over the side of the ship on leaving. But for this misdemeanor he was put under arrest by Howison, on his return from the Cascades, an indignity which Meek resented for the prisoner, by assuring Lieut. Howison that he would lose his vessel before he got out of the river. And lose her he did. Schenck was released after the vessel struck, escaping with the other officers and crew by means of small boats. Very few articles were saved from the wreck, but among those few was the stand of colors, which Lieut. Howison subsequently presented to Gov. Abernethy for the colony's encouragement and use. News of the Treaty which defined the Oregon boundary having been just received, Lieut. Howison concluded his letter to the Governor by saying: "Nor can I omit the occasion to express my gratification and pride that this relict of my late command should be emphatically the first *United States'* flag to wave over the undisputed and purely American Territory of Oregon."

The long agony was over at last; the boundary question was settled, but not to the satisfaction of the majority of the people in Oregon. They no more liked the terms of the treaty, which granted the free navigation of the Columbia to England until the expiration of the Hudson's Bay Company's charter, than they did the fixing of the boundary line at the 49th parallel. However, there was no help for it now, and after one long sigh of disappointment and chagrin, they submitted to necessity; and, rather sullenly it is true, accepted the fact that seventeen years more they must endure the odious monopoly of the Hudson's Bay Company. While a few malcontents talked quite openly of a design to take Fort Vancouver, and thus end the business of that Company, the wiser portion of the people interested themselves in the future welfare of the colony, and perhaps a few were thoughtful enough to remember that the gentlemen of the Hudson's Bay Company in Oregon had some reason to feel disappointed also, inasmuch as, contrary to their expectations, the United States had taken possession of both sides of the Columbia River.

CHAPTER XXXII

1846. THERE had been no winter since the commencement of the American settlement which had not had its
own particular causes for agitation, its colonial gossip, and
its party divisions.

The principal subjects on which the agitation, the gossip, and the divisions, were founded, this winter, were
first, the treaty, secondly, the immigration, and lastly, the
usual jealous dislike toward everything that was British.
Formerly, the news of the colony had been carried from
lip to lip alone: but now a newspaper, established in the
beginning of the year, and conducted by the "Oregon
Printing Association" at Oregon City, had become the
medium through which colonial affairs were supposed to
be made known.

And as the editor of the *Oregon Spectator* had as yet
no exchange list, the matter it contained could not but be
that which related almost entirely to Oregon affairs.   From
the following advertisement, which appeared in the first
number of the *Spectator*, we may learn that the facilities for postal communication were, at the best, indifferent.

To PERSONS WISHING TO SEND LETTERS EAST.—The postmaster-general
has contracted with Mr. H. BURNS to carry the mail from Oregon City to
Weston, in Missouri, for one trip only.   Letters mailed at any of the offices,
post paid, will be forwarded to any part of the United States.   As the mail
sent east, by Mr. BURNS, will reach Weston early in the season, it would be
advisable for those wishing to correspond with their friends in the east, to avail
themselves of the opportunity.   Postage only fifty cents on single sheets.

Through the same medium we are informed, by the following notices, that the officers of the *Modeste*, and the Hudson's Bay Company, were still exerting themselves to allay any irritation of feeling which dissatisfaction with the late treaty might have occasioned in the minds of the Americans.

THEATRE AT VANCOUVER.—That happy ship, (H. B. M. S. "Modeste,") was a scene of mirth and amusement upon Tuesday evening, the "Corps Dramatique" again performing before a fashionable and crowded audience. The musical and favorite comedy of "Love in a Village," followed by the "Mock Doctor" and the "Mayor of Garratt," were the plays of the evening, and we have to congratulate the whole performers in having so ably sustained their characters, and to thank these "tars" for the rich treat afforded us, in the *far west*, upon this occasion, as well as for the variety of attractions during the past winter.

THEATRE AT VANCOUVER.—The first performance of this season took place on the evening of the 5th instant, on board H. B. M. S. Modeste, by the same party of sailors who got up the drama so credibly, and afforded so much amusement last winter. The plays were "High life below stairs," "The deuce is in him," and "The Irish Widow;" and to do justice to these companions of the wave, the characters were, if not more ably, equally as well sustained as formerly. A numerous audience attended, (front seats graced by a beauteous circle of the fair sex,) and all appeared much gratified with the fun and mirth of these entertainments.

In addition to the theatrical entertainments, we find mention of balls, races, and picnics, extending through the year-and-a-half during which the *Modeste* remained in the river.

The *Spectator* usually contained articles on the resources of the country, intended to instruct the friends of the colony in the East, and also frequent metrical tributes to the loveliness and excellence of the new territory, contributed by enthusiastic correspondents. The average amount of poetical ability exhibited in these effusions was that of a "happy mediocrity;" and yet the local interest which attached to them made them rather attractive reading at that time. One stanza selected at random, will

25

convey the spirit of these productions, quite as well as a
more lengthy quotation :

> " Upon Mount Hood I stand,
> And with rapt gaze explore
> The valley, and that patriot band
> Upon Columbia's shore."

The author of the following, however, was not either a
dull or an unobservant writer ; and we insert his verses as
a comical bit of natural history belonging peculiarly to
Oregon.

ADVENTURES OF A COLUMBIA SALMON.

What is yon object which attracts the eye
Of the observing traveler, who ascends
Columbia's watèrs, when the summer sky
In one soft tint, calm nature's clothing blends:
As glittering in the sunbeams down it floats
'Till some vile vulture on its carcase gloats ?

'Tis a poor salmon, which a short time past,
With thousands of her finny sisters came,
By instinct taught, to seek and find at last,
The place that gave her birth, there to remain
'Till nature's offices had been discharged,
And fry from out the ova had emerged.

Her Winter spent amongst the sheltered bays
Of the salt sea, where numerous fish of prey,
With appetite keen, the number of her days
Would soon have put an end to, could but they
Have caught her ; but as they could not, she,
Spring having come, resolved to quit the sea :

And moving with the shoal along the coast, at length
She reached the outlet of her native river,
There tarried for a little to recruit her strength,
So tried of late by cold and stormy weather ;
Sporting in playful gambols o'er the banks and sands,
Chasing the tiny fish frequenting there in bands.

But ah, how little thought this simple fish,
The toils and perils she had yet to suffer,
The chance she ran of serving as a dish
For hungry white men or for Indian's supper,—
Of enemies in which the stream abounded,
When lo! she's by a fisher's net surrounded.

Partly conscious of her approaching end,
She darts with meteoric swiftness to and fro,
Striking the frail meshes, within which she's penned,
Which bid defiance to her stoutest blow:
To smaller compass by degrees the snare is drawn,
When with a leap she clears it and is gone.

Once more at large with her companions, now
Become more cautious from her late escape,
She keeps in deeper water and thinks how
Foolish she was to get in such a scrape;
As mounting further up the stream, she vies
With other fish in catching gnats and flies.

And as she on her way did thus enjoy
Life's fleeting moments, there arose a panic
Amongst the stragglers, who in haste deploy
Around their elder leaders, quick as magic,
While she unconscious of the untimely rout,
Was by a hungry otter singled out:

Vigorous was the chase, on the marked victim shot
Through the clear water, while in close pursuit
Followed her amphibious foe, who scarce had got
Near enough to grasp her, when with turns acute,
And leaps and revolutions, she so tried the otter,
He gave up the hunt with merely having bit her.

Scarce had she recovered from her weakness, when
An ancient eagle, of the bald-head kind,
Winging his dreary way to'rds some lone glen,
Where was her nest with four plump eaglets lined,
Espied the fish, which he judged quite a treat,
And just the morsel for his little ones to eat:

And sailing in spiral circles o'er the spot,
Where lay his prey, then hovering for a time,
To take his wary aim, he stooped and caught
His booty, which he carried to a lofty pine;
Upon whose topmost branches, he first adjusted
His awkward load, ere with his claws he crushed it.

"Ill is the wind that blows no person good "—
So said the adage, and as luck would have it,
A huge grey eagle out in search of food,
Who just had whet his hunger with a rabbit,
Attacked the other, and the pair together,
In deadly combat fell into the river.

Our friend of course made off, when she'd done falling
Some sixty yards, and well indeed she might;
For ne'er, perhaps, a fish got such a mauling
Since Adam's time, or went up such a height
Into the air, and came down helter-skelter,
As did this poor production of a melter.

All these, with many other dangers, she survived,
Too manifold in this short space to mention ;
So we'll suppose her to have now arrived
Safe at *the Falls*, without much more detention
Than one could look for, where so many liked her
Company, and so many Indians spiked her.

And here a mighty barrier stops her way:
The tranquil water, finding in its course
Itself beset with rising rocks, which lay
As though they said, "retire ye to your source,"
Bursts with indignant fury from its bondage, now
Rushes in foaming torrents to the chasm below.

The persevering fish then at the foot arrives,
Laboring with redoubled vigor mid the surging tide,
And finding, by her strength, she vainly strives
To overcome the flood, though o'er and o'er she tried ;
Her tail takes in her mouth, and bending like a bow
That's to full compass drawn, aloft herself doth throw;

And spinning in the air, as would a silver wand
That's bended end to end and upwards cast,
Headlong she falls amid the showering waters, and
Gasping for breath, against the rocks is dashed :
Again, again she vaults, again she tries,
And in one last and feeble effort—dies.

There was, in Oregon City, a literary society called the
Falls Association," some of whose effusions were occasionally sent to the *Spectator*, and this may have been one

of them. At all events, it is plain that with balls, the-
atres, literary societies, and politics, the colony was not
afflicted with dullness, in the winter of 1846.

But the history of the immigration this year, afforded,
perhaps, more material for talk than any one other subject. The condition in which the immigrants arrived was
one of great distress. A new road into the valley had
been that season explored, at great labor and expense, by
a company of gentlemen who had in view the aim to
lessen the perils usually encountered in descending the
Columbia. They believed that a better pass might be
discovered through the Cascade range to the south, than
that which had been found around the base of Mount
Hood, and one which should bring the immigrants in at
the upper end of the valley, thus saving them considerable travel and loss of time at a season of the year
when the weather was apt to be unsettled.

With this design, a party had set out to explore the
Cascades to the south, quite early in the spring ; but failing in their undertaking, had returned. Another company was then immediately formed, headed by a prominent member of society and the legislature. This company followed the old Hudson's Bay Company's trail,
crossing all those ranges of mountains perpendicular to
the coast, which form a triple wall between Oregon and
California, until they came out into the valley of the Hum-
boldt, whence they proceeded along a nearly level, but
chiefly barren country to Fort Hall, on the Snake River.

The route was found to be practicable, although there
was a scarcity of grass and water along a portion of it ;
but as the explorers had with great difficulty found out
and marked all the best camping grounds, and encountered first for themselves all the dangers of a hitherto unexplored region, most of which they believed they had

overcome, they felt no hesitation in recommending the new road to the emigrants whom they met at Fort Hall.

Being aware of the hardships which the immigrants of the previous years had undergone on the Snake River plains, at the crossing of Snake River, the John Day, and Des Chutes Rivers, and the passage of the Columbia, the travelers gladly accepted the tidings of a safer route to the Wallamet. A portion of the immigration had already gone on by the road to the Dalles; the remainder turned off by the southern route.

Of those who took the new route, a part were destined for California. All, however, after passing through the sage deserts, committed the error of stopping to recruit their cattle and horses in the fresh green valleys among the foot-hills of the mountains. It did not occur to them that they were wasting precious time in this way; but to this indulgence was owing an incredible amount of suffering. The California-bound travelers encountered the season of snow on the Sierras, and such horrors are recorded of their sufferings as it is seldom the task of ears to hear or pen to record. Snow-bound, without food, those who died of starvation were consumed by the living; even children were eaten by their once fond parents, with an indifference horrible to think on: so does the mind become degraded by great physical suffering.

The Oregon immigrants had not to cross the lofty Sierras; but they still found mountains before them which, in the dry season, would have been formidable enough. Instead, however, of the dry weather continuing, very heavy rains set in. The streams became swollen, the mountain sides heavy and slippery with the wet earth. Where the road led through canyons, men and women were sometimes forced to stem a torrent, breast high, and cold enough to chill the life in their veins. The cattle gave out, the wagons broke down, provisions became exhausted, and a few persons perished, while all were in the direst straits.

The first who got through into the valley sent relief to those behind; but it was weeks before the last of the worn, weary, and now impoverished travelers escaped from the horrors of the mountains in which they were so hopelessly entangled, and where most of their worldly goods were left to rot.

This unfortunate termination to their hopes of a southern road had a dispiriting influence on the colony; inasmuch, too, as some of the immigrants who had suffered most loss, were disposed to lay the blame of it upon those gentlemen who, with so much effort, had marked out the new route. It did not soften the acrimony of this class of persons to be assured that those who had arrived by the Cascades were in fully as bad a plight, in many instances, as themselves. They could not forgive the innocent first-cause of their own particular ills. Feuds grew out of their bitter indignation, which only a life-time could heal: and thus it was, that with all these impoverished new comers making demands on their sympathy, each with the tale of his own peculiar woes to relate, there was plenty of excitement among the colonists that winter.

The Oregon legislature met as usual, to hold its winter session, though the people hoped and expected it would be for the last time under the Provisional Government. There were only two "mountain-men" in the House, at this session—Meek and Newell. There were also two Hudson's Bay Company men, from the counties on the north side of the river, showing an improvement in the public sentiment, since the settlement of the boundary question. In all, there were but fifteen members. Of the three nominees for Speaker of the House, Meek was one, but failed of the election.

There was no very important business before the legislature at this session.   Considerable effort was made to get
a bill through, regulating the manufacture and sale of
wine and distilled spirituous liquors.   After considerable
discussion the bill passed the House, and was vetoed by
the Governor, but finally was passed over the veto, by a
two-thirds vote, this being the first successful attempt to
legalize the sale of ardent spirits in Oregon.

Wheat still remaining a legal tender, Meek introduced
a bill for its inspection, having probably learned from his
experience as tax collector, that the people were sometimes
inclined to cheat the government.

The Provisional Government had not provided for a divorce law suited to the wants of the country, and it was
therefore only by special act of the legislature that divorces
could be obtained.   Several applications had been made,
in the form of bills praying for a release from the bonds
of matrimony.   In every case but one these applications
came from the sterner sex, and with various success.   In
this one case, the applicant had failed to enlist the sympathies of the committee to whom her case was referred, and
there was every prospect that the legislature would adjourn without acting upon her petition.

In this emergency the lady sought out our hero, who
could never refuse a lady's request, and entreated him to
exert himself in her behalf, to procure her a divorce from
her lord no longer loved.   Accordingly the bill was prepared, but not presented to the House until the last
moment before the close of the session, when it was hurried
over, considered engrossed, read a third time, voted on
and passed in a very brief space of time, to the entire satisfaction of both Meek and his *protegé.*

CHAPTER XXXIII.

1847. There were no events to make remarkable the spring and summer of 1847. Oregon had a promising commerce growing up with California, the principal articles of export being flour and lumber. In the month of April alone there went out of the Columbia River 1736 barrels of flour, 200,000 feet of lumber, and over 200,000 shingles. Of this amount about half was furnished by the Hudson's Bay Company's mills, the remainder by the mills of the colony. Letters were received from California, giving notice that at least 20,000 barrels of flour would be needed in that country in the fall. Of this quantity the colonists expected to be able to supply one-half. Money now began to come into the colony, and the future looked promising.

To forward the cause of education, the Oregon Printing Association made a reprint of *Webster's Elementary Spelling-Book*, without so much as saying "by your leave" to the owners of the copy-right, and probably justified the theft upon the strength of the adage that "necessity knows no law."

Oregon certainly furnished, in her colonial condition, an example to the world scarcely second in interest to that of the Pilgrims of the New England colonies, such was the determined patriotism, the temperance, the industry, and the wonderful *success* of her undertakings. We have attempted, without being too diffuse, to show by what de-

grees, assisted by those whom they in their patriotism felt
bound to regard as foes, they proceeded step by step toward the goal of their desires—the founding of a new
state. Divers were the errors they committed, and rough
and unpolished was the material out of which the edifice
was to be erected; nevertheless it was well and strongly
built, the foundation being civil liberty, the superstructure
temperance, good morals, and education. These things
the colonists had struggled for, and so far had maintained,
and they were now looking for their reward. That Government which they so loved, regarding it as children regard a fond parent, and to which they had addressed so
many prayers and entreaties in all these years, was about
to take them under its fostering care, and to accept from
their hands the filial gift of a vigorous young state.

In the suspense under which they for the present remained, there was nothing to do but to go on in the path
of duty as they had heretofore done, keeping up their
present form of government until it was supplanted by a
better one. So passed the summer until the return of the
"Glorious Fourth," which, being the first national anni-
versary occuring since the news of the treaty had reached
the colony, was celebrated with proper enthusiasm.

It chanced that an American ship, the *Brutus*, Capt.
Adams, from Boston, was lying in the Wallamet, and that
a general invitation had been given to the celebrationists
to visit the ship during the day. A party of fifty or sixty,
including Meek and some of his mountain associates, had
made their calculations to go on board at the same time,
and were in fact already alongside in boats, when Captain
Adams singled out a boat load of people belonging to the
mission clique, and inviting them to come on board, ordered all the others off.

This was an insult too great to be borne by mountain-men, who resented it not only for themselves, but for the people's party of Americans to which they naturally belonged. Their blood was up, and without stopping to deliberate, Meek and Newell hurried off to fetch the twelve-pounder that had a few hours before served to thunder forth the rejoicings of a free people, but with which they now purposed to proclaim their indignation as freeman heinously insulted. The little twelve-pound cannon was loaded with rock, and got into range with the offending ship, and there is little doubt that Capt. Adams would have suffered loss at the hands of the incensed multitude, but for the timely interference of Dr. McLaughlin. On being informed of the warlike intentions of Meek and his associates, the good Doctor came running to the rescue, his white hair flowing back from his noble face with the hurry of his movements.

"Oh, oh, Mr. Joe, Mr. Joe, you must not do this! indeed, you must not do this foolish thing! Come now; come away. You will injure your country, Mr. Joe. How can you expect that ships will come here, if they are fired on? Come away, come away!"

And Meek, ever full of wagishness, even in his wrath, replied:

"Doctor, it is not that I love the Brutus less, but my dignity more."

"Oh, Shakespeare, Mr. Joe! But come with me; come with me."

And so the good Doctor, half in authority, half in kindness, persuaded the resentful colonists to pass by the favoritism of the Boston captain.

Meek was reëlected to the legislature this summer, and swam out to a vessel lying down at the mouth of the Wallamet, to get liquor to treat his constituents; from which circumstance it may be inferred that while Oregon was remarkable for temperance, there were occasions on which conviviality was deemed justifiable by a portion of her people.

Thus passed the summer. The autumn brought news of a large emigration *en route* for the new territory ; but it brought no news of good import from Congress. On the contrary the bill providing for a territorial government for Oregon had failed, because the Organic Laws of that territory excluded slavery forever from the country. The history of its failure is a part and parcel of the record of the long hard struggle of the south to extend slavery into the United States' territories.

One crumb of comfort, however, accompanied the intelligence of this disappointment; and that was a letter from the indefatigable friend of Oregon, Thomas H. Benton, of which the following is a copy :

WASHINGTON CITY, MARCH, 1847.

MY FRIENDS :—(For such I may call many of you from personal acquaintance, and all of you from my thirty years devotion to the interests of your country)—I think it right to make this communication to you at the present moment, when the adjournment of Congress, without passing the bill for your government and protection, seems to have left you in a state of abandonment by your mother country. But such is not the case. You are not abandoned ! nor will you be denied protection unless you agree to admit slavery. I, a man of the South, and a slaveholder, tell you this.

The House of Representatives, as early as the middle of January, had passed the bill to give you a Territorial Government ; and in that bill had sanctioned and legalized your Provisional Organic Act, one of the clauses of which forever prohibited the existence of slavery in Oregon. An amendment from the Senate's committee, to which this bill was referred, proposed to abrogate that prohibition ; and in the delays and vexations to which that amendment gave rise, the whole bill was laid upon the table, and lost for the session. This will be a great disappointment to you and a real calamity, already five years without law, or legal institutions for the protection of life, liberty, and property, and now doomed to wait a year longer. This is a strange and anomalous condition ! almost incredible to contemplate, and most critical to endure ! a colony of free men, four thousand miles from the Metropolitan government, and without law or government to preserve them ! But do not be alarmed, or desperate. You will not be outlawed for not admitting slavery. Your fundamental act against that institution, copied from the Ordinance of 1787—(the work of the great men of the SOUTH, in the great day of the SOUTH, prohibiting slavery in a TERRITORY far less northern than yours)—will not be abrogated! nor is that the intention of the prime mover of the amendment. Upon the record of the Judiciary committee of the Senate is the author of that amendment; but not so the fact! It is only mid-wife to it. Its author is the same mind that generated the "FIRE BRAND RESOLUTIONS," of which I send you a copy, and of which the amendment is the legitimate derivation. Oregon is not the object. The most rabid propagandist of slavery cannot expect to plant it on the shores of the Pacific, in the latitude of Wisconsin and the Lake of the Woods. A home agitation, for election and disunion purposes, is all that is intended by thrusting this fire-brand question into your bill! and, at the next session, when it is thrust in again, we will scourge it out! and pass your bill as it ought to be. I promise you this in the name of the SOUTH as well as of the NORTH; and the event will not deceive me. In the meantime, the President will give you all the protection which existing laws, and detachments of the army and navy, can enable him to extend to you; and, until Congress has time to act, your friends must rely upon you to continue to govern yourselves, as you have heretofore done, under the provisions of your own voluntary compact, and with the justice, harmony, and moderation which is due to your own character and to the honor of the American name.

I send you, by Mr. Shively, a copy of the bill of the late session, both as it passed the House of Representatives and as proposed to be amended in the Senate, with the Senate's vote upon laying it on the table, and a copy of Mr. Calhoun's resolutions—(posterior in date to the amendment, but, nevertheless, its father)—also a copy of your own Provisional Organic Act, printed by order of the Senate; all which will put you completely in possession of the proceedings of Congress on your Petition for a Territorial Government, and for the protection and security of your rights.

In conclusion, I have to assure you that the same spirit which has made me the friend of Oregon for thirty years—which led me to denounce the joint occupation treaty the day it was made, and to oppose its renewal in 1828, and to labor for its abrogation until it was terminated; the same spirit which led me to reveal the grand destiny of Oregon in articles written in 1818, and to support every measure for her benefit since—this same spirit still animates me, and will continue to do so while I live—which, I hope, will be long enough to see an emporium of Asiatic commerce at the mouth of your river, and a stream of Asiatic trade pouring into the Valley of the Mississippi through the channel of Oregon.

> Your friend and fellow citizen,
>
> THOMAS H. BENTON.

In addition to this valuable bit of comfort and of history, another letter, written by James Buchanan, Secretary of State, and conveying President Polk's regrets that no more had been done for Oregon, was presented to the colonists by its bearer, who had also brought the communication of Senator Benton. This gentleman was a Mr. Shively, one of the two postmasters appointed for Oregon Territory. Here was all that Congress, after much effort, had been able to accomplish—the appropriation of money for transporting the mails to Oregon *via* the Isthmus of Panama; the establishment of a post-office at Astoria, and another at Oregon City; and the appointment of an Indian agent, whose inefficiency was patent to all Oregon! Mr. Buchanan's letter, however, contained a promise of a regiment of mounted riflemen to protect the emigration; and war vessels to visit Oregon waters as often as practicable.

Justly dissatisfied, but not inconsolable, the colony, now that hope was extinguished for another season, returned to its own affairs. The immigration, which had arrived early this year, amounted to between four and five thousand. An unfortunate affray between the immigrants and the Indians at the Dalles, had frightened away from that station the Rev. Father Waller; and Dr. Whitman of the Waiilatpu mission had purchased the station for the Presbyterian mission, and placed a nephew of his in charge. Although, true to their original bad character, the Dalles Indians had frequently committed theft upon the passing emigration, this was the first difficulty resulting in loss of life, which had taken place. This quarrel arose out of some thefts committed by the Indians, and the unwise advice of Mr. Waller, in telling the immigrants to retaliate by taking some of the Indian horses. An Indian can see the justice of taking toll from every traveler passing through his country; but he cannot see the justice of being robbed in return; and Mr. Waller had been long enough among them to have known this savage peculiarity.   In the skirmish which followed this act of retaliation, one of the immigrants was killed, two seriously wounded, and several others driven into the mountains for safety. The chief of the Wascopams, or Dalles Indians, was killed, and several of the tribe wounded.   Fearing the design of the immigrants was to make war on them, they removed back into the mountains.   And thus was inaugurated a series of Indian difficulties which harrassed the inhabitants of the territory for the next ten years.

Following the arrival of the immigration and the extinguishment of the colony's hopes of a territorial government, a movement was put on foot among the members of the Mission party, to send a delegate to Congress, charged with instructions to that body concerning the wants and wishes of the future Territory.   The gentleman selected by the Governor, for this mission, was J. Q. Thornton, at that time Chief Justice of the colony, and a man of undoubted ability.   But as he did not go as a delegate from the legislature, and only by appointment of the Governor, with the sanction of the Mission party, there was considerable dissatisfaction with the action of Governor Abernethy, and the legislature passed certain resolutions expressive of its sense of the impropriety of "secret factions" in the colony.   The event has since proven that no harm was done, but probably considerable good, by the extraordinary delegate, who chanced to be in Washington at a critical time for the interests of Oregon.

But the manner in which the delegate was equipped for the journey is unprecedented in the annals of the whole country.   Had he been a regularly chosen delegate from the legislature,—and had the legislature a right to send a delegate to Congress, which it had not,—there was not money enough in the colonial treasury to have paid

his passage out. Nor had the Governor and his friends
money enough for this purpose. As might be conjectured
in this case, extraordinary measures had to be adopted to
raise the passage money. Subscriptions were taken in
any and every thing which could be converted into currency. One contributer gave fifteen barrels of flour; another a little money; another furnished an outfit of clothing; and the largest amount of coin raised was one hundred and fifty dollars.

Passage was secured on the bark *Whitton*, Captain
Ghelston, who agreed to carry to New York, but failed
to do so. At San Francisco the delegate made sale of
his flour and other commodities, and Captain Ghelston
obtained so favorable an opinion of the profits of a coasting trade, that when he had arrived at San Juan on the
Mexican coast, he threw up his contract to carry his passenger to New York, leaving him to proceed as best he
could. Fortunately, the United States sloop of war
Portsmouth, Captain Montgomery, was lying at this port.
She was a part of the squadron which had been guarding
the American interests in the Pacific during the previous
year; and when Captain Montgomery learned the situation of the Oregon representative, he took the liberty of
construing his instructions to "rescue American ministers
in foreign ports" from difficulties into which they might
have fallen through various causes, to mean that he was
to convey this stranded delegate to his destination, which
he immediately proceeded to do. Therefore it may be
reckoned that the whole transaction of appointing and
conveying the first Oregon delegate to Washington was
decidedly unique, as well as somewhat expensive.

Finding that it must continue yet a little longer to look
after its own government and welfare, the colony had
settled back into its wonted pursuits. The legislature

had convened for its winter session, and had hardly elected its officers and read the usual message of the Governor, before there came another, which fell upon their ears like a thunderbolt. Gov. Abernethy had sent in the following letter, written at Vancouver the day before :

FORT VANCOUVER, Dec. 7, 1847.

George Abernethy, Esq.;

SIR :—Having received intelligence, last night, by special express from Walla-Walla, of the destruction of the missionary settlement at Waiilatpu, by the Cayuse Indians of that place, we hasten to communicate the particulars of that dreadful event, one of the most atrocious which darkens the annals of Indian crime.

Our lamented friend, Dr. Whitman, his amiable and accomplished lady, with nine other persons, have fallen victims to the fury of these remorseless savages, who appear to have been instigated to this appalling crime by a horrible suspicion which had taken possession of their superstitious minds, in consequence of the number of deaths from dysentery and measles, that Dr. Whitman was silently working the destruction of their tribe by administering poisonous drugs, under the semblance of salutary medicines.

With a goodness of heart and benevolence truly his own, Dr. Whitman had been laboring incessantly since the appearance of the measles and dysentery among his Indian converts, to relieve their sufferings ; and such has been the reward of his generous labors.

A copy of Mr. McBean's letter, herewith transmitted, will give you all the particulars known to us of this indescribably painful event.

Mr. Ogden, with a strong party, will leave this place as soon as possible for Walla-Walla, to endeavor to prevent further evil ; and we beg to suggest to you the propriety of taking instant measures for the protection of the Rev. Mr. Spalding, who, for the sake of his family, ought to abandon the Clear-water mission without delay, and retire to a place of safety, as he cannot remain at that isolated station without imminent risk, in the present excited and irritable state of the Indian population.

I have the honor to be, sir, your most obedient servant,

JAMES DOUGLAS.

CHAPTER XXXIV.

1842–7. DOUBTLESS the reader remembers the disquiet felt and expressed by the Indians in the upper country in the years 1842–3, when Dr. White was among them, lest the Americans should take away their lands from them without payment. For the time they had been quieted by presents, by the advice of the Hudson's Bay Company, and by the Agent's promise that in good time the United States would send them blankets, guns, ammunition, food farming implements, and teachers to show them how to live like the whites.

In the meantime, five years having passed, these promises had not been kept. ˙Five times a large number of whites, with their children, their cattle, and wagons, had passed through their country, and gone down into the Wallamet Valley to settle. Now they had learned that the United States claimed the Wallamet valley; yet they had never heard that the Indians of that country had received any pay for it.

They had accepted the religion of the whites believing it would do them good; but now they were doubtful. Had they not accepted laws from the United States agent, and had not their people been punished for acts which their ancestors and themselves had always before committed at will? None of these innovations seemed to do them any good: they were disappointed. But the whites, or Bostons, (meaning the Americans) were coming more and more every year, so that by-and-by there would be all Bostons and no Indians.

Once they had trusted in the words of the Americans; but now they knew how worthless were their promises. The Americans had done them much harm. Years before had not one of the missionaries suffered several of their people, and the son of one of their chiefs, to be slain in his company, yet himself escaped? Had not the son of another chief, who had gone to California to buy cattle, been killed by a party of Americans, for no fault of his own? Their chief's son was killed, the cattle robbed from his party, after having been paid for; and his friends obliged to return poor and in grief.

To be sure, Dr. White had given them some drafts to be used in obtaining cattle from the immigration, as a compensation for their losses in California; but they could not make them available; and those who wanted cattle had to go down to the Wallamet for them. In short, could the Indians have thought of an American epithet to apply to Americans, it would have been that expressive word *humbug*. What they felt and what they thought, was, that they had been cheated. They feared greater frauds in the future, and they were secretly resolved not to submit to them.

So far as regarded the missionaries, Dr. Whitman and his associates, they were divided; yet as so many looked on the Doctor as an agent in promoting the settlement of the country with whites, it was thought best to drive him from the country, together with all the missionaries. Several years before Dr. Whitman had known that the Indians were displeased with his settlement among them. They had told him of it: they had treated him with violence; they had attempted to outrage his wife; had burned his property; and had more recently several times warned him to leave their country, or they should kill him.

Not that all were angry at him alike, or that any were personally very ill-disposed towards him. Everything that a man could do to instruct and elevate these savage people, he had done, to the best of his ability, together with his wife and assistants. But he had not been able, or perhaps had not attempted, to conceal the fact, that he looked upon the country as belonging to his people, rather than to the natives, and it was this fact which was at the bottom of their "bad hearts" toward the Doctor. So often had warnings been given which were disregarded by Dr. Whitman, that his friends, both at Vancouver and in the settlements, had long felt great uneasiness, and often besought him to remove to the Wallamet valley.

But although Dr. Whitman sometimes was half persuaded to give up the mission upon the representations of others, he could not quite bring himself to do so. So far as the good conduct of the Indians was concerned, they had never behaved better than for the last two years. There had been less violence, less open outrage, than formerly; and their civilization seemed to be progressing; while some few were apparently hopeful converts. Yet there was ever a whisper in the air—"Dr. Whitman must die."

The mission at Lapwai was peculiarly successful. Mrs. Spalding, more than any other of the missionaries, had been able to adapt herself to the Indian character, and to gain their confidence. Besides, the Nez Perces were a better nation than the Cayuses;—more easily controlled by a good counsel; and it seemed like doing a wrong to abandon the work so long as any good was likely to result from it. There were other reasons too, why the missions could not be abandoned in haste, one of which was the difficulty of disposing of the property. This might have been done perhaps, to the Catholics, who were establishing missions throughout the upper country; but Dr. Whitman would never have been so false to his own doctrines, as to leave the field of his labors to the Romish Church.

Yet the division of sentiment among the Indians with regard to religion, since the Catholic missionaries had come among them, increased the danger of a revolt: for in the Indian country neither two rival trading companies, nor two rival religions can long prosper side by side. The savage cannot understand the origin of so many religions.   He either repudiates all, or he takes that which addresses itself to his understanding through the senses. In the latter respect, the forms of Catholicism, as adapted to the savage understanding, made that religion a dangerous rival to intellectual and idealistic Presbyterianism. But the more dangerous the rival, the greater the firmness with which Dr. Whitman would cling to his duty.

There were so many causes at work to produce a revolution among the Indians, that it would be unfair to name any one as *the* cause.   The last and immediate provocation was a season of severe sickness among them.   The disease was measels, and was brought in the train of the immigration.

This fact alone was enough to provoke the worst passions of the savage.   The immigration in itself was a sufficient offense; the introduction through them of a pestilence, a still weightier one.   It did not signify that Dr. Whitman had exerted himself night and day to give them relief.   Their peculiar notions about a medicine-man made it the Doctor's duty to cure the sick; or made it the duty of the relatives of the dead and dying to avenge their deaths.

Yet in spite of all and every provocation, perhaps the fatal tragedy might have been postponed, had it not been for the evil influence of one Jo Lewis, a half-breed, who had accompanied the emigration from the vicinity of Fort Hall.   This Jo Lewis, with a large party of emigrants, had stopped to winter at the mission, much against Dr. Whitman's wishes; for he feared not having food enough for so many persons.   Finding that he could not prevent them, he took some of the men into his employ, and among others the stranger half-breed.

This man was much about the house, and affected to relate to the Indians conversations which he heard between Dr. and Mrs. Whitman, and Mr. Spalding, who with his little daughter, was visiting at Waiilatpu.   These conversations related to poisoning the Indians, in order to get them all out of the way, so that the white men could enjoy their country unmolested.   Yet this devil incarnate did not convince his hearers at once of the truth of his statements; and it was resolved in the tribe to make a test of Dr. Whitman's medicine.   Three persons were selected to experiment upon; two of them already sick, and the third quite well.   Whether it was that the medicine was administered in too large quantities, or whether an unhappy chance so ordered it, all those three persons died. Surely it is not singular that in the savage mind this circumstance should have been deemed decisive.   It was then that the decree went forth that not only the Doctor and Mrs. Whitman, but all the Americans at the mission must die.

On the 22d of November, Mr. Spalding arrived at Waiilatpu, from his mission, one hundred and twenty miles distant, with his daughter, a child of ten years, bringing with him also several horse-loads of grain, to help feed the emigrants wintering there.   He found the Indians suffering very much, dying one, two, three, and sometimes five in a day.   Several of the emigrant families, also, were sick with measels and the dysentery, which followed the disease. A child of one of them died the day following Mr. Spalding's arrival.

Dr. Whitman's family consisted of himself and wife, a young man named Rodgers, who was employed as a teacher, and also studying for the ministry, two young people, a brother and sister, named Bulee, seven orphaned children of one family, whose parents had died on the road to Oregon in a previous year, named Sager, Helen Mar, the daughter of Joe Meek, another little half-breed girl, daughter of Bridger the fur-trader, a half-breed Spanish boy whom the Doctor had brought up from infancy, and two sons of a Mr. Manson, of the Hudson's Bay Company.

Besides these, there were half-a-dozen other families at the mission, and at the saw-mill, twenty miles distant, five families more—in all, forty-six persons at Waiilatpu, and fifteen at the mill, who were among those who suffered by the attack. But there were also about the mission, three others, Joe Lewis, Nicholas Finlay, and Joseph Stanfield, who probably knew what was about to take place, and may, therefore be reckoned as among the conspirators.

While Mr. Spalding was at Waiilatpu, a message came from two Walla-Walla chiefs, living on the Umatilla River, to Dr. Whitman, desiring him to visit the sick in their villages, and the two friends set out together to attend to the call, on the evening of the 27th of November. Says Mr. Spalding, referring to that time: "The night was dark, and the wind and rain beat furiously upon us. But our interview was sweet. We little thought it was to be our last. With feelings of the deepest emotion we called to mind the fact, that eleven years before, we crossed this trail before arriving at Walla-Walla, the end of our seven months' journey from New York. We called to mind

the high hopes and thrilling interests which had been
awakened during the year that followed—of our successful labors and the constant devotedness of the Indians to
improvement. True, we remembered the months of deep
solicitude we had, occasioned by the increasing menacing
demands of the Indians for pay for their wood, their
water, their air, their lands. But much of this had passed
away, and the Cayuses were in a far more encouraging
condition than ever before." Mr. Spalding further relates that himself and Dr. Whitman also conversed on the
danger which threatened them from the Catholic influence.
"We felt," he says, "that the present sickness afforded
them a favorable opportunity to excite the Indians to
drive us from the country, and all the movements about
us seemed to indicate that this would soon be attempted,
if not executed." Such was the suspicion in the minds
of the Protestants. Let us hope that it was not so well
founded as they believed.

The two friends arrived late at the lodge of *Stickas*, a
chief, and laid down before a blazing fire to dry their
drenched clothing. In the morning a good breakfast was
prepared for them, consisting of beef, vegetables, and
bread—all of which showed the improvement of the Indians in the art of living. The day, being Sunday, was
observed with as much decorum as in a white man's house.
After breakfast, Dr. Whitman crossed the river to visit
the chiefs who had sent for him, namely, *Tan-i-tan*, *Five
Crows*, and *Yam-ha-wa-lis*, returning about four o'clock
in the afternoon, saying he had taken tea with the Catholic bishop and two priests, at their house, which belonged
to *Tan-i-tan*, and that they had promised to visit him in a
short time. He then departed for the mission, feeling
uneasy about the sick ones at home.

Mr. Spalding remained with the intention of visiting

the sick and offering consolation to the dying. But he soon discovered that there was a weighty and uncomfortable secret on the mind of his entertainer, *Stickas*. After much questioning, *Stickas* admitted that the thought which troubled him was that the Americans had been " decreed against" by his people ; more he could not be induced to reveal. Anxious, yet not seriously alarmed,—for these warnings had been given before many times,—he retired to his couch of skins, on the evening of the 29th, being Monday—not to sleep, however; for on either side of him an Indian woman sat down to chant the death-song —that frightful lament which announces danger and death. On being questioned they would reveal nothing.

On the following morning, Mr. Spalding could no longer remain in uncertainty, but set out for Waiilatpu. As he mounted his horse to depart, an Indian woman placed her hand on the neck of his horse to arrest him, and pretending to be arranging his head-gear, said in a low voice to the rider, "Beware of the Cayuses at the mission." Now more than ever disturbed by this intimation that it was the mission which was threatened, he hurried forward, fearing for his daughter and his friends. He proceeded without meeting any one until within sight of the lovely Walla-Walla valley, almost in sight of the mission itself, when suddenly, at a wooded spot where the trail passes through a little hollow, he beheld two horsemen advancing, whom he watched with a fluttering heart, longing for, and yet dreading, the news which the very air seemed whispering.

The two horsemen proved to be the Catholic Vicar General, Brouillet, who, with a party of priests and nuns had arrived in the country only a few months previous, and his half-breed interpreter, both of whom were known

to Mr. Spalding. They each drew rein as they approached, Mr. Spalding immediately inquiring "what news?"

"There are very many sick at the Whitman station,"
answered Brouillet, with evident embarrassment.

"How are Doctor and Mrs. Whitman?" asked Spalding
anxiously.

"The Doctor is ill—is dead," added the priest reluc-
tantly.

"And Mrs. Whitman?" gasped Spalding.

"Is dead also. The Indians have killed them."

"My daughter?" murmured the agonized questioner.

"Is safe, with the other prisoners," answered Brouillet.

"And then," says Spalding in speaking of that moment
of infinite horror, when in his imagination a picture of the
massacre, of the anguish of his child, the suffering of the
prisoners, of the probable destruction of his own family
and mission, and his surely impending fate, all rose up
before him—"I felt the world all blotted out at once, and
sat on my horse as rigid as a stone, not knowing or feeling
anything."

While this conversation had been going on the half-
breed interpreter had kept a sinister watch over the communication, and his actions had so suspicious a look that
the priest ordered him to ride on ahead. When he had
obeyed, Brouillet gave some rapid instructions to Spalding; not to go near the mission, where he could do no
good, but would be certainly murdered; but to fly, to
hide himself until the excitement was over. The men at
the mission were probably all killed; the women and
children would be spared; nothing could be done at present but to try to save his own life, which the Indians were
resolved to take.

The conversation was hurried, for there was no time to
lose. Spalding gave his pack-horse to Brouillet, to avoid

being encumbered by it; and taking some provisions which the priest offered, struck off into the woods there to hide until dark. Nearly a week from this night he arrived at the Lapwai mission, starved, torn, with bleeding feet as well as broken heart. Obliged to secrete himself by day, his horse had escaped from him, leaving him to perform his night journeys on foot over the sharp rocks and prickly cactus plants, until not only his shoes had been worn out, but his feet had become cruelly lacerated. The constant fear which had preyed upon his heart of finding his family murdered, had produced fearful havoc in the life-forces; and although Mr. Spalding had the happiness of finding that the Nez Perces had been true to Mrs. Spalding, defending her from destruction, yet so great had been the first shock, and so long continued the strain, that his nervous system remained a wreck ever afterward.

CHAPTER XXXV.

1847. WHEN Dr. Whitman reached home on that Sunday night, after parting with Mr. Spalding at the Umatilla, it was already about midnight; yet he visited the sick before retiring to rest; and early in the morning resumed his duties among them. An Indian died that morning. At his burial, which the Doctor attended, he observed that but few of the friends and relatives of the deceased were present but attributed it to the fear which the Indians have of disease.

Everything about the mission was going on as usual. Quite a number of Indians were gathered about the place; but as an ox was being butchered, the crowd was easily accounted for. Three men were dressing the beef in the yard. The afternoon session of the mission school had just commenced. The mechanics belonging to the station were about their various avocations. Young Bulee was sick in the Doctor's house. Three of the orphan children who were recovering from the measles, were with the Doctor and Mrs. Whitman in the sitting-room; and also a Mrs. Osborne, one of the emigrants who had just got up from a sick bed, and who had a sick child in her arms.

The Doctor had just come in, wearied, and dejected as it was possible for his resolute spirit to be, and had seated himself, bible in hand, when several Indians came to a side door, asking permission to come in and get some medicine. The Doctor rose, got his medicines, gave them out, and

MASSACRE OF REV. DR. WHITMAN OF THE PRESBYTERIAN MISSION.

sat down again. At that moment Mrs. Whitman was in an adjoining room and did not see what followed. *Tam-a-has*, a chief called "the murderer," came behind the Doctor's chair, and raising his tomahawk, struck the Doctor in the back of the head, stunning but not killing him.

Instantly there was a violent commotion. John Sager, one of the adopted children, sprang up with his pistol in his hand, but before he could fire it, he too was struck down, and cut and hacked shockingly. In the meantime Dr. Whitman had received a second blow upon the head, and now laid lifeless on the floor. Cries and confusion filled the house.

At the first sound, Mrs. Whitman, in whose ears that whisper in the air had so long sounded, began in agony to stamp upon the floor, and wring her hands, crying out, "Oh, the Indians, the Indians!" At that moment one of the women from an adjoining building came running in, gasping with terror, for the butchery was going on outside as well, and *Tam-a-has* and his associates were now assisting at it. Going to the room where the Doctor lay insensible, Mrs. Whitman and her terrified neighbor dragged him to the sofa and laid him upon it, doing all they could to revive him. To all their inquiries he answered by a whispered "no," probably not conscious what was said.

While this was being done, the people from every quarter began to crowd into the Doctor's house, many of them wounded. Outside were heard the shrieks of women, the yells of the Indians, the roar of musketry, the noise of furious riding, of meeting war-clubs, groans, and every frightful combination of sound, such as only could be heard at such a carnival of blood. Still Mrs. Whitman sat by her husband's side, intent on trying to rouse him to say one coherent word.

Nearer and nearer came the struggle, and she heard

some one exclaim that two of her friends were being murdered beneath the window. Starting up, she approached the casement to get a view, as if by looking she could save; but that moment she encountered the fiendish gaze of Jo Lewis the half-breed, and comprehended his guilt. "Is it *you*, Jo, who are doing this?" she cried. Before the expression of horror had left her lips, a young Indian who had been a special favorite about the mission, drew up his gun and fired, the ball entering her right breast, when she fell without a groan.

When the people had at first rushed in, Mrs. Whitman had ordered the doors fastened and the sick children removed to a room up stairs. Thither now she was herself conveyed, having first recovered sufficiently to stagger to the sofa where lay her dying husband. Those who witnessed this strange scene, say that she knelt and prayed— prayed for the orphan children she was leaving, and for her aged parents. The only expression of personal regret she was heard to utter, was sorrow that her father and mother should live to know she had perished in such a manner.

In the chamber were now gathered Mrs. Whitman, Mrs. Hayes, Miss Bulee, Catharine Sager, thirteen years of age, and three of the sick children, besides Mr. Rogers and Mr. Kimble. Scarcely had they gained this retreat when the crashing of windows and doors was heard below, and with whoops and yells the savages dashed into the sitting-room where Doctor Whitman still lay dying. While some busied themselves removing from the house the goods and furniture, a chief named *Te-lau-ka-ikt*, a favorite at the mission, and on probation for admission into the church, deliberately chopped and mangled the face of his still breathing teacher and friend with his tomahawk, until every feature was rendered unrecognizable.

The children from the school-house were brought into the kitchen of the Doctor's house about this time, by Jo Lewis, where, he told them, they were going to be shot. Mr. Spalding's little girl Eliza, was among them. Understanding the native language, she was fully aware of the terrible import of what was being said by their tormentors. While the Indians talked of shooting the children huddled together in the kitchen, pointing their guns, and yelling, Eliza covered her face with her apron, and leaned over upon the sink, that she might not see them shoot her. After being tortured in this manner for some time, the children were finally ordered out of doors.

While this was going on, a chief called *Tamt-sak-y*, was trying to induce Mrs. Whitman to come down into the sitting-room.

She replied that she was wounded and could not do so, upon which he professed much sorrow, and still desired her to be brought down, "If you are my friend *Tamt-sak-y*, come up and see me," was her reply to his professions, but he objected, saying there were Americans concealed in the chamber, whom he feared might kill him. Mr. Rogers then went to the head of the stairs and endeavored to have the chief come up, hoping there might be some friendly ones, who would aid them in escaping from the murderers. *Tamt-sak-y*, however, would not come up the stairs, although he persisted in saying that Mrs. Whitman should not be harmed, and that if all would come down and go over to the other house where the families were collected, they might do so in safety.

The Indians below now began to call out that they were going to burn the Doctor's house. Then no alternative remained but to descend and trust to the mercy of the savages. As Mrs. Whitman entered the sitting-room, leaning on one arm of Mr. Rogers, who also was wounded in the head, and had a broken arm, she caught a view of the shockingly mutilated face of her husband and fell fainting upon the sofa, just as Doctor Whitman gave a dying gasp.

Mr. Rogers and Mrs. Hayes now attempted to get the sofa, or settee, out of the house, and had succeeded in moving it through the kitchen to the door. No sooner did they appear in the open door-way than a volley of balls assailed them. Mr. Rogers fell at once, but did not die immediately, for one of the most horrid features in this horrid butchery was, that the victims were murdered by torturing degrees. Mrs. Whitman also received several gunshot wounds, lying on the settee. Francis Sager, the oldest of her adopted boys, was dragged into the group of dying ones and shot down.

The children, who had been turned out of the kitchen were still huddled together about the kitchen door, so near to this awful scene that every incident was known to them, so near that the flashes from the guns of the Indians burnt their hair, and the odor of the blood and the burning powder almost suffocated them.

At two o'clock in the afternoon the massacre had commenced. It was now growing dusk, and the demons were eager to finish their work. Seeing that life still lingered in the mangled bodies of their victims, they finished their atrocities by hurling them in the mud and gore which filled the yard, and beating them upon their faces with whips and clubs, while the air was filled with the noise of their shouting, singing, and dancing—the Indian women and children assisting at these orgies, as if the Bible had never been preached to them. And thus, after eleven years of patient endeavor to save some heathen souls alive, perished Doctor and Mrs. Whitman.

In all that number of Indians who had received daily kindnesses at the hands of the missionaries, only two showed any compassion. These two, *Ups* and *Madpool*, Walla-Wallas, who were employed by the Doctor, took the children away from the sickening sights that surrounded them, into the kitchen pantry, and there in secret tried to comfort them.

When night set in the children and families were all removed to the building called the mansion-house, where they spent a night of horror; all, except those who were left in Mrs. Whitman's chamber, from which they dared not descend, and the family of Mr. Osborne, who escaped.

On the first assault Mr. and Mrs. Osborne ran into their bedroom which adjoined the sitting-room, taking with them their three small children. Raising a plank in the floor, Mr. O. quickly thrust his wife and children into the space beneath, and then following, let the plank down to its place. Here they remained until darkness set in, able to hear all that was passing about them, and fearing to stir. When all was quiet at the Doctor's house, they stole out under cover of darkness and succeeded in reaching Fort Walla-Walla, after a painful journey of several days, or rather nights, for they dared not travel by day.

Another person who escaped was a Mr. Hall, carpenter, who in a hand to hand contest with an Indian, received a wound in the face, but finally reached the cover of some bushes where he remained until dark, and then fled in the direction of Fort Walla-Walla. Mr. Hall was the first to arrive at the fort, where, contrary to his expectations, and to all humanity, he was but coldly received by the gentleman in charge, Mr. McBean.

Whether it was from cowardice or cruelty as some alleged, that Mr. McBean rejoiced in the slaughter of the Protestant missionaries, himself being a Catholic, can never be known. Had that been true, one might have supposed that their death would have been enough, and that he

27

might have sheltered a wounded man fleeing for his life, without grudging him this atom of comfort. Unfortunately for Mr. McBean's reputation, he declined to grant such shelter willingly. Mr. Hall remained, however, twelve hours, until he heard a report that the women and children were murdered, when, knowing how unwelcome he was, and being in a half distracted state, he consented to be set across the Columbia to make his way as best he could to the Wallamet. From this hour he was never seen or heard from, the manner of his death remaining a mystery to his wife and their family of five children, who were among the prisoners at Waiilatpu.

When Mr. Osborne left the mission in the darkness, he was able only to proceed about two miles, before Mrs. Osborne's strength gave way, she lately having been confined by an untimely birth; and he was compelled to stop, secreting himself and family in some bushes. Here they remained, suffering with cold, and insufficient food, having only a little bread and cold mush which they had found in the pantry of the Doctor's house, before leaving it. On Tuesday night, Mrs. O. was able to move about three miles more: and again they were compelled to stop. In this way to proceed, they must all perish of starvation; therefore on Wednesday night Mr. O. took the second child and started with it for the fort, where he arrived before noon on Thursday.

Although Mr. McBean received him with friendliness of manner, he refused him horses to go for Mrs. Osborne and his other children, and even refused to furnish food to relieve their hunger, telling him to go to the Umatilla, and forbidding his return to the fort. A little food was given to himself and child, who had been fasting since Monday night. Whether Mr. McBean would have allowed this man to perish is uncertain: but certain it is that some base or cowardly motive made him exceedingly cruel to both Hall and Osborne.

While Mr Osborne was partaking of his tea and crackers, there arrived at the fort Mr. Stanley, the artist, whom the reader will remember having met in the mountains several years before. When the case became known to him, he offered his horses immediately to go for Mrs. Osborne. Shamed into an appearance of humanity, Mr. McBean then furnished an Indian guide to accompany Mr. O. to the Umatilla, where he still insisted the fugitives should go, though this was in the murderer's country.

A little meat and a few crackers were furnished for the supper of the travelers; and with a handkerchief for his hatless head and a pair of socks for his child's naked feet, all furnished by Mr. Stanley, Mr. Osborne set out to return to his suffering wife and children. He and his guide traveled rapidly, arriving in good time near the spot where he believed his family to be concealed. But the darkness had confused his recollection, and after beating the bushes until daylight, the unhappy husband and father was about to give up the search in despair, when his guide at length discovered their retreat.

The poor mother and children were barely alive, having suffered much from famine and exposure, to say nothing of their fears. Mrs. Osborne was compelled to be tied to the Indian in order to sit her horse. In this condition the miserable fugitives turned toward the Umatilla, in obedience to the command of McBean, and were only saved from being murdered by a Cayuse by the scornful words of the guide, who shamed the murderer from his purpose of slaughtering a sick and defenceless family. At a Canadian farm-house, where they stopped to change horses, they were but roughly received ; and learning here that *Tamt-sak-y's* lodge was near by, Mrs. Osborne refused to proceed any farther toward the Umatilla. She said, " I doubt if I can live to reach the Umatilla ; and if I must die, I may as well die at the gates of the Fort." Let us, then, turn back to the Fort."

To this the guide assented, saying it was not safe going among the Cayuses. The little party, quite exhausted, reached Walla-Walla about ten o'clock at night, and were at once admitted. Contrary to his former course, Mr. McBean now ordered a fire made to warm the benumbed travelers, who, after being made tolerably comfortable, were placed in a secret room of the fort. Again Mr. Osborne was importuned to go away, down to the Walla-met, Mr. McBean promising to take care of his family and furnish him an outfit if he would do so. Upon being asked to furnish a boat, and Indians to man it, in order that the family might accompany him, he replied that his Indians refused to go.

From all this reluctance, not only on the part of Mc-Bean, but of the Indians also, to do any act which appeared like befriending the Americans, it would appear that there was a very general fear of the Cayuse Indians, and a belief that they were about to inaugurate a general war upon the Americans, and their friends and allies. Mr. Osborne, however, refused to leave his family behind, and Mr. McBean was forced to let him remain until relief came. When it did come at last, in the shape of Mr. Ogden's party, *Stickas*, the chief who had warned Mr. Spalding, showed his kind feeling for the sufferers by removing his own cap and placing it on Mr. Osborne's head, and by tying a handkerchief over the ears of Mr. Osborne's little son, as he said, " to keep him warm, going down the river." Sadly indeed, did the little ones who suffered by the massacre at Waiilatpu, stand in need of any Christian kindness.

CHAPTER XXXVI.

1847. A FULL account of the horrors of the Waii-latpu massacre, together with the individual sufferings of the captives whose lives were spared, would fill a volume, and be harrowing to the reader ; therefore, only so much of it will be given here as, from its bearing upon Oregon history, is important to our narrative.

The day following the massacre, being Tuesday, was the day on which Mr. Spalding was met and warned not to go to the mission, by the Vicar General, Brouillet. Happening at the mission on that day, and finding the bodies of the victims still unburied, Brouillet had them hastily interred before leaving, if interment it could be called which left them still a prey to wolves. The reader of this chapter of Oregon history will always be very much puzzled to understand by what means the Catholic priests procured their perfect exemption from harm during this time of terror to the Americans. Was it that they were French, and that they came into the country *only* as mis-sionaries of a religion adapted to the savage mind, and not as settlers ? Was it at all owing to the fact that they were celibates, with no families to excite jealous feelings of comparison in the minds of their converts ?

Through a long and bitter war of words, which fol-lowed the massacre at Waiilatpu, terrible sins were charged upon the priests—no less than inciting the Indians to the murder of the Protestants, and winking at the atrocities of every kind committed by the savages. Whether they feared to enter into the quarrel, and were restrained from showing sympathy solely by this fear, is a question only themselves can determine. Certain it is, that they preserved a neutral position, when to be neutral was to seem, if not to be, devoid of human sympathies. That the event would have happened without any other provocation than such as the Americans furnished by their own reckless disregard of Indian prejudices, seems evident. The question, and the only question which is suggested by a knowledge of all the circumstances, is whether the event was helped on by an intelligent outside influence.

It was quite natural that the Protestants should wonder at the immunity from danger which the priests enjoyed; and that, not clearly seeing the reason, they should suspect them of collusion with the Indians. It was natural, too, for the sufferers from the massacre to look for some expression of sympathy from any and all denominations of Christians; and that, not receiving it, they should have doubts of the motives which prompted such reserve. The story of that time is but an unpleasant record, and had best be lightly touched upon.

The work of death and destruction did not close with the first day at Waiilatpu. Mr. Kimble, who had remained in the chamber of the Doctor's house all night, had suffered much from the pain of his broken arm. On Tuesday, driven desperate by his own sufferings, and those of the three sick children with him, one of whom was the little Helen Mar Meek, he resolved to procure some water from the stream which ran near the house. But he had not proceeded more than a few rods before he was shot down and killed instantly. The same day, a Mr. Young, from the saw-mill, was also killed. In the course of the week, Mr. Bulee, who was sick over at the mansion, was brutally murdered.

Meanwhile the female captives and children were enduring such agony as seldom falls to the lot of humanity to suffer. Compelled to work for the Indians, their feelings were continually harrowed up by the terrible sights which everywhere met their eyes in going back and forth between the houses, in carrying water from the stream, or moving in any direction whatever. For the dead were not removed until the setting in of decay made it necessary to the Indians themselves.

The goods belonging to the mission were taken from the store-room, and the older women ordered to make them up into clothing for the Indians. The buildings were plundered of everything which the Indians coveted; all the rest of their contents that could not be made useful to themselves were destroyed. Those of the captives who were sick were not allowed proper attention, and in a day or two Helen Mar Meek died of neglect.

Thus passed four or five days. On Saturday a new horror was added to the others. The savages began to carry off the young women for wives. Three were thus dragged away to Indian lodges to suffer tortures worse than death. One young girl, a daughter of Mr. Kimble, was taken possession of by the murderer of her father, who took daily delight in reminding her of that fact, and when her sorrow could no longer be restrained, only threatened to exchange her for another young girl who was also a wife by compulsion.

Miss Bulee, the eldest of the young women at the mission, and who was a teacher in the mission school, was taken to the Umatilla, to the lodge of *Five-Crows*. As has before been related, there was a house on the Umatilla belonging to *Tan-i-tan*, in which were residing at this time two Catholic priests—the Vicar-General Brouillet, and Blanchet, Bishop of Walla-Walla. To this house Miss Bulee applied

for protection, and was refused, whether from fear, or from
the motives subsequently attributed to them by some
Protestant writers in Oregon, is not known to any but
themselves. The only thing certain about it is, that Miss
Bulee was allowed to be violently dragged from their
presence every night, to return to them weeping in the
morning, and to have her entreaties for their assistance
answered by assurances from them that the wisest course
for her was to submit. And this continued for more than
two weeks, until the news of Mr. Ogden's arrival at Walla-
Walla became known, when Miss Bulee was told that if
Five-Crows would not allow her to remain at their house
altogether, she must remain at the lodge of *Five-Crows*
without coming to their house at all, well knowing what
Five-Crows would do, but wishing to have Miss Bulee's
action seem voluntary, from shame perhaps, at their own
cowardice. Yet the reason they gave ought to go for all
it is worth—that they being priests could not have a
woman about their house. In this unhappy situation did
the female captives spend three most miserable weeks.

In the meantime the mission at Lapwai had been broken
up, but not destroyed, nor had any one suffered death as
was at first feared. The intelligence of the massacre at
Waiilatpu was first conveyed to Mrs. Spalding by a Mr.
Camfield, who at the breaking out of the massacre, fled
with his wife and children to a small room in the attic of
the mansion, from the window of which he was able to
behold the scenes which followed. When night came Mr.
Camfield contrived to elude observation and descend into
the yard, where he encountered a French Canadian long
in the employ of Dr. Whitman, and since suspected to
have been privy to the plan of the murders. To him Mr.
Camfield confided his intention to escape, and obtained a
promise that a horse should be brought to a certain place

at a certain time for his use. But the Canadian failing to appear with his horse, Mr. C. set out on foot, and under cover of night, in the direction of the Lapwai mission. He arrived in the Nez Perce country on Thursday. On the following day he came upon a camp of these people, and procured from them a guide to Lapwai, without, however, speaking of what had occurred at Waiilatpu.

The caution of Mr. Camfield relates to a trait of Indian character which the reader of Indian history must bear in mind, that is, the close relationship and identity of feeling of allied tribes. Why he did not inform the Nez Perces of the deed done by their relatives, the Cayuses, was because in that case he would have expected them to have sympathized with their allies, even to the point of making him a prisoner, or of taking his life. It is this fact concerning the Indian character, which alone furnishes an excuse for the conduct of Mr. McBean and the Catholic priests. Upon it Mr. Camfield acted, making no sign of fear, nor betraying any knowledge of the terrible matter on his mind to the Nez Perces.

On Saturday afternoon Mr. C. arrived at Mrs. Spalding's house and dismissed his guide with the present of a buffalo robe. When he was alone with Mrs. Spalding he told his unhappy secret. It was then that the strength and firmness of Mrs. Spalding's character displayed itself in her decisive action. Well enough she knew the close bond between the Nez Perces and Cayuses, and also the treachery of the Indian character. But she saw that if affairs were left to shape themselves as Mr. Camfield entreated they might be left to do, putting off the evil day,—that when the news came from the Cayuses, there would be an outbreak.

The only chance of averting this danger was to inform the chiefs most attached to her, at once, and throw herself and her family upon their mercy. Her resolution was taken not an hour too soon. Two of the chiefs most relied upon happened to be at the place that very afternoon, one of whom was called *Jacob*, and the other *Eagle*. To these two Mrs. Spalding confided the news without delay, and took counsel of them. According to her hopes, they assumed the responsibility of protecting her. One of them went to inform his camp, and give them orders to stand by Mrs. S., while the other carried a note to Mr. Craig, one of our Rocky Mountain acquaintances, who lived ten miles from the mission.

Jacob and *Eagle*, with two other friendly chiefs, decided that Mrs. S. must go to their camp near Mr. Craig's; because in case the Cayuses came to the mission as was to be expected, she would be safer with them. Mrs. S. however would not consent to make the move on the Sabbath, but begged to be allowed to remain quiet until Monday. Late Saturday evening Mr. Craig came down; and Mrs. Spalding endeavored with his assistance to induce the Indians to carry an express to Cimikain in the country of the Spokanes, where Messrs. Walker and Eells had a station. Not an Indian could be persuaded to go. An effort, also, was made by the heroic and suffering wife and mother, to send an express to Waiilatpu to learn the fate of her daughter, and if possible of her husband. But the Indians were none of them inclined to go. They said, without doubt all the women and children were slain. That Mr. Spalding was alive no one believed.

The reply of Mrs. S. to their objections was that she could not believe that they were her friends if they would not undertake this journey, for the relief of her feelings under such circumstances. At length *Eagle* consented to go; but so much opposed were the others to having anything done which their relations, the Cayuses, might be displeased with, that it was nearly twenty-four hours before *Eagle* got leave to go.

On Monday morning a Nez Perce arrived from Waii-latpu with the news of what the Cayuses had done. With him were a number of Indians from the camp where Mr. Camfield had stopped for a guide, all eager for plunder, and for murder too, had not they found Mrs. Spalding protected by several chiefs. Her removal to their camp probably saved her from the fate of Mrs. Whitman.

Among those foremost in plundering the mission buildings at Lapwai were some of the hitherto most exemplary Indians among the Nez Perces. Even the chief, first in authority after Ellis, who was absent, was prominent in these robberies. For eight years had this chief, Joseph, been a member of the church at Lapwai, and sustained a good reputation during that time. How bitter must have been the feelings of Mrs. Spalding, who had a truly devoted missionary heart, when she beheld the fruit of her life's labor turned to ashes in her sight as it was by the conduct of Joseph and his family.

Shortly after the removal of Mrs. Spalding, and the pillaging of the buildings, Mr. Spalding arrived at Lapwai from his long and painful journey during which he had wandered much out of his way, and suffered many things. His appearance was the signal for earnest consultations among the Nez Perces who were not certain that they might safely give protection to him without the consent of the Cayuses. To his petition that they should carry a letter express to Fort Colville or Fort Walla-Walla, they would not consent. Their reason for refusing seemed to be a fear that such a letter might be answered by an armed body of Americans, who would come to avenge the deaths of their countrymen.

To deprive them of this suspicion, Mr. Spalding told

them that as he had been robbed of everything, he had
no means of paying them for their services to his family,
and that it was necessary to write to Walla-Walla for
blankets, and to the Umatilla for his horses. He assured
them that he would write to his countrymen to keep quiet,
and that they had nothing to fear from the Americans.
The truth was, however, that he had forwarded through
Brouillet, a letter to Gov. Abernethy asking for help
which could only come into that hostile country armed
and equipped for war. And it was fearing this, that the
Indians detained him and his family as hostages until it
became apparent what the Americans meant to do.

Happily for the captives both at Waiilatpu and elsewhere, the prompt action of the Hudson's Bay Company
averted any collision between the Indians and Americans,
until after they had been ransomed.

Late in the month of December there arrived in Oregon City to be delivered to the governor, sixty-two captives, bought from the Cayuses and Nez Perces by Hudson's Bay blankets and goods; and obtained at that price
by Hudson's Bay influence. "No other power on earth,"
says Joe Meek, the American, "could have rescued those
prisoners from the hands of the Indians;" and no man
better than Mr. Meek understood the Indian character,
or the Hudson's Bay Company's power over them.

The number of victims to the Waiilatpu massacre was
fourteen. None escaped who had not to mourn a father,
brother, son, or friend. If "the blood of the martyrs is
the seed of the church," there ought to arise on the site
of Waiilatpu a generation of extraordinary piety. As for
the people for whom a noble man and woman, and numbers of innocent persons were sacrificed, they have returned to their traditions; with the exception of the Nez
Perces, who under the leadership of their old teacher Mr.

Spalding, have once more resumed the pursuits of civilized and Christianized nations.

As early in the Spring as possible Messrs. Walker and Eells left the Cimikain mission, and settled in the Wallamet Valley, leaving the upper country entirely in the hands of the Indians for a period of several years, during which Oregon went through her Indian wars.

CHAPTER XXXVII.

1847-8. WHEN the contents of Mr. Douglas' letter to the governor became known to the citizens of the Wallamet settlement, the greatest excitement prevailed. On the reading of that letter, and those accompanying it, before the House, a resolution was immediately introduced authorizing the governor to raise a company of riflemen, not to exceed fifty in number, to occupy and hold the mission station at the Dalles, until a larger force could be raised, and such measures adopted as the government might think advisable. This resolution being sent to the governor without delay, received his approval, when the House adjourned.

A large meeting of the citizens was held that evening, which was addressed by several gentlemen, among whom was Meek, whose taste for Indian fighting was whetted to keenness by the aggravating circumstances of the Waiilatpu massacre, and the fact that his little Helen Mar was among the captives. Impatient as was Meek to avenge the murders, he was too good a mountain-man to give any rash advice. All that could be done under the existing circumstances was to trust to the Hudson's Bay Company for the rescue of the prisoners, and to take such means for defending the settlements as the people in their unarmed condition could devise.

The legislature undertook the settlement of the question of ways and means. To raise money for the carrying out of the most important measures immediately, was a task which after some consideration was entrusted to three commissioners; and by these commissioners letters were addressed to the Hudson's Bay Company, the superintendent of the Methodist mission, and to the "merchants and citizens of Oregon." The latter communication is valuable as fully explaining the position of affairs at that time in Oregon. It is dated Dec. 17th, and was as follows:

GENTLEMEN:—You are aware that the undersigned have been charged by the legislature of our provisional government with the difficult duty of obtaining the necessary means to arm, equip, and support in the field a force sufficient to obtain full satisfaction of the Cayuse Indians, for the late massacre at Waiilatpu, and to protect the white population of our common country from further aggression.

In furtherance of this object they have deemed it their duty to make immediate application to the merchants and citizens of the country for the requisite assistance.

Though clothed with the power to pledge, to the fullest extent, the faith and means of the present government of Oregon, they do not consider this pledge the only security to those who, in this distressing emergency, may extend to the people of this country the means of protection and redress.

Without claiming any special authority from the government of the United States to contract a debt to be liquidated by that power, yet, from all precedents of like character in the history of our country, the undersigned feel confident that the United States government will regard the murder of the late Dr. Whitman and his lady, as a national wrong, and will fully justify the people of Oregon in taking active measures to obtain redress for that outrage, and for their protection from further aggression.

The right of self-defence is tacitly acknowledged to every body politic in the confederacy to which we claim to belong, and in every case similar to our own, within our knowledge, the general government has promptly assumed the payment of all liabilities growing out of the measures taken by the constituted authorities, to protect the lives and property of those who reside within the limits of their districts.

If the citizens of the States and territories, east of the Rocky mountains, are justified in promptly acting in such emergencies, who are under the immediate protection of the general government, there appears no room for doubt that the lawful acts of the Oregon government will receive a like approval.

Though the Indians of the Columbia have committed a great outrage upon our fellow citizens passing through their country, and residing among them, and their punishment for these murders may, and ought to be, a prime object with every citizen of Oregon, yet, as that duty more particularly devolves upon the government of the United States, and admits of delay, we do not make this the strongest ground upon which to found our earnest appeal to you for pecuniary assistance. It is a fact well known to every person acquainted with the Indian character, that, by passing silently over their repeated thefts, robberies, and murders of our fellow-citizens, they have been emboldened to the commission of the appalling massacre at Waiilatpu. They call us women, destitute of the hearts and courage of men, and if we allow this wholesale murder to pass by as former aggressions, who can tell how long either life or property will be secure in any part of this country, or what moment the Willamette will be the scene of blood and carnage.

The officers of our provisional government have nobly performed their duty. None can doubt the readiness of the patriotic sons of the west to offer their personal services in defence of a cause so righteous. So it now rests with you, gentlemen, to say whether our rights and our fire-sides shall be defended, or not.

Hoping that none will be found to falter in so high and so sacred a duty, we beg leave, gentlemen, to subscribe ourselves,

Your servants and fellow-citizens,

JESSE APPLEGATE,
A. L. LOVEJOY,
GEO. L. CURRY,
Commissioners.

A similar letter had been addressed to the Hudson's Bay Company, and to the Methodist mission. From each of these sources such assistance was obtained as enabled the colony to arm and equip the first regiment of Oregon riflemen, which in the month of January proceeded to the Cayuse country. The amount raised, however, was very small, being less than five thousand dollars, and it became imperatively necessary that the government of the United States should be called upon to extend its aid and protection to the loyal but distressed young territory.

In view of this necessity it was resolved in the legislature to send a messenger to carry the intelligence of the massacre to Gov. Mason of California, and through him to the commander of the United States squadron in the Pacific, that a vessel of war might be sent into the Columbia River, and arms and ammunition borrowed for the present emergency, from the nearest arsenal. For this duty was chosen Jesse Applegate, Esq., a gentleman who combined in his character and person the ability of the statesman with the sagacity and strength of the pioneer. Mr. Applegate, with a small party of brave men, set out in midwinter to cross the mountains into California, but such was the depth of snow they encountered that traveling became impossible, even after abandoning their horses, and they were compelled to return.

The messenger elected to proceed to the United States was Joseph L. Meek, whose Rocky Mountain experiences eminently fitted him to encounter the dangers of such a winter journey, and whose manliness, firmness, and ready wit stood him instead of statesmanship.

On the 17th December Meek resigned his seat in the House in order to prepare for the discharge of his duty as messenger to the United States. On the 4th of January, armed with his credentials from the Oregon legislature, and bearing dispatches from that body and the Governor to the President, he at length set out on the long and perilous expedition, having for traveling companions Mr. John Owens, and Mr. George Ebbarts—the latter having formerly been a Rocky Mountain man, like himself.

At the Dalles they found the first regiment of Oregon Riflemen, under Major Lee, of the newly created army of Oregon. From the reports which the Dalles Indians brought in of the hostility of the Indians beyond the Des Chutes River it was thought best not to proceed before the arrival of the remainder of the army, when all the forces would proceed at once to Waiilatpu. Owing to various delays, the army, consisting of about five hundred men, under Colonel Gilliam, did not reach the Dalles until late in January, when the troops proceeded at once to the seat of war.

28

The reports concerning the warlike disposition of the Indians proved to be correct. Already, the Wascopams or Dalles Indians had begun robbing the mission at that place, when Colonel Lee's arrival among them with troops had compelled them to return the stolen property. As the army advanced they found that all the tribes above the Dalles were holding themselves prepared for hostilities. At Well Springs, beyond the Des Chutes River, they were met by a body of about six hundred Indians to whom they gave battle, soon dispersing them, the superior arms and equipments of the whites tending to render timid those tribes yet unaccustomed to so superior an enemy. From thence to Waiilatpu the course of the army was unobstructed.

In the meantime the captives had been given up to the Hudson's Bay Company, and full particulars of the massacre were obtained by the army, with all the subsequent abuses and atrocities suffered by the prisoners. The horrible details were not calculated to soften the first bitterness of hatred which had animated the volunteers on going into the field. Nor was the appearance of an armed force in their midst likely to allay the hostile feelings with which other causes had inspired the Indians. Had not the captives already been removed out of the country, no influence, not even that of the Hudson's Bay Company, could have prevailed to get them out of the power of their captors then. Indeed, in order to treat with the Cayuses in the first place, Mr. Ogden had been obliged to promise peace to the Indians, and now they found instead of peace, every preparation for war. However, as the army took no immediate action, but only remained in their country to await the appearance of the commissioners appointed by the legislature of Oregon to hold a council with the chiefs of the various tribes, the Cayuses were forced to observe the outward semblance of amity while these councils were pending.

Arrived at Waiilatpu, the friends and acquaintances of Dr. Whitman were shocked to find that the remains of the victims were still unburied, although a little earth had been thrown over them. Meek, to whom, ever since his meeting with her in the train of the fur-trader, Mrs. Whitman had seemed all that was noble and captivating, had the melancholy satisfaction of bestowing, with others, the last sad rite of burial upon such portions of her once fair person as murder and the wolves had not destroyed. Some tresses of golden hair were severed from the brow so terribly disfigured, to be given to her friends in the Wallamet as a last and only memorial. Among the State documents at Salem, Oregon, may still be seen one of these relics of the Waiilatpu tragedy.

Not only had Meek to discover and inter the remains of Dr. and Mrs. Whitman, but also of his little girl, who was being educated at the mission, with a daughter of his former leader, Bridger.

This sad duty performed, he immediately set out, escorted by a company of one hundred men under Adjutant Wilcox, who accompanied him as far as the foot of the Blue Mountains. Here the companies separated, and Meek went on his way to Washington.

CHAPTER XXXVIII.

1848. MEEK's party now consisted of himself, Ebbarts, Owens, and four men, who being desirous of returning to the States took this opportunity. However, as the snow proved to be very deep on the Blue Mountains, and the cold severe, two of these four volunteers became discouraged and concluded to remain at Fort Boise, where was a small trading post of the Hudson's Bay Company.

In order to avoid trouble with the Indians he might meet on the western side of the Rocky mountains, Meek had adopted the red belt and Canadian cap of the employees of the Hudson's Bay Company; and to this precaution was owing the fact of his safe passage through the country now all infected with hostility caught from the Cayuses. About three days' travel beyond Fort Boise, the party met a village of Bannack Indians, who at once made warlike demonstrations; but on seeing Meek's costume, and receiving an invitation to hold a 'talk', desisted, and received the travelers in a friendly manner. Meek informed the chief, with all the gravity which had won for him the name of "*shiam shuspusia*" among the Crows in former years, that he was going on the business of the Hudson's Bay Company to Fort Hall; and that Thomas McKay was a day's march behind with a large trading party, and plenty of goods. On the receipt of this good news, the chief ordered his braves to fall back, and permit the party to pass. Yet, fearing the deception might be discovered, they thought it prudent to travel day and night until they reached Fort Hall.

At this post of the Hudson's Bay Company, in charge of Mr. Grant, they were kindly received, and stopped for a few hours of rest.   Mr. Grant being absent, his wife provided liberally for the refreshment of the party, who were glad to find themselves even for a short interval under a roof, beside a fire and partaking of freshly cooked food. But they permitted themselves no unnecessary delay. Before night they were once more on their way, though snow had now commenced to fall afresh, rendering the traveling very difficult.   For two days they struggled on, their horses floundering in the soft drifts, until further progress in that manner became impossible.   The only alternative left was to abandon their horses and proceed on snow-shoes, which were readily constructed out of willow sticks.

Taking only a blanket and their rifles, and leaving the animals to find their way back to Fort Hall, the little party pushed on.   Meek was now on familiar ground, and the old mountain spirit which had once enabled him to endure hunger, cold, and fatigue without murmuring, possessed him now.   It was not without a certain sense of enjoyment that he found himself reduced to the necessity of shooting a couple of pole-cats to furnish a supper for himself and party.   How long the enjoyment of feeling want would have lasted is uncertain, but probably only long enough to whet the appetite for plenty.

To such a point had the appetites of all the party been whetted, when, after several days of scarcity and toil, followed by nights of emptiness and cold, Meek had the agreeable surprise of falling in with an old mountain comrade on the identical ground of many a former adventure, the head-waters of Bear River.   This man, whom Meek

was delighted to meet, was Peg-leg Smith, one of the
most famous of many well-known mountain-men.   He
was engaged in herding cattle in the valley of Thomas'
Fork, where the tall grass was not quite buried under
snow, and had with him a party of ten men.

Meek was as cordially received by his former comrade
as the unbounded hospitality of mountain manners rendered it certain he would be.   A fat cow was immediately
sacrificed, which, though not buffalo meat, as in former
times it would have been, was very good beef, and furnished a luxurious repast to the pole-cat eaters of the
last several days.   Smith's camp did not lack the domestic element of women and chidren, any more than had
the trapper's camps in the flush times of the fur-trade.
Therefore, seeing that the meeting was most joyful, and
full of reminiscences of former winter camps, Smith
thought to celebrate the occasion by a grand entertainment.   Accordingly, after a great deal of roast beef had
been disposed of, a dance was called for, in which white
men and Indian women joined with far more mirth and
jollity than grace or ceremony.   Thus passed some hours
of the night, the bearer of dispatches seizing, in true
mountain style, the passing moment's pleasure, so long as
it did not interfere with the punctilious discharge of his
duty.   And to the honor of our hero be it said, nothing
was ever allowed to interfere with that.

Refreshed and provided with rations for a couple of
days, the party started on again next morning, still on
snow-shoes, and traveled up Bear River to the head-waters
of Green River, crossing from the Muddy fork over to
Fort Bridger, where they arrived very much fatigued but
quite well in little more than three days' travel.   Here
again it was Meek's good fortune to meet with his former
leader, Bridger, to whom he related what had befallen

him since turning pioneer. The meeting was joyful on both sides, clouded only by the remembrance of what had brought it about, and the reflection that both had a personal wrong to avenge in bringing about the punishment of the Cayuse murderers.

Once more Meek's party were generously fed, and furnished with such provisions as they could carry about their persons. In addition to this, Bridger presented them with four good mules, by which means the travelers were mounted four at a time, while the fifth took exercise on foot ; so that by riding or walking, turn about, they were enabled to get on very well as far as the South Pass. Here again for some distance the snow was very deep, and two of their mules were lost in it. Their course lay down the Sweetwater River, past many familiar hunting and camping grounds, to the Platte River. Owing to the deep snows, game was very scarce, and a long day of toil was frequently closed by a supperless sleep under shelter of some rock or bank, with only a blanket for cover. At Red Buttes they were so fortunate as to find and kill a single buffalo, which, separated from the distant herd, was left by Providence in the path of the famished travelers.

On reaching the Platte River they found the traveling improved, as well as the supply of game, and proceeded with less difficulty as far as Fort Laramie, a trading post in charge of a French trader named Papillion. Here again fresh mules were obtained, and the little party treated in the most hospitable manner. In parting from his entertainer, Meek was favored with this brief counsel:

"There is a village of Sioux, of about six hundred lodges, a hundred miles from here. Your course will bring you to it. Look out for yourself, and don't make a Gray muss of it!"—which latter clause referred to the affair of 1837, when the Sioux had killed the Indian escort of Mr. Gray.

When the party arrived at Ash Hollow, which they meant to have passed in the night, on account of the Sioux village, the snow was again falling so thickly that the party had not perceived their nearness to the village until they were fairly in the midst of it. It was now no safer to retreat than to proceed; and after a moment's consultation, the word was given to keep on. In truth, Meek thought it doubtful whether the Sioux would trouble themselves to come out in such a tempest, and if they did so, that the blinding snow-fall was rather in his favor. Thus reasoning, he was forcing his mule through the drifts as rapidly as the poor worried animal could make its way, when a head was protruded from a lodge door, and "Hallo, Major!" greeted his ear in an accent not altogether English.

On being thus accosted, the party came to a halt, and Meek was invited to enter the lodge, with his friends. His host on this occasion was a French trader named Le Bean, who, after offering the hospitalities of the lodge, and learning who were his guests, offered to accompany the party a few miles on its way. This he did, saying by way of explanation of this act of courtesy, "The Sioux are a bad people; I thought it best to see you safe out of the village." Receiving the thanks of the travelers, he turned back at night-fall, and they continued on all night without stopping to camp, going some distance to the south of their course before turning east again, in order to avoid any possible pursuers.

Without further adventures, and by dint of almost constant travel, the party arrived at St. Joseph, Mo., in safety, in a little over two months, from Portland, Oregon. Soon afterwards, when the circumstances of this journey became known, a steamboat built for the Missouri River trade was christened the *Joseph L. Meek*, and bore for a motto, on her pilot-house, "The quickest trip yet," in reference both to Meek's overland journey and her own steaming qualities.

As Meek approached the settlements, and knew that he must soon be thrown into society of the highest official grade, and be subjected to such ordeals as he dreaded far more than Indian fighting, or even traveling express across a continent of snow, the subject of how he was to behave in these new and trying positions very frequently occurred to him. He, an uneducated man, trained to mountain life and manners, without money, or even clothes, with nothing to depend on but the importance of his mission and his own mother wit, he felt far more keenly than his careless appearance would suggest, the difficulties and awkwardness of his position.

"I thought a great deal about it," confesses the Col. Joseph L. Meek of to-day, "and I finally concluded that as I had never tried to act like anybody but myself, I would not make myself a fool by beginning to ape other folks now. So I said, 'Joe Meek you always have been, and Joe Meek you shall remain; go ahead, Joe Meek!'"

In fact, it would have been rather difficult putting on fine gentleman airs, in that old worn-out hunting suit of his, and with not a dollar to bless himself. On the contrary, it needed just the devil-may-care temper which naturally belonged to our hero, to carry him through the remainder of his journey to Washington. To be hungry, ill-clad, dirty, and penniless, is sufficient in itself for the subduing of most spirits; how it affected the temper of the messenger from Oregon we shall now learn.

When the weary little party arrived in St. Joseph, they repaired to a hotel, and Meek requested that a meal should be served for all, but frankly confessing that they had no money to pay. The landlord, however, declined furnishing guests of his style upon such terms, and our travelers were forced to go into camp below the town. Meek now bethought himself of his letters of introduction. It chanced that he had one from two young men among the Oregon volunteers, to their father in St. Joseph. Stopping a negro who was passing his camp, he inquired whether such a gentleman was known to him; and on learning that he was, succeeded in inducing the negro to deliver the letter from his sons.

This movement proved successful. In a short space of time the gentleman presented himself, and learning the situation of the party, provided generously for their present wants, and promised any assistance which might be required in future. Meek, however, chose to accept only that which was imperatively needed, namely, something to eat, and transportation to some point on the river where he could take a steamer for St. Louis. A portion of his party chose to remain in St. Joseph, and a portion accompanied him as far as Independence, whither this same St. Joseph gentleman conveyed them in his carriage.

While Meek was stopping at Independence, he was recognized by a sister, whom he had not seen for nineteen years; who, marrying and emigrating from Virginia, had settled on the frontier of Missouri. But he gave himself no time for family reunion and gossip. A steamboat that had been frozen up in the ice all winter, was just about starting for St. Louis, and on board of this he went, with an introduction to the captain, which secured for him every privilege the boat afforded, together with the kindest attention of its officers.

When the steamer arrived in St. Louis, by one of those fortuitous circumstances so common in our hero's career,

he was met at the landing by Campbell, a Rocky Mountain trader who had formerly belonged to the St. Louis
Company. This meeting relieved him of any care about
his night's entertainment in St. Louis, and it also had another effect—that of relieving him of any further care
about the remainder of his journey; for, after hearing
Meek's story of the position of affairs in Oregon and his
errand to the United States, Campbell had given the
same to the newspaper reporters, and Meek, like Byron,
waked up next morning to find himself famous.

Having telegraphed to Washington, and received the
President's order to come on, the previous evening, our
hero wended his way to the levee the morning after his

MEEK AS STEAMBOAT RUNNER.

arrival in St. Louis. There were two steamers lying side
by side, both up for Pittsburg, with runners for each,

striving to outdo each other in securing passengers. A bright thought occurred to the moneyless envoy — he would earn his passage!

Walking on board one of the boats, which bore the name of *The Declaration*, himself a figure which attracted all eyes by his size and outlandish dress, he mounted to the hurricane deck and began to harrangue the crowd upon the levee, in the voice of a Stentor:

"This way, gentlemen, if you please. Come right on board the *Declaration*. I am the man from Oregon, with dispatches to the President of these United States, that you all read about in this morning's paper. Come on board, ladies and gentlemen, if you want to hear the news from Oregon. I've just come across the plains, two months from the Columbia River, where the Injuns are killing your missionaries. Those passengers who come aboard the *Declaration* shall hear all about it before they get to Pittsburg. Don't stop thar, looking at my old wolf-skin cap, but just come aboard, and hear what I've got to tell!"

The novelty of this sort of solicitation operated capitally. Many persons crowded on board the *Declaration* only to get a closer look at this picturesque personage who invited them, and many more because they were really interested to know the news from the far off young territory which had fallen into trouble. So it chanced that the *Declaration* was inconveniently crowded on this particular morning.

After the boat had got under way, the captain approached his roughest looking cabin passenger and inquired in a low tone of voice if he were really and truly the messenger from Oregon.

"Thar's what I've got to show for it;" answered Meek, producing his papers.

" Well, all I have to say is, Mr. Meek, that you are the best runner this boat ever had; and you are welcome to your passage ticket, and anything you desire besides."

Finding that his bright thought had succeeded so well, Meek's spirit rose with the occasion, and the passengers had no reason to complain that he had not kept his word. Before he reached Wheeling his popularity was immense, notwithstanding the condition of his wardrobe. At Cincinnati he had time to present a letter to the celebrated Doctor ——, who gave him another, which proved to be an ' open sesame' wherever he went thereafter.

On the morning of his arrival in Wheeling it happened that the stage which then carried passengers to Cumberland, where they took the train for Washington, had already departed. Elated by his previous good fortune our ragged hero resolved not to be delayed by so trivial a circumstance; but walking pompously into the stage office inquired, with an air which must have smacked strongly of the mock-heroic, if he " could have a stage for Cumberland ?"

The nicely dressed, dignified elderly gentleman who managed the business of the office, regarded the man who proffered this modest request for a moment in motionless silence, then slowly raising the spectacles over his eyes to a position on his forehead, finished his survey with unassisted vision. Somewhat impressed by the manner in which Meek bore this scrutiny, he ended by demanding " who are you ?"

Tickled by the absurdity of the tableau they were enacting, Meek straightened himself up to his six feet two, and replied with an air of superb self assurance—

" I am Envoy extraordinary and minister plenipotentiary from the Republic of Oregon to the Court of the United States !"

After a pause in which the old gentleman seemed to be recovering from some great surprise, he requested to see the credentials of this extraordinary envoy. Still more surprised he seemed on discovering for himself that the personage before him was really a messenger from Oregon to the government of the United States. But the effect was magical. In a moment the bell-rope was pulled, and in an incredibly short space of time a coach stood at the door ready to convey the waiting messenger on his way to Washington.

In the meantime in a conversation with the stage agent, Meek had explained more fully the circumstances of his mission, and the agent had become much interested. On parting, Meek received a ticket to the Relay House, with many expressions of regret from the agent that he could ticket him no farther.

"But it is all the same," said he; "you are sure to go through."

"Or run a train off the track," rejoined Meek, as he was bowed out of the office.

It happened that there were some other passengers waiting to take the first stage, and they crowded into this one, glad of the unexpected opportunity, but wondering at the queer looking passenger to whom the agent was so polite. This scarcely concealed curiosity was all that was needed to stimulate the mad-cap spirits of our so far "conquering hero." Putting his head out of the window just at the moment of starting, he electrified everybody, horses included, by the utterance of a war-whoop and yell that would have done credit to a wild Camanche. Satisfied with the speed to which this demoniac noise had excited the driver's prancing steeds, he quietly ensconced himself in his corner of the coach and waited for his fellow passengers to recover from their stunned sensations.

When their complete recovery had been effected, there followed the usual questioning and explanations, which ended in the inevitable lionizing that was so much to the taste of this sensational individual.

On the cars at Cumberland, and at the eating-houses, the messenger from Oregon kept up his sensational character, indulging in alternate fits of mountain manners, and again assuming a disproportionate amount of grandeur; but in either view proving himself very amusing. By the time the train reached the Relay House, many of the passengers had become acquainted with Meek, and were prepared to understand and enjoy each new phase of his many-sided comicality.

The ticket with which the stage agent presented him, dead-headed him only to this point. Here again he must make his poverty a jest, and joke himself through to Washington. Accordingly when the conductor came through the car in which he, with several of his new acquaintances were sitting, demanding tickets, he was obliged to tap his blanketed passenger on the shoulder to attract his attention to the "ticket, sir!"

"*Ha ko any me ca, hanch?*" said Meek, starting up and addressing him in the Snake tongue.

"Ticket, sir!" repeated the conductor, staring.

"*Ka hum pa, hanch?*" returned Meek, assuming a look which indicated that English was as puzzling to him, as Snake to other people.

Finding that his time would be wasted on this singular passenger, the conductor went on through the train; returning after a time with a fresh demand for his ticket. But Meek sustained his character admirably, and it was only through the excessive amusement of the passengers that the conductor suspected that he was being made the subject of a practical joke. At this stage of affairs it was

privately explained to him who and what his waggish customer was, and tickets were no more mentioned during
the journey.

On the arrival of the train at Washington, the heart of
our hero became for a brief moment of time " very little."
He felt that the importance of his mission demanded some
dignity of appearance—some conformity to established
rules and precedents. But of the latter he knew absolutely nothing ; and concerning the former, he realized
the absurdity of a dignitary clothed in blankets and a
wolf-skin cap. ' Joe Meek I must remain,' said he to himself, as he stepped out of the train, and glanced along the
platform at the crowd of porters with the names of their
hotels on their hat-bands. Learning from inquiry that
Coleman's was the most fashionable place, he decided that
to Coleman's he would go, judging correctly that it was
best to show no littleness of heart even in the matter of
hotels.

HAPTER XXXIX.

1848. When Meek arrived at Coleman's it was the dinner hour, and following the crowd to the dining saloon, he took the first seat he came to, not without being very much stared at. He had taken his cue and the staring was not unexpected, consequently not so embarrassing as it might otherwise have been. A bill of fare was laid beside his plate. Turning to the colored waiter who placed it there, he startled him first by inquiring in a low growling voice—

"What's that boy?"

"Bill of fare, sah," replied the "boy," who recognized the Southerner in the use of that one word.

"Read!" growled Meek again. "The people in *my* country can't read."

Though taken by surprise, the waiter, politely obedient, proceeded to enumerate the courses on the bill of fare. When he came to game——

"Stop thar, boy!" commanded Meek, "what kind of game?"

"Small game, sah."

"Fetch me a piece of antelope," leaning back in his chair with a look of satisfaction on his face.

" Got none of that sah; don't know what that ar' sah."

"Don't know!" with a look of pretended surprise. "In *my* country antelope and deer ar' small game; bear and buffalo ar' large game. I reckon if you haven't got one,

29

you havn't got the other, either. In that case you may fetch me some beef."

The waiter disappeared grinning, and soon returned with the customary thin and small cut, which Meek eyed at first contemptuously, and then accepting it in the light of a sample swallowed it at two mouthfuls, returning his plate to the waiter with an approving smile, and saying loud enough to be overheard by a score of people——

"Boy, that will do. Fetch me about four pounds of the same kind."

By this time the blanketed beef-eater was the recipient of general attention, and the "boy" who served him comprehending with that quickness which distinguishes servants, that he had no ordinary backwoodsman to deal with, was all the time on the alert to make himself useful. People stared, then smiled, then asked each other "who is it?" loud enough for the stranger to hear. Meek looked neither to the right nor to the left, pretending not to hear the whispering. When he had finished his beef, he again addressed himself to the attentive "boy."

"That's better meat than the old mule I eat in the mountains."

Upon this remark the whispering became more general, and louder, and smiles more frequent.

"What have you got to drink, boy?" continued Meek, still unconscious. "Isn't there a sort of wine called—some kind of *pain*?"

"Champagne, sah?"

"That's the stuff, I reckon; bring me some."

While Meek drank his champagne, with an occasional aside to his faithful attendant, people laughed and wondered "who the devil it was." At length, having finished his wine, and overhearing many open inquiries as to his identity, the hero of many bear-fights slowly arose, and

addressing the company through the before-mentioned
" boy," said :

" You want to know who I am ?"

" If you please, sah; yes, if you please, sah, for the
sake of these gentlemen present," replied the " boy," answering for the company.

" Wall then," proclaimed Meek with a grandiloquent
air quite at variance with his blanket coat and unkempt
hair, yet which displayed his fine person to advantage, " I
am Envoy Extraordinary and Minister Plenipotentiary from
the Republic of Oregon to the Court of the United
States!"

With that he turned and strode from the room. He
had not proceeded far, however, before he was overtaken
by a party of gentlemen in pursuit. Senator Underwood
of Kentucky immediately introduced himself, calling the
envoy by name, for the dispatch from St. Louis had prepared the President and the Senate for Meek's appearance
in Washington, though it had not advised them of his
style of dress and address. Other gentlemen were introduced, and questions followed questions in rapid succession.

When curiosity was somewhat abated, Meek expressed
a wish to see the President without delay. To Underwood's question as to whether he did not wish to make his
toilet before visiting the White House, his reply was,
" business first, and toilet afterwards."

" But," said Underwood, " even your business can wait
long enough for that."

" No, that's your mistake, Senator, and I'll tell you why:
I can't dress, for two reasons, both good ones. I've not
got a cent of money, nor a second suit of clothes."

The generous Kentuckian offered to remove the first of

the objections on the spot, but Meek declined. "I'll see the President first, and hear what he has to say about my mission." Then calling a coach from the stand, he sprang into it, answering the driver's question of where he would be taken, with another inquiry.

"Whar should a man of *my* style want to go?—to the White House, of course!" and so was driven away amid the general laughter of the gentlemen in the portico at Coleman's, who had rather doubted his intention to pay his respects to the President in his dirty blankets.

He was admitted to the Presidential mansion by a mulatto of about his own age, with whom he remembered playing when a lad, for it must be remembered that the Meeks and Polks were related, and this servant had grown up in the family. On inquiring if he could see the President, he was directed to the office of the private Secretary, Knox Walker, also a relative of Meek's on the mother's side.

On entering he found the room filled with gentlemen waiting to see the President, each when his turn to be admitted should arrive. The Secretary sat reading a paper, over the top of which he glanced but once at the new comer, to ask him to be seated. But Meek was not in the humor for sitting. He had not traveled express for more than two months, in storm and cold, on foot and on horseback, by day and by night, with or without food, as it chanced, to sit down quietly now and wait. So he took a few turns up and down the room, and seeing that the Secretary glanced at him a little curiously, stopped and said:

"I should like to see the President immediately. Just tell him if you please that there is a gentleman from Oregon waiting to see him on very important business."

At the word *Oregon*, the Secretary sprang up, dashed his paper to the ground, and crying out "Uncle Joe!" came forward with both hands extended to greet his long lost relative.

"Take care, Knox! don't come too close," said Meek stepping back, "I'm ragged, dirty, and—lousy."

"TAKE CARE, KNOX."

But Walker seized his cousin's hand, without seeming fear of the consequences, and for a few moments there was an animated exchange of questions and answers, which Meek at last interrupted to repeat his request to be admitted to the President without delay. Several times the Secretary turned to leave the room, but as often came back with some fresh inquiry, until Meek fairly refused to say another word, until he had delivered his dispatches.

When once the Secretary got away he soon returned with a request from the President for the appearance of the Oregon messenger, all other visitors being dismissed for that day. Polk's reception proved as cordial as Walker's had been. He seized the hand of his newly found relative, and welcomed him in his own name, as well as that of messenger from the distant, much loved, and long neglected Oregon. The interview lasted for a couple of hours. Oregon affairs and family affairs were talked over together; the President promising to do all for Oregon that he could do; at the same time he bade Meek make himself at home in the Presidential mansion, with true southern hospitality.

But Meek, although he had carried off his poverty and all his deficiencies in so brave a style hitherto, felt his assurance leaving him, when, his errand performed, he stood, in the presence of rank and elegance, a mere mountain-man in ragged blankets, whose only wealth consisted of an order for five hundred dollars on the Methodist mission in New York, unavailable for present emergencies. And so he declined the hospitalities of the White House, saying he "could make himself at home in an Indian wigwam in Oregon, or among the Rocky Mountains, but in the residence of the chief magistrate of a great nation, he felt out of place, and ill at ease."

Polk, however, would listen to no refusal, and still further abashed his Oregon cousin by sending for Mrs. Polk and Mrs. Walker, to make his acquaintance. Says Meek:

"When I heard the silks rustling in the passage, I felt more frightened than if a hundred Blackfeet had whooped in my ear. A mist came over my eyes, and when Mrs. Polk spoke to me I couldn't think of anything to say in return."

But the ladies were so kind and courteous that he soon began to see a little, though not quite plainly while their visit lasted. Before the interview with the President and his family was ended, the poverty of the Oregon envoy became known, which led to the immediate supplying of all his wants. Major Polk was called in and introduced; and to him was deputed the business of seeing Meek "got up" in a style creditable to himself and his relations. Meek avers that when he had gone through the hands of the barber and tailor, and surveyed himself in a full length mirror, he was at first rather embarrassed, being under the impression that he was being introduced to a fashionable and decidedly good-looking gentleman, before whose over. powering style he was disposed to shrink, with the old familiar feeling of being in blankets.

But Meek was not the sort of man to be long in getting used to a situation however novel or difficult. In a very short time he was *au fait* in the customs of the capital. His perfect frankness led people to laugh at his errors as eccentricities; his good looks and natural *bonhomie* procured him plenty of admirers; while his position at the White House caused him to be envied and lionized at once.

On the day following his arrival the President sent in a message to Congress accompanied by the memorial from the Oregon legislature and other documents appertaining to the Oregon cause. Meek was introduced to Benton, Oregon's indefatigable friend, and received from him the kindest treatment; also to Dallas, President of the Senate; Douglas, Fremont, Gen. Houston, and all the men who had identified themselves with the interests of the West.

It will be remembered that only a short time previous to the Waiilatpu massacre a delegate had left Oregon for Washington, by ship around Cape Horn, who had been accredited by the governor of the colony only, and that the legislature had subsequently passed resolutions expressive of their disapproval of "secret factions," by which was meant the mission party, whose delegate Mr. Thornton was.

It so happened that, by reason of the commander of the *Portsmouth* having assumed it to be a duty to convey Mr. Thornton from La Paz, where through the infidelity of the Captain of the *Whitton*, he was stranded, he was enabled to reach the States early in the Spring, arriving in fact a week or two before Meek reached Washington. Thus Oregon had two representatives, although not entitled to any: nor had either a right to a seat in either House; yet to one this courtesy was granted, while the two together controlled more powerful influences than were ever before or since brought to bear on the fate of any single territory of the United States. While Mr. Thornton sat among Senators as a sort of consulting member or referee, but without a vote; Meek had the private ear of the President, and mingled freely among members of both Houses, in a social character, thereby exercising a more immediate influence than his more learned coadjutor. Happily their aims were not dissimilar, although their characters were; and the proper and prudish mission delegate, though he might often be shocked by the private follies of the legislative messenger from Oregon, could find no fault with the manner in which he discharged his duty to their common country.

The bill to admit Oregon as a territory which had been so long before Congress, and failed only because certain southern Senators insisted on an amendment allowing slave property to be introduced into that territory, was again under discussion in the Senate. The following extract from a speech of Benton's, delivered May 31st, before the Senate, shows how his energies were taxed in support of the Oregon cause—a cause which he had fostered from its infancy, and which he never deserted until his efforts to extend the United States government to the Pacific Ocean were crowned with success:—

" Only three or four years ago, the whole United States seemed to be inflamed with a desire to get possession of Oregon. It was one of the absorbing and agitating questions of the continent. To cbtain exclusive possession of Oregon, the greatest efforts were.made, and it was at length obtained. What next? After this actual occupation of the entire continent, and having thus obtained exclusive possession of Oregon in order that we might govern it, we have seen session after session of Congress pass away without a single thing being done for the government of a country, to obtain possession of which we were willing to go to war with England !

Year after year, and session after session have gone by, and to this day the laws of the United States have not been extended over that Territory. In the mean time, a great community is growing up there, composed at this time of twelve thousand souls—persons from all parts of the world, from Asia as well as from Europe and America—and which, till this time, have been preserved in order by compact among themselves. Great efforts have been made to preserve order—most meritorious efforts, which have evinced their anxiety to maintain their own reputation and that of the country to which they belong. Their efforts have been eminently meritorious ; but we all know that voluntary governments cannot last—that they are temporary in their very nature, and must encounter rude shocks and resistance, under which they must fall. Besides the inconvenience resulting from the absence of an organized government, we are to recollect that there never yet has been a civilized settlement in territory occupied by the aboriginal inhabitants, in which a war between the races has not occurred. Down to the present moment, the settlers in Oregon had escaped a conflict with the Indians. Now the war between them is breaking out ; and I cannot resist the conviction, that if there had been a regularly organized government in that country, immediately after the treaty with Great Britain, with a military force to sustain it,—for a government in such a region, so remote, would be nothing without military force,—the calamities now impending over that country might have been averted.

But no government was established; and now all these evils are coming upon these people, as everybody must have foreseen they would come ; and in the depth of winter, they send to us a special messenger, who makes his way across the Rocky Mountains at a time when almost every living thing perished in the snow—when the snow was at such a depth that nothing could penetrate to the bottom of it. He made his way across, however, and brings these complaints which we now hear. They are in a suffering condition. Not a moment of time is to be lost. If the bill were passed this instant,—this morning, as I hoped it would be,—it would require the utmost degree of vigor in the execution of it to be able to send troops across the Rocky Mountains before the season of deep snow. They should cross the mountains before the month of September. I was in hopes then, that on this occasion, there would be nothing to delay action—that we should all have united in deploring that for years the proposition to give these people government and laws has been defeated by the introduction of a question of no practical consequence, but which has had the effect of depriving these people of all government, and bringing about the massacres which have taken place, and in which the benevolent missionary has fallen in the midst of his labors. All the calamities which have taken place in that country have resulted from mixing up this question, which has not a particle of practical value, with all the measures which have been introduced for the organization of a government in Oregon. All the laws passed by the Congress of the United States can have no effect on the question of slavery there. In that country there is a law superior to any which Congress can pass on the subject of slavery. There is a law of climate, of position, and of Nature herself, against it. Besides, the people of the country itself, by far the largest number of whom have gone out from slave-holding States, many of them from the State of Missouri, in their organic law, communicated to Congress more than a year ago, and printed among our documents at the last session, declare that the law of nature is against slavery in that region. Who would think of carrying slaves to the Lake of the Woods? and what would anybody think of a law of Congress which should say that slavery should or should not exist there? I was in hopes, then, that this bill would be allowed to pass through this morning. And it was in order to avoid any delay that I did not make a separate bill to raise the regiments necessary to sustain the government there. I did hope, that on this occasion—when a great political measure of the highest importance is pending, which has been delayed for years, and which delay has brought on the massacres of which we now hear—this question, which has already produced these calamities, would not have been introduced, and that some other opportunity would have been taken for its discussion. There will be opportunities enough for its discussion. The doors of legislation are open to it as a separate measure. I trust, even now, that this question will not be permitted to delay our action. The delay of a few days here will be the delay of a year in Oregon. Delay at all now, is delay not for a week or a month, but for a year, during all which time these calamities will continue.

*   *   *   *   *   *   *   *   *

With respect to the question itself, I am ready to meet it in every shape and form. Let me here say, that no gentleman on this floor must assume to be the representative of the fifteen slave-holding States. I assume to represent one— no more than one—and if I can satisfy my constituents, my duty is performed. I invade no gentleman's bailiwick, and no one shall invade mine. Let every one speak for himself. This Federal Government was made for something else than to have this pestiferous question constantly thrust upon us to the interruption of the most important business. I am willing to vote down this question at this moment; I am willing to take it up and act upon it in all its extent and bearings, at the proper time, when its consideration will not interrupt and destroy important measures. What I protest against is, to have the real business of the country—the pressing, urgent, crying business of the country— stopped, prostrated, defeated, by thrusting this question upon us. We read in Holy Writ, that a certain people were cursed by the plague of frogs, and that the plague was everywhere. You could not look upon the table but there were frogs; you could not sit down at the banquet but there were frogs; you could not go to the bridal couch and lift the sheets but there were frogs! We can see nothing, touch nothing, have no measures proposed, without having this pestilence thrust before us. Here it is, this black question, forever on the table, on the nuptial couch—everywhere! So it was not in the better days of the Republic. I remember the time when no one would have thought of asking a public man what his views were on the extension of slavery, any more than what was the length of his foot; and those were happy days which, although gone by, are remembered, and may, perhaps, be brought back.

We ought to vote down this amendment as a thing which should not be allowed to interrupt our action. Our action should not be delayed a single moment. This cruel war, which cannot continue in Oregon without extending to California, must be stopped without delay. Oregon and California must be saved from the desolation of an Indian war. Whatever opinions may be entertained upon the subject of slavery, let us agree on this point, that we will give law and government to the people of Oregon, and stop, if we can, the progress of this Indian war."

This was the tone which the friends of Oregon preserved through that last session of Congress in which the Oregon bill was under discussion.

In the meantime our hero was making the most of his advantages. He went to dinners and champagne suppers, besides giving an occasional one of the latter. At the presidential levees he made himself agreeable to witty and distinguished ladies, answering innumerable questions about Oregon and Indians, generally with a veil of reserve between himself and the questioner whenever the inquiries became, as they sometimes would, disagreeably searching. Again the spirit of perversity and mischief led him to make his answers so very direct as to startle or bewilder the questioner.

On one occasion a lady with whom he was promenading a drawing-room at some Senator's reception, admiring his handsome physique perhaps, and wondering if any woman owned it, finally ventured the question—was he married?

"Yes, indeed," answered Meek, with emphasis, "I have a wife and several children.."

"Oh dear," exclaimed the lady, "I should think your wife would be *so* afraid of the Indians!"

"Afraid of the Indians!" exclaimed Meek in his turn; "why, madam, she is an Indian herself!"

No further remarks on the subject were ventured that evening; and it is doubtful if the lady did not take his answer as a rebuke to her curiosity rather than the plain truth that it was.

Meek found his old comrade, Kit Carson, in Washington, staying with Fremont at the house of Senator Benton. Kit, who had left the mountains as poor as any other of the mountain-men, had no resource at that time except the pay furnished by Fremont for his services as guide and explorer in the California and Oregon expeditions; where, in fact, it was Carson and not Fremont who deserved fame as a path-finder. However that may be, Carson had as little money as men of his class usually have, and needed it as much. So long as Meek's purse was supplied, as it generally was, by some member of the family at the White House, Carson could borrow from him. But one being quite as careless of money as the other, they were sometimes both out of pocket at the same time. In that case the conversation was apt to take a turn like this:

Carson.   Meek, let me have some money, can't you?

Meek.   I hav 'nt got any money, Kit.

Carson.   Go and get some.

Meek.   D——n it, whar am I to get money from?

Carson.   Try the "contingent fund," can't you?

Truth to tell the contingent fund was made to pay for a good many things not properly chargeable to the necessary expenditures of "Envoy Extraordinary" like our friend from Oregon.

The favoritism with which our hero was everywhere received was something remarkable, even when all the circumstances of his relationship to the chief magistrate, and the popularity of the Oregon question were considered. Doubtless the novelty of having a bear-fighting and Indian-fighting Rocky Mountain man to lionize, was one great secret of the furore which greeted him wherever he went; but even that fails to account fully for the enthusiasm he awakened, since mountain-men had begun to be pretty well known and understood, from the journal of Fremont and other explorers. It could only have been the social genius of the man which enabled him to overcome the impediments of lack of education, and the associations of half a lifetime. But whatever was the fortunate cause of his success, he enjoyed it to the full. He took excursions about the country in all directions, petted and spoiled like any "curled darling" instead of the six-foot-two Rocky Mountain trapper that he was.

In June he received an invitation to Baltimore, tendered by the city council, and was received by that body with the mayor at its head, in whose carriage he was conveyed to Monument Square, to be welcomed by a thousand ladies, smiling and showering roses upon him as he passed. And kissing the roses because he could not kiss the ladies, he bowed and smiled himself past the festive groups waiting to receive the messenger from Oregon. Music, dining, and the parade usual to such occasions distinguished this day, which Meek declares to have been the proudest of his life; not denying that the beauty of the Baltimore ladies contributed chiefly to produce that impression.

On the fourth of July, Polk laid the corner stone of the National Monument. The occasion was celebrated with great *eclat*, the address being delivered by Winthrop, the military display, and the fire-works in the evening being unusually fine. In the procession General Scott and staff rode on one side of the President's carriage, Col. May and Meek on the other,—Meek making a great display of horsemanship, in which as a mountain-man he excelled.

A little later in the summer Meek joined a party of Congressmen who were making campaign speeches in the principal cities of the north. At Lowell, Mass., he visited the cotton factories, and was equally surprised at the extent of the works, and the number of young women employed in them. Seeing this, the forewoman requested him to stop until noon and see the girls come out. As they passed in review before him, she asked if he had made his choice.

"No," replied the gallant Oregonian, "it would be impossible to choose, out of such a lot as that; I should have to take them all."

If our hero, under all his gaity smothered a sigh of regret that he was not at liberty to take *one*—a woman like those with whom for the first time in his life he was privileged to associate—who shall blame him? The kind of life he was living now was something totally different to anything in the past. It opened to his comprehension delightful possibilities of what might have been done and enjoyed under other circumstances, yet which now never could be done or enjoyed, until sometimes he was ready to fly from all these allurements, and hide himself again in the Rocky Mountains. Then again by a desperate effort, such thoughts were banished, and he rushed more eagerly than before into every pleasure afforded by the present moment, as if to make the present atone for the past and the future.

The kindness of the ladies at the White House, while it was something to be grateful for, as well as to make him envied, often had the effect to disturb his tranquility by the suggestions it gave rise to. Yet he was always de-

A MOUNTAIN-MAN IN CLOVER.

manding it, always accepting it. So constantly was he the attendant of his lady cousins in public and in private, riding and driving, or sauntering in the gardens of the presidential mansion, that the less favored among their acquaintances felt called upon to believe themselves aggrieved. Often, as the tall form of our hero was seen with a lady on either arm promenading the gardens at evening, the question would pass among the curious but uninitiated—" Who is that?" And the reply of some jealous grumbler would be—" It is that d——d Rocky Mountain man," so loud sometimes as to be overheard by the careless trio, who smothered a laugh behind a hat or a fan.

And so passed that brief summer of our hero's life. A great deal of experience, of sight-seeing, and enjoyment had been crowded into a short few months of time. He had been introduced to and taken by the hand by the most celebrated men of the day. Nor had he failed to meet with men whom he had known in the mountains and in Oregon. His old employer, Wilkes, who was ill in Washington, sent for him to come and tell " some of those Oregon lies" for his amusement, and Meek, to humor him, stretched some of his good stories to the most wonderful dimensions.

But from the very nature of the enjoyment it could not last long; it was too vivid and sensational for constant wear. Feeling this, he began to weary of Washington, and more particularly since he had for the last few weeks been stopping away from the White House. In one of his restless moods he paid a visit to Polk, who detecting the state of his mind asked laughingly——

" Well, Meek, what do you want now?"

" I want to be franked."

" How long will five hundred dollars last you?"

"About as many days as there ar' hundreds, I reckon."

"You are shockingly extravagant, Meek. Where do you think all this money is to come from?"

"It is not my business to know, Mr. President," replied Meek, laughing, "but it *is* the business of these United States to pay the expenses of the messenger from Oregon, isn't it?"

"I think I will send you to the Secretary of War to be franked, Meek; his frank is better than mine. But no, stay; I will speak to Knox about it this time. And you must not spend your money so recklessly, Meek; it will not do—it will not do."

Meek thanked the President both for the money and the advice, but gave a champagne supper the next night, and in a week's time was as empty-handed as ever. Washington manners were in some respects too much like mountain manners for five hundred dollars to go a great ways.

CHAPTER XL.

We must go back a little way and take up the thread of Oregon's political history as it relates to the persons and events of which we have been writing. However irregular had been the appointment of a delegate for Oregon, while still unrecognized by the general government, and however distasteful as a party measure the appointment of Mr. Thornton had been to a majority of the people of Oregon, there was nevertheless sufficient merit in his acts, since events had turned out as they had, to reconcile even his enemies to them. For what did it concern the people who procured or helped to procure the blessings they asked for, so only that they were made sure of the blessings.

Mr. Thornton had done what he could in Washington to secure for Oregon the things desired by her citizens. Immediately on his arrival he had prepared, at the instance of Mr. Polk, a memorial to Congress setting forth the condition of the country and the wants of the colony. In addition to this he had prayed for the passage of a law organizing a territorial government, and donating land-claims. To be sure Congress had been memorialized on these subjects for years, and all to no purpose. But there was a decided advantage in having a man versed in law and conversant with legal forms as well as territorial wants, to assist in getting up the bills concerning Oregon. Besides, Thornton was a conscientious man, and would not agree to a fraud.

30

The territorial bill was gotten up among the friends of Oregon in the Free-Soil party, and had incorporated into it the ordinance of 1787, prohibiting slavery, and this was so not only because the free-soilers desired it, but because the people of Oregon desired it. But a few sagacious Southern members had conceived the idea of making Mr. Thornton responsible for the expunging of the obnoxious clause, by trying to convince him that the bill could never be passed with the ordinance of 1787 in it, and that would he, Thornton, but consent to have it stricken out, they were assured that the friends of free-soil would allow it to pass for the sake of waiting, expectant Oregon. So reasoned Calhoun and others.

Thornton, however, was both too wise and too faithful to be humbugged in that specious manner. He assured Mr. Calhoun that in the first place he had no authority to consent to the expunging of the ordinance of 1787; in the second place, that the people of Oregon would wait for a territorial government until they could obtain one which promised them free institutions; and in the third place, that he did not believe the free-soil party would ever allow the bill to pass, amended as Mr. Calhoun proposed; therefore that had he the authority to consent to the amendment, he should gain nothing, but lose all by doing so.

Thus, through the almost entire summer, the friends and the enemies of free-soil quarreled and schemed over Oregon. Not that any were really opposed to the extension of the Government over that territory, but only that the Southern members objected to more free soil.

The President was very anxious that the bill should pass in some shape during his administration. Benton of Missouri, was eager for its passage as it was. Butler of South Carolina, fiercely opposed to it. Numerous were the skirmishes which these two Senators had over the

Oregon question; and a duel would, in one instance, have resulted, had not the arrest of the parties put a termination to the affair.

The land bill too, gave considerable trouble; not from any opposition it encountered, but because nobody knew how much land to give each settler. Some Congressmen, in the magnificence of their generosity and compassion, were for granting one thousand acres to every white male settler of the territory. The committee who had this bill in hand, on consulting the two Oregon representatives, were informed that the proposed donation was altogether too large, and it was subsequently reduced.

The close of the session was at hand and nothing had been done except to talk. Congress was to adjourn at noon on Monday, August 14th, and it was now Saturday the 12th. The friends of Oregon were anxious; the two waiting Oregonians nearly desperate. On this morning of the 12th, the friends of the bill, under Benton's lead, determined upon obtaining a vote on the final passage of the bill; resolving that they would not yield to the usual motions for delay and adjournments, but that they would, if necessary, sit until twelve o'clock Monday.

On the other hand, the southern members, finding that no motion for adjournment could be made to prevail, Butler, of South Carolina, moved that the Senate go into executive session. This was done because under the rules of the Senate, the Oregon bill would necessarily give place to the business of the executive session. And the business to which Senator Butler proposed to call the attention of the senate was certain conduct of the gentleman from Missouri, which he characterized as dishonorable.

At the word "dishonorable" Benton sprang to his feet, exclaiming—"You lie, sir! you lie!! I cram the lie down your throat!!!" at the same time advancing toward Butler with his fist clenched and raised in a threatening manner. Butler on his part seemed very willing to engage in a personal conflict, awaiting his antagonist with the genuine game look which has formerly been supposed to be one of the signs of good southern blood.

But a fight on the floor of the Senate between two of its white-haired members could not be suffered to go on, the combatants being separated by the other Senators. who crowded in between. The eyes of Butler burned fiercely as he said to Benton over the heads of his officious friends,—

"I will see you, sir, at another time and place!"

"Very well, sir;" returned Benton: "but you will do well to understand that when I fight, I fight for a funeral!"

That this affair did not terminate in a funeral was probably owing to the arrest of the parties.

At ten o'clock Saturday evening, order having been restored, and no adjournment having yet prevailed, Senator Foote of Mississippi, arose and commenced to speak in a manner most irritatingly drawling and dull; saying that since there was to be no adjournment before twelve o'clock Monday noon, he proposed to entertain to the best of his ability the grave deliberative body before him.

Commencing at the creation of Adam, he gave the Bible Story—the creation of Eve; the fall of man; the history of the children of Israel; the stories of the prophets; ecclesiastical history,—only yielding the floor for a motion, at intervals of an hour each, continuing to drawl through the time hour after hour.

Sleepy senators betook themselves to the anteroom to lunch, to drink, to talk to the waiting ones, and to sleep. But whenever a motion was made, a page aroused the sleepers and they took their seats and voted.

Thus wore the night away.   The Sabbath morning's sun arose, and still Foote was in the midst of his Bible disquisitions.   At length, two hours after sunrise, a consultation was held between Butler, Mason, Calhoun, Davis and Foote, which resulted in the announcement that no further opposition would be offered to taking the vote upon the final passage of the Oregon bill.   The vote was then taken, the bill passed, and the weary senate adjourned, to meet again on Monday for a final adjournment.

After the adjournment on Sunday morning, Benton in alluding to the scene between himself and the senator from South Carolina, said, "he did not blame Judge Butler so much as he might ; because that d——d scoundrel Calhoun was urging Butler to it, while he himself sat saying nothing, and doing nothing, but looking as demure as a courtesan at a christening."

Truly "such are the compliments that pass when gentlemen meet."

The Land bill, or Donation act, as it is generally known, failed of being passed at this session, simply because it had to wait for the Territorial bill to be passed, being supplementary to it, and because after the passage of that bill there was no time to take up the other.

As Thornton had been chiefly instrumental in getting the Donation bill into shape, it was a severe disappointment, in not having it passed at the same session with the Territorial bill, and having to return to Oregon without this welcome present to the people of the new territory.

Collamer of Vermont, sympathizing with the failure of the Donation Law, proposed to Thornton to draw up a new bill including some amendments suggested by him, and to forward the same to his (Collamer's) address, promising to see what could be done with it thereafter.   This

Thornton did, and also carried a copy of it home to Oregon, and placed it in the hands of Oregon's first delegate to Congress, who, after making a few alterations in the bill, adopted and claimed it for his own. The bill thus amended and re-amended, became a law in September, 1850; and of that law we shall have occasion to speak hereafter.

CHAPTER XLI.

1848–9. THE long suspense ended, Meek prepared to
return to Oregon, if not without some regrets, at the same
time not unwillingly. His restless temper, and life-long
habits of unrestrained freedom began to revolt against the
conventionality of his position in Washington. Besides,
in appointing officers for the new territory, Polk had made
him United States Marshal, than which no office could
have suited him better, and he was as prompt to assume
the discharge of its duties, as all his life he had been to
undertake any duty to which his fortunes assigned him.

On the 20th of August, only six days after the passage
of the territorial bill, he received his papers from Buchanan, and set off for Bedford Springs, whither the family
from the White House were flown to escape from the suf-
focating air of Washington in August. He had brought
his papers to be signed by Polk, and being expected by
the President found everything arranged for his speedy
departure ; Polk even ordering a seat for him in the up-
coming coach, by telegraph. On learning this from the
President, at dinner, when the band was playing, Meek
turned to the leader and ordered him to play "Sweet
Home," much to the amusement of his lady cousins, who
had their own, views of the sweets of a home in Oregon.
A hurried farewell, spoken to each of his friends sepa-
rately, and Oregon's new Marshal was ready to proceed
on his long journey toward the Pacific.

The occasion of Polk's haste in the matter of getting Meek started, was his anxiety to have the Oregon government become a fact before the expiration of his term of office. The appointment of Governor of the new territory had been offered to Shields, and declined. Another commission had been made out, appointing General Joseph Lane of Indiana, Governor of Oregon, and the commission was that day signed by the President and given to Meek to be delivered to Lane in the shortest possible time. His last words to the Marshal on parting were— " God bless you, Meek. Tell Lane to have a territorial government organized during my administration."

Of the ten thousand dollars appropriated by Congress " to be expended under the direction of the President, in payment for services and expenses of such persons as had been engaged by the provisional government of Oregon in conveying communications to and from the United States; and for purchase of presents for such Indian tribes as the peace and quiet of the country required"— Thornton received two thousand six hundred dollars, Meek seven thousand four hundred, and the Indian tribes none. Whether the President believed that the peace and quiet of the country did not require presents to be made to the Indians, or whether family credit required that Meek should get the lion's share, is not known. However that may be, our hero felt himself to be quite rich, and proceeded to get rid of his superfluity, as will hereafter be seen, with his customary prodigality and enjoyment of the present without regard to the future.

Before midnight on the day of his arrival at the springs, Meek was on his way to Indiana to see General Lane. Arriving at the Newburg landing one morning at day-break, he took horse immediately for the General's residence at Newburg, and presented him with his commission soon after breakfast. Lane sat writing, when Meek, introducing himself, laid his papers before him.

"Do you accept?" asked Meek.

"Yes," answered Lane.

"How soon can you be ready to start?"

"In fifteen minutes!" answered Lane, with military promptness.

Three days, however, were actually required to make the necessary preparations for leaving his farm and proceeding to the most remote corner of the United States territory.

At St. Louis they were detained one day, waiting for a boat to Leavenworth, where they expected to meet their escort. This one day was too precious to be lost in waiting by so business-like a person as our hero, who, when nothing more important was to be done generally was found trying to get rid of his money. So, on this occasion, after having disburdened himself of a small amount in treating the new Governor and all his acquaintances, he entered into negotiations with a peddler who was importuning the passengers to buy everything, from a jack-knife to a silk dress.

Finding that Nat. Lane, the General's son, wanted a knife, but was disposed to beat down the price, Meek made an offer for the lot of a dozen or two, and thereby prevented Lane getting one at any price. Not satisfied with this investment, he next made a purchase of three whole pieces of silk, at one dollar and fifty cents per yard. At this stage of the transaction General Lane interfered sufficiently to inquire "what he expected to do with that stuff?"

"Can't tell," answered Meek; "but I reckon it is worth the money."

"Better save your money," said the more prudent Lane.

But the incorrigible spendthrift only laughed, and threatened to buy out the Jew's entire stock, if Lane persisted in preaching economy.

At St. Louis, besides his son Nat., Lane was met by Lieut. Hawkins, who was appointed to the command of the escort of twenty-five riflemen, and Dr. Hayden, surgeon of the company. This party proceeded to Leavenworth, the point of starting, where the wagons and men of Hawkins' command awaited them. At this place, Meek was met by a brother and two sisters who had come to look on him for the first time in many years. The two days' delay which was necessary to get the train ready for a start, afforded an opportunity for this family reunion, the last that might ever occur between its widely separated branches, new shoots from which extend at this day from Virginia to Alabama, and from Tennessee to California and Oregon.

By the 10th of September the new government was on its way to Oregon in the persons of Lane and Meek. The whole company of officers, men, and teamsters, numbered about fifty-five; the wagons ten; and riding-horses, an extra supply for each rider.

The route taken, with the object to avoid the snows of a northern winter, was from Leavenworth to Santa Fe, and thence down the Rio Grande to near El Paso; thence northwesterly by Tucson, in Arizona; thence to the Pimas village on the Gila River; following the Gila to its junction with the Colorado, thence northwesterly again to the Bay of San Pedro in California. From this place the company were to proceed by ship to San Francisco; and thence again by ship to the Columbia River.

On the Santa Fe trail they met the army returning from Mexico, under Price, and learned from them that they could not proceed with wagons beyond Santa Fe.

The lateness of the season, although it was not attended
with snow, as on the northern route it would have been,
subjected the travelers nevertheless to the strong, cold
winds which blow over the vast extent of open country
between the Missouri River and the high mountain range
which forms the water-shed of the continent.   It also
made it more difficult to subsist the animals, especially
after meeting Price's army, which had already swept the
country bare.

On coming near Santa Fe, Meek was riding ahead of
his party, when he had a most unexpected encounter.
Seeing a covered traveling carriage drawn up under the
shade of some trees growing beside a small stream, not
far off from the trail, he resolved, with his usual love of
adventure, to discover for himself the character of the
proprietor.   But as he drew nearer, he discovered no
one, although a camp-table stood under the trees, spread
with refreshments, not only of a solid, but a fluid nature.
The sight of a bottle of cognac induced him to dismount,
and he was helping himself to a liberal glass, when a
head was protruded from a covering of blankets inside
the carriage, and a heavy bass voice was heard in a polite
protest :

"Seems to me, stranger, you are making free with my
property !"

"Here's to you, sir," rejoined the purloiner; "it isn't
often I find as good brandy as that,"—holding out the
glass admiringly,—"but when I do, I make it a point of
honor not to pass it."

"May I inquire your name, sir?" asked the owner of
the brandy, forced to smile at the good-humored audacity
of his guest.

"I couldn't refuse to give my name after that,"—re-
placing the glass on the table,—"and I now introduce

myself as Joseph L. Meek, Esq., Marshal of Oregon, on my way from Washington to assist General Lane in establishing a territorial Government west of the Rocky Mountains."

"Meek!—what, not the Joe Meek I have heard my brothers tell so much about?"

"Joe Meek is my name; but whar did your brothers know me?" inquired our hero, mystified in his turn.

"I think you must have known Captain William Sublette and his brother Milton, ten or twelve years ago, in the Rocky Mountains," said the gentleman, getting out of the carriage, and approaching Meek with extended hand.

A delighted recognition now took place. From Solomon Sublette, the owner of the carriage and the cognac, Meek learned many particulars of the life and death of his former leaders in the mountains. Neither of them were then living; but this younger brother, Solomon, had inherited Captain Sublette's wife and wealth at the same time. After these explanations, Mr. Sublette raised the curtains of the carriage again, and assisted to descend from it a lady, whom he introduced as his wife, and who exhibited much gratification in becoming acquainted with the hero of many a tale recited to her by her former husband, Captain Sublette.

In the midst of this pleasant exchange of reminiscences, the remainder of Meek's party rode up, were introduced, and invited to regale themselves on the fine liquors with which Mr. Sublette's carriage proved to be well furnished. This little adventure gave our hero much pleasure, as furnishing a link between the past and present, and bringing freshly to mind many incidents already beginning to fade in his memory.

At Santa Fe, the train stopped to be overhauled and reconstructed. The wagons having to be abandoned, their contents had to be packed on mules, after the manner of mountain or of Mexican travel and transportation. This change accomplished, with as little delay as possible, the train proceeded without any other than the usual difficulties, as far as Tucson, when two of the twenty-five riflemen deserted, having become suddenly enamored of liberty, in the dry and dusty region of southern Arizona.

Lieutenant Hawkins, immediately on discovering the desertion, dispatched two men, well armed, to compel their return. One of the men detailed for this duty belonged to the riflemen, but the other was an American, who, with a company of Mexican packers, had joined the train at Santa Fe, and was acting in the capacity of pilot. In order to fit out this volunteer for the service, always dangerous, of retaking deserting soldiers, Meek had lent him his Colt's revolvers. It was a vain precaution, however, both the men being killed in attempting to capture the deserters ; and Meek's pistols were never more heard of, having fallen into the murderous hands of the runaways.

Drouth now began to be the serious evil with which the travelers had to contend. From the Pimas villages westward, it continually grew worse, the animals being greatly reduced from the want both of food and water. At the crossing of the Colorado, the animals had to be crossed over by swimming, the officers and men by rafts made of bulrushes. Lane and Meek being the first to be ferried over, were landed unexpectedly in the midst of a Yuma village. The Indians, however, gave them no trouble, and, except the little artifice of drowning some of the mules at the crossing, in order to get their flesh to eat, committed neither murders nor thefts, nor any outrage whatever.

It was quite as well for the unlucky mules to be

drowned and eaten as it was for their fellows to travel on over the arid desert before them until they starved and perished, which they nearly all did. From the Colorado on, the company of Lieut. Hawkins became thoroughly demoralized. Not only would the animals persist in dying, several in a day, but the soldiers also persisted in deserting, until, by the time he reached the coast, his forlorn hope was reduced to three men. But it was not the drouth in their case which caused the desertions: it was rumors which they heard everywhere along the route, of mines of gold and silver, where they flattered themselves they could draw better pay than from Uncle Sam's coffers.

The same difficulty from desertion harassed Lieutenant-Colonel Loring in the following summer, when he attempted to establish a line of posts along the route to Oregon, by the way of Forts Kearney, Laramie, and through the South Pass to Fort Hall. His mounted rifle regiment dwindled down to almost nothing. At one time, over one hundred men deserted in a body : and although he pursued and captured seventy of them, he could not keep them from deserting again at the first favorable moment. The bones of many of those gold-seeking soldiers were left on the plains, where wolves had stripped the flesh from them ; and many more finally had rude burial at the hands of fellow gold-seekers : but few indeed ever won or enjoyed that for which they risked everything.

On arriving at Cook's wells, some distance beyond the Colorado, our travelers found that the water at this place was tainted by the body of a mule which had lost its life some days before in endeavoring to get at the water. This was a painful discovery for the thirsty party to make. However, there being no water for some distance ahead, General Lane boiled some of it, and made coffee of it,

GOVERNOR LANE AND MARSHAL MEEK EN-ROUTE TO OREGON.

remarking that "maggots were more easily swallowed cooked than raw!"

And here the writer, and no doubt, the reader too, is compelled to make a reflection. Was the office of Governor of a Territory at fifteen hundred dollars a year, and Indian agent at fifteen hundred more, worth a journey of over three thousand miles, chiefly by land, even allowing that there had been no maggots in the water? *Quien sabe?*

Not far from this locality our party came upon one hundred wagons abandoned by Major Graham, who had not been able to cross the desert with them. Proceeding onward, the riders eventually found themselves on foot, there being only a few animals left alive to transport the baggage that could not be abandoned. So great was their extremity, that to quench their thirst the stomach of a mule was opened to get at the moisture it contained. In the horror and pain of the thirst-fever, Meek renewed again the sufferings he had undergone years before in the deserts inhabited by Diggers, and on the parched plains of the Snake River.

About the middle of January the Oregon Government, which had started out so gaily from Fort Leavenworth, arrived weary, dusty, foot-sore, famished, and suffering, at William's Ranch on the Santa Anna River, which empties into the Bay of San Pedro. Here they were very kindly received, and their wants ministered to.

At this place Meek developed, in addition to his various accomplishments, a talent for speculation. While overhauling his baggage, the knives and the silk which had been purchased of the *peddler* in St. Louis, were brought to light. No sooner did the senoritas catch a glimpse of the shining fabrics than they went into raptures over them, after the fashion of their sex. Seeing the state of mind

to which these raptures, if unheeded, were likely to reduce the ladies of his house, Mr. Williams approached
Meek delicately on the subject of purchase. But Meek,
in the first flush of speculative shrewdness declared that
as he had bought the goods for his own wife, he could not
find it in his heart to sell them.

However, as the senoritas were likely to prove inconsolable, Mr. Williams again mentioned the desire of his family
to be clad in silk, and the great difficulty, nay, impossi-
bility, of obtaining the much coveted fabric in that part
of the world, and accompanied his remarks with an offer
of ten dollars a yard for the lot. At this magnificent offer
our hero affected to be overcome by regard for the feelings of the senoritas, and consented to sell his dollar and
a-half silks for ten dollars per yard.

In the same manner, finding that knives were a desirable article in that country, very much wanted by miners
and others, he sold out his dozen or two, for an ounce
each of gold-dust, netting altogether the convenient little
profit of about five hundred dollars. When Gen. Lane
was informed of the transaction, and reminded of his objections to the original purchase, he laughed heartily.

"Well, Meek," said he, "you were drunk when you
bought them, and by —— I think you must have been
drunk when you sold them; but drunk or sober, I will
own you can beat me at a bargain."

Such bargains, however, became common enough about
this time in California, for this was the year memorable in
California history, of the breaking out of the gold-fever,
and the great rush to the mines which made even the
commonest things worth their weight in gold-dust.

Proceeding to Los Angelos, our party, once more comfort-
ably mounted, found traveling comparatively easy. At this
place they found quartered the command of Maj. Graham,

whose abandoned wagons had been passed at the *Hornella* on the Colorado River. The town, too, was crowded with miners, men of every class, but chiefly American adventurers, drawn together from every quarter of California and Mexico by the rumor of the gold discovery at Sutter's Fort.

On arriving at San Pedro, a vessel—the *Southampton*, was found ready to sail. She had on board a crowd of fugitives from Mexico, bound to San Francisco, where they hoped to find repose from the troubles which harassed that revolutionary Republic.

At San Francisco, Meek was surprised to meet about two hundred Oregonians, who on the first news of the gold discovery the previous autumn, had fled, as it is said men shall flee on the day of judgment—leaving the wheat ungathered in the fields, the grain unground in the mills, the cattle unherded on the plains, their tools and farming implements rusting on the ground—everything abandoned as if it would never more be needed, to go and seek the shining dust, which is vainly denominated "filthy lucre." The two hundred were on their way home, having all either made something, or lost their health by exposure so that they were obliged to return. But they left many more in the mines.

Such were the tales told in San Francisco of the wonderful fortunes of some of the miners that young Lane became infected with the universal fever and declared his intention to try mining with the rest. Meek too, determined to risk something in gold-seeking, and as some of the teamsters who had left Fort Leavenworth with the company, and had come as far as San Francisco, were very desirous of going to the mines, Meek fitted out two or three with pack-horses, tools, and provisions, to accompany young Lane. For the money expended in the outfit he

31

was to receive half of their first year's profits. The result of this venture was three pickle-jars of gold-dust,
which were sent to him by the hands of Nat. Lane, the
following year; and which just about reimbursed him for
the outlay.

At San Francisco, Gen. Lane found the U. S. Sloop of
War, the *St. Mary's;* and Meek insisted that the Oregon
government, which was represented in their persons, had
a right to require her services in transporting itself to its
proper seat. But Lane, whose notions of economy extended, singularly enough, to the affairs of the general
government, would not consent to the needless expendi-
ture. Meek was rebellious, and quoted Thornton, by
whom he was determined not to be outdone in respect of
expense for transportation. Lane insisted that his dignity
did not require a government vessel to convey him to
Oregon. In short the new government was very much
divided against itself, and only escaped a fall by Meek's
finding some one, or some others, else, on whom to play
his pranks.

The first one was a Jew peddler who had gentlemen's
clothes to sell. To him the Marshal represented himself
as a United States Custom officer, and after frightening
him with a threat of confiscating his entire stock, finally
compromised with the terrified Israelite by accepting a
suit of clothes for himself. After enjoying the mortifica-
tion of spirit which the loss inflicted on the Jew, for twenty-four hours, he finally paid him for the clothes, at the
same time administering a lecture upon the sin and danger of smuggling.

The party which had left Leavenworth for Oregon
nearly six months before, numbering fifty-five, now numbered only seven. Of the original number two had been
killed, and all the rest had deserted to go to the mines.

There remained only Gen. Lane, Meek, Lieut. Hawkins and Hayden, surgeon, besides three soldiers. With this small company Gen. Lane went on board the *Jeanette*, a small vessel, crowded with miners, and destined for the Columbia River. As the *Jeanette* dropped down the Bay, a salute was fired from the *St. Mary's* in honor of Gen. Lane, and appropriated to himself by Marshal Meek, who seems to have delighted in appropriating to himself all the honors in whatever circumstances he might be placed; the more especially too, if such assumption annoyed the General.

After a tedious voyage of eighteen days the *Jeanette* arrived in the Columbia River. From Astoria the party took small boats for Oregon City, a voyage of one hundred and twenty miles; so that it was already the 2d of March when they arrived at that place, and only one day was left for the organization of the Territorial Government before the expiration of Polk's term of office. Gen. Lane's economy had nearly defeated Polk's great desire.

CHAPTER XLII.

1849. IF this were a novel which we were writing, we should fix upon this point in our story to write—"And so they were married, and lived together happily ever after;" placing the FINIS directly after that sentence. For have we not brought Oregon through all the romantic adventures and misadventures of her extraordinary youth, and ushered her upon the stage of action a promising young Territory? As for our hero, he too has arrived at the climax of his individual glory and success, a point at which it might be wise to leave him.

But a regard for the eternal fitness of things compels us to gather up again the dropped threads of some portions of our story, and follow them to their proper winding up. We promise, however, to touch as lightly as possible upon the Territorial history of Oregon; for her political record here becomes, what the political record of too many other Territories has been, a history of demagogueism. With this preface we proceed to finish our narrative.

On the 2d of March Gen. Lane arrived at Oregon City, and was introduced to Gov. Abernethy, by Marshal Meek. On the 3d, there appeared the following—

PROCLAMATION.

In pursuance of an act of Congress, approved the 14th of August, in the year of our Lord 1848, establishing a Territorial Government in the Territory of Oregon:

I, Joseph Lane, was, on the 18th day of August, in the year 1848, appointed

Governor in and for the Territory of Oregon. I have therefore thought it proper to issue this, my proclamation, making known that I have this day entered upon the discharge of the duties of my office, and by virtue thereof do declare the laws of the United States extended over, and declared to be in force in said Territory, so far as the same, or any portion thereof, may be applicable.

Given under my hand at Oregon City, in the Territory of Oregon, this 3d day of March, Anno Domini 1849. JOSEPH LANE.

Thus Oregon had one day, under Polk, who, take it all in all, had been a faithful guardian of her interests.

Shortly after the appearance of the proclamation of Gov. Lane, Meek was sworn into office, and gave the required securities. All the other Territorial officers present in the Territory, or as fast as they arrived, took the oath of office; courts were established, and the new government moved on. Of the Presidential appointees who accepted, were William T. Bryant of Indiana, Chief Justice O. C. Pratt of Illinois, and Peter H. Burnett of Oregon, Associate Justices of the District Court: John Adair of Kentucky, Collector for the District of Oregon: and Kintzinge Pritchett of Pennsylvania, Secretary of State.

The condition in which Gov. Lane found the new Territory was not so sad as might reasonably be conjectured from the fears of its inhabitants fifteen months previous. Intimidated by the presence of the volunteers in the upper country, the Indians had remained quiet, and the immigration of 1848 passed through their country without being disturbed in any manner. So little apprehension was felt concerning an Indian war at this time that men did not hesitate to leave their homes and families to go to the gold fields of California.

In the month of August, 1848, the *Honolulu*, a vessel of one hundred and fifty tons, owned in Boston, carrying a consignment of goods to a mercantile house in Portland, arrived at her anchorage in the Wallamet, *via* San Francisco, California. Captain Newell, almost before he had discharged freight, commenced buying up a cargo of flour and other provisions. But what excited the wonder of the Oregonians was the fact that he also bought up all manner of tools such as could be used in digging or cutting, from a spade and pickaxe, to a pocket-knife. This singular proceeding naturally aroused the suspicions of a people accustomed to have something to suspect. A demand was made for the *Honolulu's* papers, and these not being forthcoming, it was proposed by some of the prudent ones to tie her up. When this movement was attempted, the secret came out. Captain Newell, holding up a bag of gold-dust before the astonished eyes of his persecutors, cried out—

"Do you see that gold? D——n you, I will depopulate your country! I know where there is plenty of this stuff, and I am taking these tools where it is to be found."

This was in August, the month of harvest. So great was the excitement which seized the people, that all classes of men were governed by it. Few persons stopped to consider that this was the time for producers to reap golden harvests of precious ore, for the other yellow harvest of grain which was already ripe and waiting to be gathered. Men left their grain standing, and took their teams from the reapers to pack their provisions and tools to the mines.

Some men would have gladly paid double to get back the spades, shovels, or picks, which the shrewd Yankee Captain had purchased from them a week previous. All implements of this nature soon commanded fabulous prices, and he was a lucky man who had a supply.

The story of the gold-fever which began in the fall and winter of '48, and raged with such violence through '49, is too familiar to everybody to need repeating here. Only as it affected the fortunes of Oregon need it be mentioned.

Its immediate effect was to give an impetus to business in the Territory which nothing else ever could have done; to furnish a market for all sorts of produce, and employment for every kind of industry, to bring money into circulation in place of wheat and beaver-skins, and for a time to make the country extremely prosperous.

One of the last acts of the Provisional Government had been to authorize the weighing, assaying, and coining of gold—an act which was rendered necessary by the great amount of "dust" in circulation, and the influx of the debased South American coins. An association of gentlemen taking the matter in hand, bore all the expense of the dies, machinery, and labor, coining only about ten thousand dollars in the summer of '49. They succeeded in raising the price of "dust" from eleven to sixteen dollars per ounce, and stopping   the influx of South American coins. The gentlemen who conferred a great benefit on Oregon, were Kilborne, Magruder, Rector,

BEAVER-MONEY.

Campbell, and Smith. This money went by the name of "Beaver-money," owing to the design on the dies, which referred to the previous beaver currency.

But the ultimate effect of the California gold discoveries was to put a check upon the prosperity of Oregon. The emigration from the states, instead of going to Oregon as formerly, now turned off to California. Men soon discovered the fertile quality of California soil, and while the majority dug for gold a sufficient number went to farming to make, together with the imports from the east, almost a supply for the yearly hordes of gold seekers. The fame of the California climate, the fascinations of the ups and downs of fortune's wheel in that country, and many other causes, united to make California, and not Oregon, the object of interest on the Pacific coast; and the rapidity with which California became self-supporting removed from Oregon her importance as a source of supplies. Therefore, after a few years of rather extraordinary usefulness and consequent good fortune, the Territory relapsed into a purely domestic and very quiet young State. This change in its federal status was not altogether acceptable to Oregonians. They had so long been accustomed to regard themselves as the pets of a great and generous, but rather neglectful Republic, from whose hands all manner of favors were to be of right demanded, because they had sustained for so long a time the character of good children, without any immediate reward—that now when a rival darling sprang into vigorous life and excessive favor, almost at once, their jealousy rankled painfully. So naughty and disagreeable a passion as jealousy is its own punishment, as the Oregonian of to-day would do well to remember, while he does what he can to show to the world that his State, by its splendid resources, fully justifies all the outlay of patriotism and ardor which distinguished its early history.

But to return to our mutton. Although Gov. Lane did not find an Indian war on his hands immediately on assuming the duties of his office, there was yet plenty to do in getting the government organized, appointing officers to take the census, ordering elections, and getting the run of Oregon politics, to occupy his attention for the first three months of his administration.

The change in the government had not by any means changed the objects and aims of the different parties in Oregon. Now, as before, there was a Mission party, strong in money and influence; now, as before, the term

"Hudson's Bay man" was used by the Mission party to bring odium upon any aspirant to office, or even business success, who, not being intimidated by their interdict, ventured to be employed professionally by Dr. McLaughlin, or in any way to show regard for him. As there were always a certain number independent enough to act from free will or conviction, there was in consequence still a Hudson's Bay party. Between these two, as before, there stood a third party, who added itself to or subtracted itself from the other two, as its purposes and interests required. As there were haters of Dr. McLaughlin in two of the parties it did not require a great amount of shrewdness to inform a man that on this point might turn his political fortunes.

This discovery was made very early after his arrival in the Territory by Gov. Lane, as well as by Judge Bryant, and others, and used at times by them when there was an object to be gained by it, although neither of these dignitaries declared themselves openly as good haters of the Doctor.

Dr. McLaughlin, on the settlement of the boundary question, seeing that the London Company found much fault with him for having "encouraged the settlement of Oregon by the Americans," went to England to see the Directors and have the matter understood between himself and them. Finding on hearing his explanation, that while doing nothing to encourage settlement, he could not permit the immigrants of the first few years to suffer after their arrival, and that out of charity only he had done what was done for their relief, the Company still blamed him, the Doctor then said to the Directors, "Gentlemen, I will serve you no longer." Sixty thousand dollars, expended in helping American settlers was charged to his private account. This amount was afterwards remitted, but the debt was heavily felt at the time.

On his return to Oregon, and on the establishment of a Territorial government, the Doctor determined to take out naturalization papers, and become an American citizen. But no sooner had the government been organized than new complications arose in the Doctor's case. Judge Bryant had been but a few days in the Territory before he purchased from the Mission Milling Company the Island in the river opposite Oregon City, which was occupied by their mills, but which formed a part of the original claim of Dr. McLaughlin. Thus the Chief Justice assumed at once the same attitude towards him which the Mission and the Milling Company had done; and as the island was contained in Judge Bryant's district, and only two Judges were at that time in the Territory, the Doctor felt constrained to seek advice from such Americans as were his friends. Although some believed that his best chance of holding his original claim, was to depend upon his possessory rights under the treaty of 1846, others counseled him to take out his naturalization papers and secure himself in the rights of an American citizen. This he did at last, on the 30th of May, 1849.

We have spoken in a previous chapter of Mr. Thurston, in connection with the Donation Act. It is related of this gentleman that when he left Iowa for Oregon, he confided to his personal friends his resolve to be "in Congress or in h—" two years after reaching that Territory. Like other ambitious new-comers, he soon discovered what side to take with certain influential persons, concerning the Hudson's Bay Company, which was but another name for Dr. McLaughlin.

Mr. Thurston did not hesitate to ask the Doctor to vote for him, for delegate to Congress, which, however, the Doctor did not do, as one of his friends was up for the same office. But when he was finally elected to Congress, fortunately within the two years to which he had limited himself—Mr. Thurston took ground which betrayed by what influences he had been placed in the coveted position.

Mr. Thornton having returned to Oregon sometime in May had made the acquaintance of the candidate for Congress, and feeling some anxiety with regard to the Land Bill, which he had expended considerable thought and labor upon, conversed freely with Mr. Thurston upon the subject, and finally, on his election, presented him with a copy of his bill; the same, with certain alterations, that could not strictly be called amendments, which afterwards became the Donation Law.

But the notable section of Mr. Thurston's bill, which finally became a law, was that one which was intended to secure him future political favors, by earning him the gratitude of the anti-Hudson's Bay party, and all others whose private interests he subserved. This was the section which exempted from the benefits of the act the Oregon City claim, in the following words. "That there be, and hereby is granted to the Territory of Oregon, two townships, one north and one south of the Columbia River, to aid in establishing a University, to be selected by the Assembly, and approved by the Surveyor General. *Also the Oregon City claim, except those lots sold previous to March 4th, 1849.*"

In order to secure the passage of this part of the land bill, Mr. Thurston addressed a letter to the House of Representatives, of which he was a member, containing the following assertions:—that it was the Methodist Mission which first took the Oregon City claim; that they were driven from it by a fear of having the savages of Oregon let loose upon them; that a number of citizens of Oregon had been successively driven from it, by the power of the Hudson's Bay Company; that Dr. McLaughlin had already sold lots to the amount of $200,000, enough for a foreigner to make out of American territory; and that the Doctor had not taken out naturalization papers, but was an Englishman at heart, and still identified with the Hudson's Bay Company. Mr. Thurston's letter contained many more assertions equally false—but those just given relate more particularly to the eleventh section of the Donation Act.

Mr. Thurston's reason for asking to have all sales of lots made before the fourth of March, 1849, confirmed, he declared to be to prevent litigation. Dr. McLaughlin, he said, ought to be made to pay for those lots, but "not wishing to create any litigation, the committee concluded to quiet the whole matter by confirming those lots."

He further stated that the Doctor had upon the Oregon City claim "a flouring mill, granaries, two double saw-mills, a large number of houses, stores, and other buildings, to which he *may* be entitled by virtue of his possessory rights under the treaty of 1846. For only a part of these improvements, which he may thus hold, he has been urged during the past year to take $250,000."

Mr. Thurston sees no harm in taking this property, so valuable in his estimation, which comprises the earnings of a whole life-time spent in devotion to business in an Indian country, away from all that men commonly esteem desirable, from the proper owner. On the contrary he makes an eloquent appeal to the House to save this valuable estate to the people of Oregon wherewith to educate the rising generations.

Still further, so great is his fear that some portion of his property may be left to the Doctor, he asks that the Island portion of the claim, which he confesses is only a pile of rocks, of no value except for the improvements on it, may be " confirmed to George Abernethy, his heirs or assigns;"

assigning as a reason that when the mission was driven from Oregon City, it took refuge on this pile of rocks, and having built a mill, afterwards sold it to Mr. Abernethy, one of the stockholders. Nothing is said about the mill having been resold to Judge Bryant; but Judge Bryant could not object to having the Island confirmed to him through Mr. Abernethy.

And here we may as well sever one of the threads in our story. When it became known that by an act of Congress Oregon City was reserved from the right of even an American citizen to claim, and that only after years of waiting would the title by possessory right be settled either for or against him, the old Doctor's heart was broken.

He still continued to reside upon his claim, but the uncertainty of title prevented any sales of property. The ingratitude of those whom he had assisted when assistance was life itself to them, their refusals to pay what had been lent them, and their constant calumniations, so bore upon his spirits that his strength failed rapidly under them, and for the last few years of his life he fancied himself reduced to poverty, though he was still in possession of his improvements.

An example of the extent to which some men carried their anti-McLaughlin principles may be found in the following story which was related to us by the gentleman mentioned in it. The doctor one day stood upon the street conversing with Mr. Thornton, who had been his legal adviser in some instances, another gentleman also being present. Their conversation was rudely interrupted by a fourth individual, who set upon Mr. Thornton with every manner of abuse and vile epithet for being seen in communication with the " d——d old Hudson's Bay, Jesuitical rascal," and much more to the same effect. To this assault, Thornton, who had a great command of language, replied in a manner which sent the man about his business. Then turning to the Doctor, he said:

"Doctor, I will lay a wager that man is one of your debtors, who never intends to pay, and takes it out in abuse."

"Yes, yes," answered the Doctor, trying to suppress his nervousness; "when he came to Oregon he was naked and hungry. I gave him assistance to the amount of four hundred dollars. He is rich now; has land and herds, and everything in abundance; but he hates me on account of that four hundred dollars. That is the way with most of them!"

Dr. McLaughlin died September, 1857, and is buried in the Catholic church-yard in Oregon City. Five years after his death the State of Oregon restored to his heirs the property which it had so long wrongfully withheld. As for the demagogue who embittered the last days of a good man, for political advancement, he did not live to enjoy his reward. His health, delicate at the best, was very much undermined at last by discovering that he received more blame than praise, even among his former supporters, for the eleventh section of the Donation Law. He became very ill on his return, and died at Acapulco, Mexico, without reaching home.

Very many persons have confirmed what his admirer, Meek, says of Dr. McLaughlin, that he deserved to be called the FATHER OF OREGON.

CHAPTER XLIII.

1850–4. THE Territorial law of Oregon combined the offices of Governor and Indian Agent. One of the most important acts which marked Lane's administration was that of securing and punishing the murderers of Dr. and Mrs. Whitman. The Indians of the Cayuse tribe to whom the murderers belonged, were assured that the only way in which they could avoid a war with the whites was to deliver up the chiefs who had been engaged in the massacre, to be tried and punished according to the laws of the whites. Of the two hundred Indians implicated in the massacre, five were given up to be dealt with according to law. These were the five chiefs, *Te-lou-i-kite*, *Tam-a-has*, *Klok-a-mas*, *Ki-am-a-sump-kin*, and *I-sa-i-a-cha-lak-is*.

These men might have made their escape; there was no imperative necessity upon them to suffer death, had they chosen to flee to the mountains. But with that strange magnanimity which the savage often shows, to the astonishment of Christians, they resolved to die for their people rather than by their flight to involve them in war.

Early in the summer of 1850, the prisoners were deliv. ered up to Gov. Lane, and brought down to Oregon City, where they were given into the keeping of the marshal. During their passage down the river, and while they were incarcerated at Oregon City, their bearing was most proud and haughty. Some food, more choice than their prisoner's fare, being offered to one of the chiefs at a camp of the guard, in their transit down the Columbia, the proud savage rejected it with scorn.

"What sort of heart have you," he asked, "that you offer food to me, whose hands are red with your brother's blood?"

And this, after eleven years of missionary labor, was all the comprehension the savage nature knew of the main principle of Christianity,—forgiveness, or charity toward our enemies.

At Oregon City, Meek had many conversations with them. In all of these they gave but one explanation of their crime. They feared that Dr. Whitman intended, with the other whites, to take their land from them; and they were told by Jo Lewis, the half-breed, that the Doctor's medicine was intended to kill them off quickly, in order the sooner to get possession of their country. None of them expressed any sorrow for what had been done; but one of them, *Ki-am-a-sump-kin*, declared his innocence to the last.

In conversations with others, curious to gain some knowledge of the savage moral nature, *Te-lou-i-kite* often puzzled these students of Indian ethics. When questioned as to his motive for allowing himself to be taken, *Te-lou-i-kite* answered:

"Did not your missionaries tell us that Christ died to save his people? So die we, to save our people!"

Notwithstanding the prisoners were pre-doomed to death, a regular form of trial was gone through. The Prosecuting Attorney for the Territory, A. Holbrook, conducted the prosecution: Secretary Pritchett, Major Runnels, and Captain Claiborne, the defence. The fee offered by the chiefs was fifty head of horses. Whether it was compassion, or a love of horses which animated the defence, quite an effort was made to show that the murderers were not guilty.

The presiding Justice was O. C. Pratt—Bryant having resigned. Perhaps we cannot do better than to give the Marshal's own description of the trial and execution, which is as follows: "Thar war a great many indictments, and a great many people in attendance at this court. The Grand Jury found true bills against the five Indians, and they war arraigned for trial. Captain Claiborne led off for the defence. He foamed and ranted like he war acting a play in some theatre. He knew about as much law as one of the Indians he war defending; and his gestures were so powerful that he smashed two tumblers that the Judge had ordered to be filled with cold water for him. After a time he gave out mentally and physically. Then came Major Runnels, who made a very good defence. But the Marshal thought they must do better, for they would never ride fifty head of horses with them speeches.

Mr. Pritchett closed for the defence with a very able argument; for he war a man of brains. But then followed Mr. Holbrook, for the prosecution, and he laid down the case so plain that the jury were convinced before they left the jury-box. When the Judge passed sentence of death on them, two of the chiefs showed no terror; but the other three were filled with horror and consternation that they could not conceal.

After court had adjourned, and Gov. Lane war gone South on some business with the Rogue River Indians, Secretary Pritchett came to me and told me that as he war now acting Governor he meant to reprieve the Indians. Said he to me, 'Now Meek, I want you to liberate them Indians, when you receive the order.'

32

'Pritchett,' said I, 'so far as Meek is concerned, he would do anything for you.'

This talk pleased him; he said he 'war glad to hear it; and would go right off and write the reprieve.'

'But,' said I, 'Pritchett, let us talk now like men. I have got in my pocket the death-warrant of them Indians, signed by Gov. Lane. The Marshal will execute them men, as certain as the day arrives.'

Pritchett looked surprised, and remarked—'That war not what you just said, that you would do anything for me.'

Said I, 'you were talking then to Meek,—not to the Marshal, who always does his duty.' At that he got mad and left.

When the 3d of June, the day of execution, arrived, Oregon City was thronged with people to witness it. I brought forth the five prisoners and placed them on a drop. Here the chief, who always declared his innocence, *Ki-am-i-sump-kin*, begged me to kill him with my knife,— for an Indian fears to be hanged,—but I soon put an end to his entreaties by cutting the rope which held the drop, with my tomahawk. As I said 'The Lord have mercy on your souls,' the trap fell, and the five Cayuses hung in the air. Three of them died instantly. The other two struggled for several minutes; the Little Chief, *Tam-a-has*, the longest. It was he who was cruel to my little girl at the time of the massacre; so I just put my foot on the knot to tighten it, and he got quiet. After thirty-five minutes they were taken down and buried."

Thus terminated a tragic chapter in the history of Oregon. Among the services which Thurston performed for the Territory, was getting an appropriation of $100,000, to pay the expenses of the Cayuse war. From the Spring of 1848, when all the whites, except the Catholic missionaries, were withdrawn from the upper country, for a period of several years, or until Government had made treaties with the tribes east of the Cascades, no settlers were permitted to take up land in Eastern Oregon. During those years, the Indians, dissatisfied with the encroachments which they foresaw the whites would finally make upon their country, and incited by certain individuals who had suffered wrongs, or been punished for their own offences at the hands of the whites, finally combined, as it was supposed from the extent of the insurrection, and Oregon was involved in a three years Indian war, the history of which would fill a volume of considerable size.

When Meek returned to Oregon as marshal, with his fine clothes and his newly acquired social accomplishments, he was greeted with a cordial acknowledgment of his services, as well as admiration for his improved appearance. He was generally acknowledged to be the model of a handsome marshal, when clad in his half-military dress, and placed astride of a fine horse, in the execution of the more festive duties of marshal of a procession on some patriotic occasion.

But no amount of official responsibility could ever change him from a wag into a "grave and reverend seignior." No place nor occasion was sacred to him when the wild humor was on him.

At this same term of court, after the conviction of the Cayuse chiefs, there was a case before Judge Pratt, in which a man was charged with selling liquor to the Indians. In these cases Indian evidence was allowed, but the jury-room being up stairs, caused a good deal of annoyance in court ; because when an Indian witness was wanted up stairs, a dozen or more who were not wanted would follow. The Judge's bench was so placed that it commanded a full view of the staircase and every one passing up or down it.

A call for some witness to go before the jury was fol

lowed on this occasion, as on all others, by a general rush
of the Indians, who were curious to witness the proceedings.   One fat old squaw had got part way up the stairs,
when the Marshal, full of wrath, seized her by a leg and
dragged her down flat, at the same time holding the fat

MEEK AS UNITED STATES MARSHAL.

member so that it was pointed directly toward the Judge.
A general explosion followed this *pointed* action, and the
Judge grew very red in the face.

"Mr. Marshal, come within the bar!" thundered the
Judge.

Meek complied, with a very dubious expression of
countenance.

"I must fine you fifty dollars," continued the Judge;
"the dignity of the Court must be maintained."

When court had adjourned that evening, the Judge
and the Marshal were walking toward their respective
lodgings.   Said Meek to his Honor:

" Why did you fine me so heavily to-day ?"

" I *must* do it," returned the Judge. " I must keep up the dignity of the Court; I must do it, if I pay the fines myself."

" And you *must* pay all the fines you lay on the marshal, of course," answered Meek.

" Very well," said the Judge; " I shall do so."

" All right, Judge. As I am the proper disbursing officer, you can pay that fifty dollars to me—and I'll take it now."

At this view of the case, his Honor was staggered for one moment, and could only swing his cane and laugh faintly. After a little reflection, he said :

" Marshal, when court is called to-morrow, I shall remit your fine; but don't you let me have occasion to fine you again !"

After the removal of the capital to Salem, in 1852, court was held in a new building, on which the carpenters were still at work. Judge Nelson, then presiding, was much put out by the noise of hammers, and sent the marshal more than once, to request the men to suspend their work during those hours when court was in session, but all to no purpose. Finally, when his forbearance was quite exhausted, he appealed to the marshal for advice.

" What shall I do, Meek," said he, " to stop that infernal noise ?"

" Put the workmen on the Grand Jury," replied Meek.

" Summon them instantly !" returned the Judge. They were summoned, and quiet secured for that term.

At this same term of court, a great many of the foreign born settlers appeared, to file their intention of becoming American citizens, in order to secure the benefits of the Donation Law. Meek was retained as a witness, to swear to their qualifications, one of which was, that they were possessed of good moral characters. The first day there were about two hundred who made declarations, Meek witnessing for most of them. On the day following, he declined serving any longer.

"What now?" inquired the Judge; "you made no objections yesterday."

"Very true," replied Meek; "and two hundred lies are enough for me. I swore that all those mountain-men were of 'good moral character,' and I never knew a mountain-man of that description in my life! Let Newell take the job for to-day."

The "job" was turned over to Newell; but whether the second lot was better than the first, has never transpired.

During Lane's administration, there was a murder committed by a party of Indians at the Sound, on the person of a Mr. Wallace. Owing to the sparse settlement of the country, Governor Lane adopted the original measure of exporting not only the officers of the court, but the jury also, to the Sound district. Meek was ordered to find transportation for the court *in toto*, jury and all. Boats were hired and provisioned to take the party to the Cowelitz Landing, and from thence to Fort Steilacoom, horses were hired for the land transportation.

The Indians accused were five in number—two chiefs and three slaves. The Grand Jury found a true bill against the two chiefs, and let the slaves go. So few were the inhabitants of those parts, that the marshal was obliged to take a part of the grand jury to serve on the petite jury. The form of a trial was gone through with, the Judge delivered his charge, and the jury retired.

It was just after night-fall when these worthies betook themselves to the jury-room. One of them curled himself up in a corner of the room, with the injunction to the others to "wake him up when they got ready to hang them d——d rascals." The rest of the party spent four or five hours betting against monte, when, being sleepy also, they waked up their associate, spent about ten minutes in arguing their convictions, and returned a verdict of "guilty of murder in the first degree."

The Indians were sentenced to be hung at noon on the following day, and the marshal was at work early in the morning preparing a gallows. A rope was procured from a ship lying in the sound. At half-past eleven o'clock, guarded by a company of artillery from the fort, the miserable savages were marched forth to die. A large number of Indians were collected to witness the execution; and to prevent any attempt at rescue, Captain Hill's artillery formed a ring around the marshal and his prisoners. The execution was interrupted or delayed for some moments, on account of the frantic behavior of an Indian woman, wife of one of the chiefs, whose entreaties for the life of her husband were very affecting. Having exhausted all her eloquence in an appeal to the nobler feelings of the man, she finally promised to leave her husband and become his wife, if he, the marshal, would spare her lord and chief.

She was carried forcibly out of the ring, and the hanging took place. When the bodies were taken down, Meek spoke to the woman, telling her that now she could have her husband; but she only sullenly replied, "You have killed him, and you may bury him."

This excursion of the Oregon court footed up a sum of about $4,000, of which the marshal paid $1,000 out of his own pocket. When, in the following year, Lane was sent to Congress, Meek urged him to ask for an appropriation to pay up the debt. Lane made no effort to do so, probably because he did not care to have the illegality of the proceeding commented upon.

Lane's career in Oregon, before the breaking out of the rebellion, the betrayal of his secession proclivities, and supposed actual conspiracy against the Government, was that of a successful politician. Having been appointed so near the close of Polk's administration, he was succeeded, on the coming into office of General Taylor, by General John P. Gaines, who arrived in Oregon in August, 1850. In 1851, General Lane was elected delegate to Congress, and returned to Oregon as Governor, by Franklin Pierce, in 1853. He was appointed in March, arrived at Salem May 16th, resigned the 19th, was elected to Congress July 7th, returning again to Oregon, where he at present resides, on the expiration of his term. His mileage alone amounted to $10,000, besides the expenses of his first overland journey. John W. Davis was next appointed Governor, by President Pierce. He arrived in Salem April 1st, 1854, and resigned in August. A trip to Oregon, with the mileage, appeared to be quite the fashion of territorial times.

CHAPTER XLIV.

WHILE Meek was in Washington, he had been dubbed with the title of Colonel, which title he still bears, though during the Indian war of 1855–56, it was alternated with that of Major. During his marshalship he was fond of showing off his titles and authority to the discomfiture of that class of people who had "put on airs" with him in former days, when he was in his transition stage from a trapper to a United States Marshal.

While Pratt was Judge of the District Court, a kidnaping case came before him. The writ of *habeas corpus* having been disregarded by the Captain of the *Melvin*, who was implicated in the business, Meek was sent to arrest him, and also the first mate. Five of the *Melvin's* sailors were ordered to be summoned as witnesses, at the same time.

Meek went on board with his summons, marched forward, and called out the names of the men. Every man came up as he was summoned. When they were together, Meek ordered a boat lowered for their conveyance to Oregon City. The men started to obey, when the Captain interfered, saying that the boat should not be taken for such a purpose, as it belonged to him.

"That is of no consequence at all," answered the smiling marshal. "It is a very good boat, and will suit our purpose very well. Lower away, men?"

The men quickly dropped the boat. As it fell, they

were ordered to man it. When they were at the oars, the mate was then invited to take a seat in it, which he did, after a moment's hesitation, and glancing at his superior officer. Meek then turned to the Captain, and extended the same invitation to him. But he was reluctant to accept the courtesy, blustering considerably, and declaring his intention to remain where he was. Meek slowly drew his revolver, all the time cool and smiling.

"I don't like having to urge a gentleman too hard," he said, in a meaning tone; "but thar is an argument that few men ever resist. Take a seat, Captain."

The Captain took a seat; the idlers on shore cheered for "Joe Meek"—which was, after all, his most familiar title; the Captain and mate went to Oregon City, and were fined respectively $500 and $300; the men took advantage of being on shore to desert; and altogether, the master of the *Melvin* felt himself badly used.

About the same time news was received that a British vessel was unloading goods for the Hudson's Bay Company, somewhere on Puget Sound. Under the new order of affairs in Oregon, this was smuggling. Delighted with an opportunity of doing the United States a service, and the British traders an ill turn, Marshal Meek immediately summoned a *posse* of men and started for the Sound. On his way he learned the name of the vessel and Captain, and recognized them as having been in the Columbia River some years before. On that occasion the Captain had ordered Meek ashore, when, led by his curiosity and general love of novelty, he had paid a visit to this vessel. This information was "nuts" to the marshal, who believed that "a turn about was fair play."

With great dispatch and secrecy he arrived entirely unexpected at the point where the vessel was lying, and proceeded to board her without loss of time. The Captain and officers were taken by surprise and were all aghast at this unlooked for appearance. But after the first moment of agitation was over, the Captain recognized Meek, he being a man not likely to be forgotten, and thinking to turn this circumstance to advantage, approached him with the blandest of smiles and the most cordial manner, saying with forced frankness—

"I am sure I have had the pleasure of meeting you before. You must have been at Vancouver when my vessel was in the river, seven or eight years ago. I am very happy to have met with you again."

"Thar is some truth in that remark of yours, Captain," replied Meek, eyeing him with lofty scorn; "you *did* meet me at Vancouver several years ago. But I was nothing but 'Joe Meek' at that time, and you ordered me ashore. Circumstances are changed since then. I am now Colonel Joseph L. Meek, United States Marshal for Oregon Territory; and you sir, are only a d——d smuggler! Go ashore, sir!"

The Captain saw the point of that concluding "go ashore, sir!" and obeyed with quite as bad a grace as 'Joe Meek' had done in the first instance.

The vessel was confiscated and sold, netting to the Government about $40,000, above expenses. This money, which fell into bad hands, failed to be accounted for. Nobody suspected the integrity of the marshal, but most persons suspected that he placed too much confidence in the District Attorney, who had charge of his accounts. On some one asking him, a short time after, what had become of the money from the sale of the smuggler, he seemed struck with a sudden surprise:

"Why," said he, looking astonished at the question, "thar was barly enough for the officers of the court!"

This answer, given as it was, with such apparent simplicity, became a popular joke; and "barly enough" was quoted on all occasions.

The truth was, that there was a serious deficiency in Meek's account with the Government, resulting entirely from his want of confidence in his own literary accomplishments, which led him to trust all his correspondence and his accounts to the hands of a man whose talents were more eminent than his sense of honor. The result of this misplaced confidence was a loss to the Government, and to himself, whom the Government held accountable. Contrary to the general rule of disbursing officers, the office made him poor instead of rich; and when on the incoming of the Pierce administration he suffered decapitation along with the other Territorial officers, he was forced to retire upon his farm on the Tualatin Plains, and become a rather indifferent tiller of the earth.

The breaking out of the Indian war of 1855–6, was preceded by a long period of uneasiness among the Indians generally. The large emigration which crossed the plains every year for California and Oregon was one cause of the disturbance; not only by exciting their fears for the possession of their lands, but by the temptation which was offered them to take toll of the travelers. Difficulties occurred at first between the emigrants and Indians concerning stolen property. These quarrels were followed, probably the subsequent year, by outrages and murder on the part of the Indians, and retaliation on the part of volunteer soldiers from Oregon. When once this system of outrage and retaliation on either side, was begun, there was an end of security, and war followed as an inevitable consequence. Very horrible indeed were the acts perpetrated by the Indians upon the emigrants to Oregon, during the years from 1852 to 1858.

But when at last the call to arms was made in Oregon,

it was an opportunity sought, and not an alternative forced upon them, by the politicians of that Territory. The occasion was simply this. A party of lawless wretches from the Sound Country, passing over the Cascade Mountains into the Yakima Valley, on their way to the Upper Columbia mines, found some Yakima women digging roots in a lonely place, and abused them. The women fled to their village and told the chiefs of the outrage; and a party followed the guilty whites and killed several of them in a fight.

Mr. Bolin, the Indian sub-agent for Washington went to the Yakima village, and instead of judging of the case impartially, made use of threats in the name of the United States Government, saying that an army should be sent to punish them for killing his people. On his return home, Mr. Bolin was followed and murdered.

The murder of an Indian agent was an act which could not be overlooked. Very properly, the case should have been taken notice of in a manner to convince the Indians that murder must be punished. But, tempted by an opportunity for gain, and encouraged by the somewhat reasonable fears of the white population of Washington and Oregon, Governor G. L. Curry, of the latter, at once proclaimed war, and issued a call for volunteers, without waiting for the sanction or assistance of the general Government. The moment this was done, it was too late to retract. It was as if a torch had been applied to a field of dry grass. So simultaneously did the Indians from Puget Sound to the Rocky Mountains, and from the Rocky Mountains to the southern boundary of Oregon send forth the war-whoop, that there was much justification for the belief which agitated the people, that a combination among the Indians had been secretly agreed to, and that the whites were all to be exterminated.

Volunteer companies were already raised and sent into the Indian country, when Brevet Major G. O. Haller arrived at Vancouver, now a part of the United States. He had been as far east as Fort Boise to protect the incoming immigration; and finding on his return that there was an Indian war on hand, proceeded at once to the Yakima country with his small force of one hundred men, only fifty of whom were mounted. Much solicitude was felt for the result of the first engagement, every one knowing that if the Indians were at first successful, the war would be long and bloody.

Major Haller was defeated with considerable loss, and notwithstanding slight reinforcements, from Fort Vancouver, only succeeded in getting safely out of the country. Major Raines, the commanding officer at Vancouver, seeing the direction of events, made a requisition upon Governor Curry for four of his volunteer companies to go into the field. Then followed applications to Major Raines for horses and arms to equip the volunteers; but the horses at the Fort being unfit for service, and the Major unauthorized to equip volunteer troops, there resulted only misunderstandings and delays. When General Wool, at the head of the Department in San Francisco, was consulted, he also was without authority to employ or receive the volunteers; and when the volunteers, who at length armed and equipped themselves, came to go into the field with the regulars, they could not agree as to the mode of fighting Indians; so that with one thing and another, the war became an exciting topic for more reasons than because the whites were afraid of the Indians. As for General Wool, he was in great disfavor both in Oregon and Washington because he did not believe there ever had existed the necessity for a war; and that therefore he bestowed what assistance was at his command very grudg-

ingly.   General Wool, it was said, was jealous of the volunteers; and the volunteers certainly cared little for the
opinion of General Wool.

However all that may be, Col. Meek gives it as his opinion that the old General was right.   " It makes me think,"
said he, " of a bear-fight I once saw in the Rocky Mountains, where a huge old grizzly was surrounded by a pack
of ten or twelve dogs, all snapping at and worrying him.
It made him powerful mad, and every now and then he
would make a claw at one of them that silenced him at
once."

The Indian war in Oregon gave practice to a number of
officers, since become famous, most prominent among
whom is Sheridan, who served in Oregon as a Lieutenant.
Grant himself, was at one time a Captain on that frontier.
Col. Wright, afterwards Gen. Wright, succeeded Major
Raines at Vancouver, and conducted the war through its
most active period.   During a period of three years there
were troops constantly occupied in trying to subdue the
Indians in one quarter or another.

As for the volunteers they fared badly.   On the first
call to arms the people responded liberally.   The proposition which the Governor made for their equipment was
accepted, and they turned in their property at a certain
valuation.   When the war was over and the property sold,
the men who had turned it in could not purchase it without paying more for it in gold and silver than it was valued at when it was placed in the hands of the Quarter-
master.   It was sold, however, and the money enjoyed by
the shrewd political speculators, who thought an Indian
war a very good investment.

Meek was one of the first to volunteer, and went as a
private in Company A.   On arriving at the Dalles he was
detailed for special service by Col. J. W. Nesmith, and

sent out as pilot or messenger, whenever any such duty was required. He was finally placed on Nesmith's staff, and given the title of Major. In this capacity, as in every other, he was still the same alert and willing individual that we have always seen him, and not a whit less inclined to be merry when an opportunity offered.

While the army was in the Yakima country, it being an enemy's country, and provisions scarce, the troops sometimes were in want of rations. But Meek had not forgotten his mountain craft, and always had something to eat, if anybody did. One evening he had killed a fat cow which he had discovered astray, and was proceeding to roast a twenty-pound piece before his camp-fire, when a number of the officers called on him. The sight and savory smell of the beef was very grateful to them.

"Major Meek," said they in a breath, "we will sup with you to-night."

"I am very sorry, gentlemen, to decline the honor," returned Meek with a repetition of the innocent surprise for which he had so often been laughed at, "but I am very hungry, and thar is barly enough beef for one man!"

On hearing this sober assertion, those who had heard the story laughed, but the rest looked rather aggrieved. However, the Major continued his cooking, and when the beef was done to a turn, he invited his visitors to the feast, and the evening passed merrily with jests and camp stories.

After the army went into winter-quarters, Nesmith having resigned, T. R. Cornelius was elected Colonel. One of his orders prohibited firing in camp, an order which as a good mountaineer the Major should have remembered. But having been instructed to proceed to Salem without delay, as bearer of dispatches, the Major committed the

error of firing his gun to see if it was in good condition
for a trip through the enemy's country. Shortly after he
received a message from his Colonel requesting him to
repair to his tent. The Colonel received him politely, and
invited him to breakfast with him. The aroma of coffee
made this invitation peculiarly acceptable—for luxuries
were scarce in camp—and the breakfast proceeded for
some time very agreeably. When Meek had breakfasted,
Colonel Cornelius took occasion to inquire if the Major
had not heard his order against firing in camp. " Yes,"
said Meek. " Then," said the Colonel, " I shall be
obliged to make an example of you."

While Meek stood aghast at the idea of punishment, a
guard appeared at the door of the tent, and he heard
what his punishment was to be, " Mark time for twenty
minutes in the presence of the whole regiment."

" When the command "forward! was given," says Meek,
" you might have seen somebody step off lively, the officer counting it off, 'left, left.' But some of the regiment
grumbled more about it than I did. I just got my horse
and my dispatches and left for the lower country, and
when I returned I asked for my discharge, and got it."

And here ends the career of our hero as a public man.
The history of the young State, of which he is so old a
pioneer furnishes ample material for an interesting volume,
and will sometime be written by an abler than our sketchy
pen. One thing only it occurs to us to state in connection with it, that while many Northern men went, as Gen.
Lane did, into the rebellion against the Government, our
nobler Virginian was ever sternly loyal.

The chief excitement of Col. Meek's life at present, is
in his skirmishes with the Nazerene and other preachers
in his neighborhood. They seem not to be able to see
him treading so gently the downhill of life, when they

33

fear he may "go to the pit" prepared for mountain-men. In this state of mind they preach at him on every possible occasion, whether suitable or not, and usually he takes it pleasantly enough. But when their attacks become too personal, he does as did the bear to whom he likened Gen. Wool, he "hits one a claw that silences him."

Being very much annoyed on one occasion, not very long since, by the stupid and vulgar speech of a "preacher" whom he complimented by going to hear, he deliberately marched up to the preacher's desk, took the frightened little orator on his hip, and carried him out of the house, to the mingled horror, amazement, and amusement of the congregation.

We think that a man who at fifty-eight is able to perform such a feat, is capable of achieving fresh laurels, and need not retire upon those he has won.

CHAPTER XLV.

It was no part of the original intention of the author of the foregoing narrative to extend the work beyond the personal adventures of one man, and such portions of collateral history as were necessary to a perfect understanding of the times and events spoken of. But since the great interest which the public have taken in the opening of the first Pacific Railroad has become apparent, it has been deemed expedient to subjoin some facts concerning the Western Division of the Northern Pacific Railroad, now in contemplation, and to become a reality, probably, within an early day.

The Northern Pacific Road will have its eastern end somewhere on Lake Superior, and its western terminus at a point on Puget's Sound not yet determined. As that portion of the road lying west of Fort Union, on the Missouri River, traverses much of the country spoken of in the adventures of the fur-traders, as well as all the northern part of what was once the Oregon Territory, whose early history we have already given, it will not be found altogether irrelevant to enter into a brief description of the country so soon to be opened to the traveling public. Hitherto we have roamed it in imagination as the fur-traders did, bent only on beaver-skins and adventure. Now we will briefly consider it as a country fit for the permanent settlement of industrious Peoples seeking homes for themselves and the coming generations.

WESTERN OREGON.—To commence with the oldest settled portion of the original Oregon Territory, we will
first describe that portion of the present State of Oregon
technically known as Western Oregon. All that portion
of the State of Oregon lying west of the Cascade Mountains, is comprised in three principal valleys—the Wallamet,* the Umpqua, and the Rogue River Valleys—and in
a narrow strip of country lying along the coast, and separated from the valleys by the Coast range of mountains.
These two ranges of mountains, the Cascades, high and
almost inaccessible on the east, and the Coast range, separating it from the sea on the west, make of Western Oregon a country with a very peculiar geography. With
the Columbia River for a northern boundary, and with
three transverse ranges of mountains to the south, separating the several valleys, the situation of Western Oregon
is isolated and unique.

The Wallamet River takes its rise in the Cascade Mountains, flowing westwardly for some distance, when it takes
a course almost directly north, and falls into the Columbia
in about latitude 45° 30', and longitude 45° 40'. The
whole length of this river is probably not over one hundred and seventy-five miles ; and the extent of its valley
proper is in the neighborhood of one hundred and twenty-
five miles in length, by from sixty to eighty in breadth.
Numerous tributaries flow into the Wallamet from either
side, making the country both fertile and agreeable.

The Wallamet Valley is mostly open prairie land, ready
for the plowshare. At the northern end of it, however,
and within a few miles of the Columbia, there are dense
forests of fir, pine, yew, and cedar, on all the high and
dry lands, while the bottom-lands along the streams are

---

* Incorrectly spelled on the maps, *Willamette.*

covered with a fine growth of oak, ash, maple, cotton-
wood, alder, and willow. But as we travel southward
from the Columbia, the timber along the Wallamet becomes less dense, until finally we come to the beautiful
open prairies, only half hidden from view by a thin fringe
of low trees. and picturesquely dotted here and there by
groves of oak and fir intermingled.

The Prairies of Western Oregon do not resemble the
immense flat plains of Illinois ; but are rather gently undulating, and bear a strong likeness to the " oak openings" of Michigan and Wisconsin. Instead of being continuous levels, they are divided by low ranges of hills,
covered with oak timber, low and spreading, and draped,
like the trees of the Sacramento Valley, with a long
hanging gray moss, that floats lightly on the summer
wind, as if celebrating the delightful mildness and beauty
of the scene.

The Wallamet, although navigable for one hundred and
thirty miles from its mouth, is, like all the rivers west of
the Rocky Mountains, troubled with rapids, and narrowed
in some places to little more than the width of the passing
steamer. In the latter part of summer, steamers cannot
ascend it beyond Salem, the capital of the State. Of its
ten principal tributaries, most of them are navigable for
considerable distances, and all of them furnish abundant
water-power.

The Falls of the Wallamet, about twenty-five miles
from its junction with the Columbia, furnish the greatest
water-power in the State, as also some fine scenery.
Above the falls, the water spreads out into a wide, deep
basin, and runs slowly and smoothly until within a half-
mile of the falls, when its width diminishes, its velocity
increases, and in its haste it turns back upon itself, forming dangerous eddies, until at length, forced forward, it

makes the plunge of more than twenty feet, into a boiling whirlpool below, and breaks into foam along a ledge of volcanic rock stretching from shore to shore. The spray, dashed up by the descent of the water, forms a beautiful rainbow, besides being a means of cooling the hot air of the summer noon at Oregon City, which is situated along the rocky bluffs at this point of the river.

The navigation of the river thus interrupted, formerly necessitated a portage of a couple of miles at Oregon City; but recently the People's Transportation Company have erected a strong basin on the east side of the river, which permits their boats to come so close together that the passengers and freight have only to pass through the Company's warehouse to be transferred.

The amount of agricultural land in the Wallamet Valley is estimated at about three million acres. This estimate leaves out large bodies of land in the foot-hills of the mountains, on either side, more suitable for grazing than for farming purposes.

The Soil of the Wallamet Valley is of excellent quality. Upon the prairies it consists of gray, calcareous, sandy loam, especially adapted to the cultivation of cereals, particularly of wheat, barley, and oats. It is exceedingly mellow and easily worked, and is not affected by drouth. Along the banks of the river, and the streams tributary to it, the soil consists of various decomposed earths, sand, and vegetable matter, deposited there in seasons of freshet, and is of the most fertile description. The soil of the foot-hills is a dark clay loam, mixed with vegetable mold in the small intervening valleys. Excellent grasses are produced, though this kind of soil suffers more from drouth than that of the prairies.

The Climate of the Wallamet Valley is mild and agreeable. The seasons are two,—the wet and the dry. The rainy season usually commences in November, although frequently it holds off, except a few light showers, until December. The rains continue pretty constantly until about the last of January, when there is a clearing up of three or four weeks. This interval is the real winter season, and is sometimes cold, with frozen ground, or snow, though generally the Oregon winters are not characterised either by cold or snow to any great amount. After this "clear spell" comes a second season of rains which may clear up by the first of March, or not until April. It is not an unusual thing for gardening to be commenced in February; but the result of this early gardening is not always sure.

When the rains of winter have passed, there are occasional showers until the first of July, after which there is a dry period of four months. This dry season instead of being oppressive, as would be the case in the Atlantic States, is most delightful. Sufficient moisture is borne in from the sea, over the tops of the Coast range to make the air of a fine coolness and freshness, and not enough to make it humid. Thus there is a fine, dry, cool air, with a moderate temperature, and a dry warm earth, which makes an Oregon summer the most charming season to be experienced in any part of the world. The nights are always cool enough to make a blanket necessary. The mornings bright and not too hot—the heated term during dog-days only extending over the hours from 12 M. to 4 P. M.

That a climate such as this must be healthful is undeniable. During the falling of the rains there is little or no sickness. Just after the rain ceases falling, and before the earth becomes dry, the rapid evaporation causes colds and coughs to the careless or the inexperienced. Through the dry season there is little sickness except in certain localities where, as in all new countries, malaria is formed by the exposure to the sun of new or submerged soils.

One of the faults, so to speak, of Western Oregon, is its mildness of climate. The agricultural population are prone to be negligent in providing for that irregular, and uncertainly certain occasional visitation, a "hard winter." Therefore the stock-raiser who has his several hundred head of cattle and horses ranging his one or two thousand acres of uplands, and who, trusting in Providence, makes no sufficient provision for a month or six weeks of feeding, is liable once in five to eight years, to lose nearly all of his stock. Did this same stock-raiser have to get his cattle through seven months of winter as many eastern farmers do, he might come at last to be willing to provide for the possible six weeks. Cattle in Oregon generally look poor in the spring, because the farmers allow them to shift for themselves all through the rainy season, which they should not do. For this reason, Western Oregon, although naturally the best of dairy countries, furnishes little butter and cheese, and that often of a poor quality. An influx of Central New York dairymen would greatly benefit the state, and develop one of its surest means of wealth.

The Productions of the Wallamet Valley are wheat, oats, barley, rye, wool, and fruits. All of the grains grow abundantly, and are of unusual excellence. The same is true of such fruits as apples, pears, plums, cherries, currants, gooseberries, strawberries, blackberries, raspberries, etc. In fact all fruits do well in Western Oregon, except grapes, peaches, apricots, nectarines, and that class of fruits which love a dry and hot climate. Grapes and peaches can be raised with sufficient care, but are not a natural crop like the first mentioned fruits. Corn is not raised as a crop, on account of the cool nights, which are not favorable to its ripening.

The Umpqua Valley is that portion of Western Oregon

next south of the Wallamet Valley, being divided from it by a range of mountains bearing the Indian name of Calapooya. It is a region not so well fitted for grain-raising as the Wallamet valley, but is perhaps superior as a fruit-growing and wool-raising section. The valley is watered by the Umpqua River, and is broken up into numerous hills and valleys, in the most picturesque manner. It is one of the most beautiful portions of the Pacific Coast, being rolling, well, without being densely wooded, and having a very agreeable climate, with rather less rain than falls in the lower altitude of the Wallamet.

The Rogue River Valley is another division of Western Oregon, divided from the Umpqua valley by a range of mountains bearing the name of Umpqua. It resembles the country just described in general, but has a climate which is a happy mixture of Californian dryness and Oregonian moisture. It is not considered a grain-growing country to any great extent; not from any inadaptability of the soil, but because it is a very superior grazing and fruit-growing country, and has also a considerable mining notoriety. It is separated from northern California by the Liskiyan range of mountains, and watered by the Rogue River and its northern tributaries.

The Coast Country consists of a strip of land from five to twelve miles wide, lying between the westernmost range of mountains in Oregon, and the sea. It contains several counties, whose chief agricultural merits consist in the excellence of their grasses and vegetables. Fruit too, grows very well in the Coast counties. Hops and honey, as well as butter, are among their chief farming products. But the greatest wealth of the Coast counties is probably to be derived from the heavy forests of timber which cover the mountain sides; and from the mines of coal and copper which underlie them.

A number of points have already become quite famous for business along the coast; Coose Bay for its coal and lumber; Tilamook for its oysters; and Yaquina for its good harborage, and easy access through a fine natural pass to the heart of the Wallamet valley. The port of Umpqua once promised to become a point of some import-ance, but latterly has fallen into neglect from the difficulty of communicating thence with the interior.

The climate of the Coast counties is cooler and more moist than that of the valleys to the eastward, on account of their contiguity to the sea. Their soil is deep, black, and rich, supporting an immense growth of shrubbery, and ferns from ten to fourteen feet in height. The prai-rie spots are covered with grass, and so are the hill-sides wherever the timber is not too dense. Though the mean temperature of the Coast counties is lower than that of the interior, it is also more even; and the sea-fogs in summer as well as the rains in winter serve to keep the natural grasses in excellent condition. In short every circum-stance seems to point to the Coast counties of Oregon as the great dairy region of the Pacific Coast, as the valleys of the interior are the granaries, and the hill-sides the sheep-pastures.

Good feed the year round, grain enough for the wants of the farmer, plenty of cold mountain water, abundance of timber, plenty of game and fish, are all inducements to the settler who wishes to make himself a permanent home on the Pacific Slope. These, added to the wealth yet to be developed in mines and lumber at every opening where a vessel of a hundred tons can enter, make the future of these now almost vacant Coast counties look inviting.

Resume of the Soil, Climate and Resources of Western Oregon.—From the foregoing general description of West-ern Oregon it will be seen that the country lying between the Cascade Mountains and the Coast range, consists of one valley containing about as much agricultural land of the best quality as would make a State of the size of Connecticut, and two other smaller valleys, with a less proportion of farming land, and a greater proportion of hill and pasture lands. Also that between the Coast range and the ocean is a strip of country wide enough for a tier of counties, peculiarly adapted to grazing purposes, yet not without considerable arable land.

No one can survey the Wallamet Valley without being struck with its beauty and its fertility, and many are found who pronounce it the most beautiful spot in America. Its beauty consists in the agreeable intermixture of level or rolling prairies, with ranges of low hills, dotted with oak timber, in the multitude of its winding rivers, along which grow a skirting of graceful trees, and in the grandeur of the mountains which guard it alike from the heat of the eastern deserts, and the cold of the northern ocean. Its fertility is evident from the mighty forests which mantle the hills in everlasting green, and from the grassy plains which year after year clothe the valley with renewed verdure, as well as from the golden harvest fields which man has interspersed among the universal green.

The question which first suggests itself is concerning the durability of the soil which produces so well in a wild state. A sketch of the history of agriculture in Oregon will serve to point to an answer.

Many portions of Oregon have been cultivated for a period of twenty-five years without any of those aids to the soil, or that care in preparation and cultivation which is thought necessary to keep up the quality of soils in other farming States. This thriftless mode of farming was the result, partly of an absence of laborers and good farming utensils, for the first fifteen years of the occupation of Oregon by a farming community. From the necessity of poor farming grew the habit. It was found that the earth would continue to produce when only half-cultivated, hence farmers grew indolent from too great security. The great regularity of the seasons too, by which the maturing of crops became a certainty, contributed to this general indifference, for it is an established fact that in order to work well, men must be in some sort compelled to work.

Another reason why farmers have not put themselves upon their mettle in a generous emulation, was, that for many years farm products were worth little or nothing for want of a market. All these reasons conspired to confirm a habit of indifferent cultivation, which accident and the condition of the country first forced upon them. Yet these same lands do not appear to have suffered very materially from this long course of impoverishment.

Yet another cause of poor farming has been in the fact of so large bodies of land having been held as single farms. It is impossible, of course, for one family to cultivate a mile square of land. Hence a little grain was scratched in on one portion of the claim, and a little more on another, and all so scattered, and carelessly done that no first-rate crops could possibly be obtained.

The soil of the prairies is of a dark gray color, is mellow, and not affected by drouth. It is especially adapted to cereals, and grows vegetables and fruits well, but not so well as the more alluvial soil formed immediately along the banks of the rivers and streams. It is found, too, that that portion of the prairie which grows ferns, and the land which skirts the oak groves, or has been cleared of timber, is more favorable to fruit-growing than the more compact soil of the prairie. The timbered lands everywhere, are productive, excepting occasional clay ridges where pines are found. The prairies still furnish grass in abundance for hay, but not of such quality nor in such quantity as the swamps, swales, and beaver-dams near the rivers and in the heavy timber when drained and cleared.

Of the several varieties of soil in Western Oregon, there are none that are not sufficiently productive to invite labor with a promise of reward. The whole face of the country is productive, and wherever the hillsides are not too steep to pitch a tent, those things needed by man may be made to grow abundantly.

Climate, however, and the shape of the country govern men in their selection of occupations. The grain-farmer will keep to the valleys; the fruit grower will occupy the gentle slopes of the lowest hills; the stock-raiser will settle among the foot-hills, and take his sheep to the mountains; while the dairy-man will seek those spots where grass is good for the longest period of time, and where the temperature favors the making of good, solid and sweet butter and cheese.

The nights in Western Oregon are always cool, and sleep becomes a regular refreshment. It is owing to the low temperature of the nights that corn and some varieties of fruit have commonly failed. However the proper cultivation will yet produce those things in a sufficient abundance. Good corn has been raised in Western Oregon, and peaches of splendid size and flavor occasionally find their way to market. Apples, cherries, and plums of unequalled size and excellence grow in astonishing profusion.

The winters of Western Oregon, though rainy, are generally mild. The principal hardship of the rainy season consists in simply enduring the monotony of the dull sky and constant rain. It is, however, a favorable climate for the farmer, since he is not forced to work hard all the summer to raise what his stock will need to eat through the winter. A fortnight's feed usually suffices for the wintering of cattle.

The following tables show the comparative mean temperatures of three points in Oregon, with four in other States; also the number of rainy days in Oregon and Illinois, respectively:

TABLE I.—*Showing Comparative Mean Temperatures.*

TIME.	Astoria, Oregon.	Corvallis, Oregon.	Dalles, East'n Oregon.	Augusta, Illinois.	Hazelwood, Min.	San Diego, Cal.	Albany, N. Y.	Dubuque, Iowa.
Years of Observation	1⅓	1⅙	3⅓	11⅞	2	5½	24	3⅞
Spring Temperature	51.16	52.19	53.00	51.34	42.33	59.97	47.61	47.36
Summer "	61.36	67.13	70.36	72.51	69.95	71.08	70.17	71.42
Autumn "	53.55	53.41	52.21	53.38	42.60	64.36	50.01	50.34
Winter "	42.43	39.27	35.59	29.80	13.06	52.29	25.83	25.88
Whole Time "	52.13	53.00	52.79	51.76	41.97	61.93	48.41	48.75

The only point in Eastern Oregon, whose temperature is exhibited in this table, is Dalles, which, situated as it is, immediately at the base of the Cascade Mountains, does not fairly represent the temperature of the extensive valleys farther east, which constitute the agricultural region of that country. The summer, in most of those valleys, as well as on the table-lands, is much warmer than at the Dalles. The winter temperature, it will be observed, is much higher than that of other States in the same latitude, while that of the spring is nearly the same, and the summer not quite so high.

TABLE II.—*Showing the Number of Rainy Days during the Winter, at Astoria, Oregon, Wallamet Valley, Oregon, and Peoria, Illinois, respectively.*

MONTH.	Astoria, Oregon.			Wallamet Valley, O.	Peoria, Ill.	
	1857–8	1858–9	1859–60	1856–7	1856–7	1857–8
November.	21	16	19	9	9	16
December.	25	14	15	13	10	7
January.	17	19	19	15	4	6
February . . . . -	9	20	17	6	10	8
Total	72	69	70	43	33	37

This table includes all rainy days, without reference to whether it rained all day, or only a part. It also includes snowy days, very few of which are seen in Oregon, in an ordinary winter.

The climate of Oregon has proven to be a healthful one during a thirty years' residence of some of the earliest missionaries and settlers. So far as natural causes are concerned, there appears to be none for the promotion of disease, if we except the tendency to pulmonary and rheumatic diseases for which both California and Oregon are famed, and which no doubt is to be credited to the cold winds from the ocean. These winds in themselves are a sanitary provision of nature, and serve to give the Pacific coast a climate generally free from miasmatic and pestilential diseases; but it is necessary for sensitive constitutions to guard against the rapid change of temperature which they effect when they come sweeping in from the sea, suddenly displacing the warm air of the valleys. With proper care, and attention to the most manifest laws of health, the physical man has a better opportunity for magnificent development, on the Pacific coast, than in any other part of the American continent.

While the winters of Western Oregon are dull and disagreeable, the summers are proportionately delightful. The general temperature of the days is mild and agreeable, the air bright and clear, warmer in the afternoons than in the mornings, invariably ; yet falling again to an invigorating coolness in the evening. *Sultriness* is almost never experienced in this part of Oregon. The greatest heat of summer has not that enervating effect which the summer-heats have in the Atlantic States. It is frequently remarked by the farmers here that their cattle can endure to work right on under the hottest sun of summer without showing signs of exhaustion, as they would have done in those States from which they were brought.

From the peculiarities of the soil, seasons, and climate of Western Oregon, it becomes necessary for the farmer to practice modes of culture especially adapted to it, and to conform to other seed-time than that he may have been accustomed to in other States. Much can undoubtedly be learned from old Oregon farmers; but a careful observation from year to year, with a little judicious experiment, will, we hope, develop among the newer settlers a better manner of farming than that formerly practiced in Oregon, when one year's cultivation was made to answer for three years' crops—the two latter of which were of course self-sown.

While the yield of wheat is perhaps no greater than that of the Genesee valley, or the rich prairies of Indiana or southwestern Michigan, the crop is far more sure, from the absence of insects, rust, winter-killing, etc. Perhaps not more than twice since the settlement of the Wallamet Valley has the wheat crop been injured by rain in harvest time. As a general thing the straw is short and stout, and the grain is never laid down by summer tempests of wind and rain.

Peas sown broadcast, with or without oats, bring a product about equal to wheat; and are the best crop for fattening hogs, requiring little labor, and producing a fine quality of pork by turning the hogs into the field in the fall and letting them fatten there. Bacon brings a high price in the mines, and is one of the most valuable possessions of the farmer. The rapid increase of sheep in Oregon gives the sheep-raiser a large surplus every year above what he can afford to keep for their wool, and of this surplus quite a number every year may be sold for mutton at home, or driven to the mines, where they command a good price.

The whole country west of the Rocky Mountains is favorably adapted to fruit-growing, and no portion of it more so than Western Oregon. Trees of three years' growth bend to the earth under their burdens of fruit. Before the tree matures its strength it bears at a rate so wonderful that without artificial support the branches split away from the main tree. Apple trees less than two inches in diameter, with branches no more than three-quarters of an inch in thickness are so crowded with apples as to leave very little of the stock visible. We have counted forty large apples on a limb of the thickness mentioned above, and no more than four feet and a half long,—a mere rod. Plum and pear trees bear in the same manner. Cherries are equally prolific, but peaches seldom crowd the tree in Western Oregon, though they do in Eastern Oregon. Probably the best treatment to give young fruit trees in Oregon would be to pull off the greater portion of the fruit for the first year or two in order that the trees might mature their strength. No doubt it would also add to the flavor of the fruit, though that seems to be always excellent.

"Wild berries are very abundant, some of which are peculiarly delicious. The berries are strawberries, dewberries, whortleberries, sallalberries, black and

34

yellow raspberries, gooseberries, juneberries, and cranberries. The cranberries are good, but found in abundance only in the vicinity of the ocean; the june, salmon, and gooseberries are not particularly desirable; the dew, sallal, and raspberries are choice, and quite abundant; and the straw and whortleberries are extremely abundant and delicious. The prairies may be truly said to be literally red with strawberries, and the timbered openings blue with whortleberries, in their season. The season of ripe strawberries is from three to six weeks, and that of whortleberries from six to ten weeks. The whortleberry bush, except in the mountains, like the Umpqua plum shrub, is borne prostrate upon the earth's grassy covering, from the weight of its delicious fruit. The wild strawberry of Oregon is larger and better than any we have ever seen, except the largest of the large garden cultivated English strawberry. The whortleberry has more acidity than those of unshaded growth, growing east of the mountains. English gooseberries and currants are cultivated here with success."

The native grasses of Western Oregon are blue-grass, and red and white clover. The grass formerly grew very tall on the prairies but has been so much eaten off and trampled out by numerous herds of cattle, that it is now much shorter. When sown in favorable situations, timothy will grow to a height of between five and six feet.

The timber of Western Oregon consists of pine, fir, cedar, oak, spruce, hemlock, cotton-wood, cherry, and maple. Probably there is no country in the world where timber grows so strikingly straight and beautiful, and to such gigantic altitude and dimensions as in Oregon. Two hundred feet is but a moderate height for the growth of firs, cedars, and spruce, and they frequently attain a much greater altitude. We have seen elder growing in Oregon three feet in circumference, and hazel thirty inches in circumference, and of the height of forty feet. Black alder and a species of laurel grow to what would be termed, in most countries, large trees—logs of alder have been obtained thirty-two inches in diameter, and of the laurel four feet in diameter. In Western Oregon groves of timber are found skirting and separating prairies; but the immense timber districts are mainly confined to the neighborhood of the coast of the Pacific, to the Coast, Cascade and Blue ranges of mountains, and the immediate vicinity of the rivers.

The fir is seen almost solely on the western slope of the Cascade Mountains, along the Columbia River from where it breaks through that range until it passes through the coast range, on the eastern slope of the Coast Mountains, and along the rivers and upon the mountains almost any where between the summits of these two principal ranges. It is everywhere slightly mixed with spruce, hemlock, cedar, and yew. The pine is generally found in ridges or patches by itself, except on the west side of the Coast range where it grows with hemlock, spruce, and cedar. Willow grows along all the streams, and acquires considerable size. Ash, oak, maple, cotton-wood, and alder also grow wherever the ground is low and moist.

The shrubbery of Oregon is very beautiful and in great variety. There are several varieties of alder, bearing, severally, light purple, scarlet and orange colored berries. The wild cherry is a light and graceful tree, having a small, clear scarlet fruit, that is very beautiful, and exceedingly bitter. The tree-whortleberry has a very diminutive leaf, almost round, and a small crimson berry tasting much like a barberry. There are two smaller whortleberry shrubs corresponding to those of the Atlantic States, called swamp and mountain whortleberries. There are several varieties of wild currants, one of which is useless as a fruit, but is most beautiful as a flowering shrub. White spirea, and golden honeysuckle thrust their white or golden blossoms through every thicket, and with the white syringa and wild rose, festoon the river banks and hill sides until they seem one bed of bloom. The handsome shrubbery, and the abundant wild flowers of Oregon, atone greatly for the want of greater variety in the forest tints; and the ease with which flowers may be cultivated for the adornment of homes is one of the greatest recommendations of the climate. Nature has been lavish, though man may be indifferent. If ever a wilderness might be made to blossom as the rose, that wilderness is Oregon. Few of the old settlers of Oregon have cared, however, to take advantage of the facilities afforded them for beautifying their homesteads, and it is more common to find a house without garden or shrubbery than with either; a peculiarity as strange as it is inexcusable.

Though Western Oregon is especially adapted to agricultural and pastoral pursuits, the present indications of mineral wealth make it almost certain that the miner's pick, as well as the farmer's plow, must furrow the face of mother Earth, west of the Cascade Mountains. This discovery was not sought after by the people of Oregon, who were firmly fixed in their belief that it was as an agricultural and manufacturing State that they were to achieve their highest destiny. But when gold and silver, iron, coal, and copper, are knocking for admittance as State resources, they cannot and will not be denied. They will be accepted as aids to manufactures and commerce; and will be taken in connection with forests of splendid timber and rivers of unfailing water-power, as the means by which Oregon is to acquire her future status as one of the most important States of the Union.

Since the repeated tests by which the Santiam gold-bearing quartz has been found to yield $160 to the ton, other discoveries have been made, and will continue to be made in the Cascade Mountains. Already the mining town of Quartzville has started up in the Santiam district, and another town called Copperopolis, about ten miles to the southeast has sprung into existence near the copper mines. Discoveries of gold have recently been made in

Clackamas County; but as no actual test has yet been made of the quality of the ores, we cannot speak of their value.

It is sufficient to say that enough is known of the mineral resources of Western Oregon to warrant the investment of large amounts of capital; and that discoveries have only just begun to be made.

As to the price of farming lands in the Wallamet valley, they vary from three to fifteen dollars, including improvements. Many excellent farms may be had at from three to five dollars per acre; the owners selling out in order to remove with their children into towns, where they can be educated. These lands in a few years will be worth fifty dollars per acre, and we trust it will not be long before the population will be sufficiently dense to insure good schools throughout the State. The Oregon Central Railroad, now in course of construction, will do much to bring out the resources of the interior, and the time is not distant when lands in Western Oregon will bring a high price.

Sheep-raising and Manufacture of Woolen Goods. Wm. Lair Hill, in his prize essay, read before the Oregon State Fair, for 1862, says:—

"If Oregon has a specialty, it is her pre-eminence as a wool-growing country. Until recently, very little attention has been paid to the matter of sheep-raising; but it has now become one of the staple interests of the State. Sheep thrive better here than in any other State. Disease amongst them is exceedingly rare. They increase here faster than in the east, and the wool is of excellent quality."

In a similar essay, read before the Oregon State Fair for 1863, by John Minto, Esq., the following passages occur:—

"For the health of sheep, dry upland pasture is necessary. Taking the whole of Oregon into view, nine-tenths of the State may be pronounced of that character. For the feeding of sheep for wool-raising purposes, short sweet grasses and open woodland pastures are deemed best; and full three-fourths of the surface of the State is composed of hills and plains yielding such grasses; and a large portion of it is open woodland. For the growth of a long, even, strong, and flexible staple of wool, a mild, even climate (with proper feeding) is considered best, and that Oregon possesses in a remarkable degree. In fact, the climate and natural grasses of Oregon seem to be a natural combination of the peculiarities of England and Spain, in those particulars, especially the climate.

"Over twenty years ago, Mr. Peale, a naturalist who accompanied Commodore Wilkes' expedition to this coast gave it as his opinion that 'the country would become famous for its production of fine wool,' for the reason that 'the evenness of the climate enables the fur-bearing animals found here to carry their fine covering during the summer months, whereas under greater variations between the seasons, the same animals usually shed their furs, or they become mixed with hair during summer;' and for the further reason that the 'physical geography and natural grasses of the country make it a natural sheep pasture.'

"Experience goes far to show Mr. Peale's opinion correct. In a conversation between the writer and Mr. Henry Perkins, Chief Wool Stapler in the woolen factory at Salem, (a gentleman who has had a large and varied experience in assorting wool,) the latter said that he had never handled the wool from any country, which as a whole, was equal to that of Oregon as a combing wool; and that during a term of three years as wool stapler in a De Laine factory in Boston, Mass., he deemed that he did well when he could get from the bulk assorted 30 per cent. of wool fit for combing and manufacturing into that fabric. Of the wool he was then receiving—the crop of 1863, as it came in indiscriminately—Mr. P. said he could get from 50 to 60 per cent. of good combing wool. He further said if wools were properly assorted here and the combing portion graded and baled and marked according to its quality, and shipped to New York or Boston, it would soon draw the attention of De Laine manufacturers to this country as a source of supply for this most valuable kind of wool. We have further practical proof of the superiority of Oregon wool, in the fact that San Francisco papers as late as July last, quoted Oregon wool as selling three cents per pound above California wool sold on the same day.

"The fact of the superiority of Oregon wool is an encouraging circumstance to those engaged, or about to engage in raising it. But they will never reap the full benefit of it so long as they allow the business men of California to put their crops into market: so long as this is the case, the fact will be used to spread the fame of California, as a wool-producing country, and so long will Oregon dwell in the shadow of California, and feel the blighting influence. This is the inevitable result, even without any effort on the part of California merchants. It goes from their port in their shipping mart; the buyer cares no more but to know that he is receiving a good article for his money, and it would be too much to expect the California merchant to inform his customer that it was the product of another state. * * *

"The success of the woolen manufactory at Salem, started under more adverse circumstances than, it is believed, will ever again exist on this coast, shows plainly that a De Laine factory would be eminently successful here where such goods are worn throughout the year.*

" And there is no doubt that there is many a farmer in the Middle and West-ern States, who, worn down by the debilitating influences of miasmatic climates, would get a new lease of life by changing his location and becoming a sheep-raiser under the clear skies and pure air of Eastern Oregon. *   *   *   *   *

" There are at present more promising inducements for the Oregon farmer to turn his attention to the raising of sheep and wool (where his lands are of a suitable kind,) than any other branch of farming, for the reasons: 1st. That in that occupation the farmer can get along with less hired help, which is al-ways hard to get of a reliable kind, and will continue to be, so long as the dis-covery of new gold mines continues. 2d. Sheep eat nearer to the ground and a greater variety of plants, and consequently require less labor in providing them food than any other domestic animal which yields anything like the re-turn which they yield. 3d. There are two products from sheep, for either of which there is a greater prospective market than for any other farm product we can raise. We have already glanced at the condition of the market with re-gard to wool. ' It is the only thing raised by the farmers of Oregon that con-tains enough value in proportion to its weight to bear the expense of transpor-tation to the Atlantic States. It is the only product that cannot be raised cheaper in the Atlantic States than here. It is the only product of the soil of Oregon (gold excepted) which we can send to the Eastern seaboard in ex-change for the clothing, boots and shoes, machinery, iron, etc., etc., which we must buy there or elsewhere until we can build up manufactures of our own.' And manufactures we must have, unless we can contentedly remain utterly de-pendent upon the manufacturing skill of other communities, subject to the in-conveniences of interruption in time of war, and the always increasing cost of transportation, which, as the producers of the raw material and consumers of the manufactured article, we must pay all the cost of, according to the amount of our consumption. The market for good wool-bearing stock sheep is only to be measured by the extent of the country yet unoccupied and fit for grazing pur-poses lying between the Pacific Ocean and the western base of the Rocky Mountains. The market for mutton will be in accordance with the increase of population; it can be produced cheaper and will always sell higher than beef until the country is glutted with wool-bearing flocks.

" Oregon lies on the western edge of an immense extent of country—reach-ing from Mexico to the British line; from Kansas to the Pacific Ocean—which, with the exception of the belt between the Cascade Mountains and the ocean, covered by parts of California, Oregon, and Washington Territory, is fitted for pastoral pursuits only. She has within her own borders a large portion of the best of that natural pasture. Within that, and almost surrounded by it, she has the largest compact body of good wheat land on the Pacific slope; which,

---

* Since the above was written a large factory at Oregon City has commenced manufacturing de laines, and several kinds of cloths.

surrounded and intermingled with never-failing water-power, makes the Willamette Valley adapted by nature for the cheap support of a dense manufacturing population, in a three-fold greater degree than ever was either Old or New England. She may, if her citizens will it, do her full share of first supplying all the region drained by the waters of the Columbia River with stock sheep, and then manufacture the wool raised from them and their increase. She may become to the north-west coast of America what England is now to the world, and what New England is to the United States in the power of their manufacturing commerce—following the settlements as they spread to the East and North with her improved stock and woolen fabrics."

Since Mr. Minto wrote his able essay on Sheep-raising, further facts have come to light concerning the quality of wool raised in the Eastern portion of Oregon. It has been well ascertained that the alkaline properties of the grass on which the sheep feed in some portions of Eastern Oregon, as well as the dust which settles upon them, has a deteriorating effect upon the wool; and that so far no good fleeces have been obtained from those regions. Undoubtedly the very best sheep-pastures are to be found on the Western side of the Cascade Mountains; though many valuable sheep-ranges may yet be discovered in the territory lying east of the Cascades and west of the Rocky Mountains.

Timber and Lumbering.—The State of Oregon, although in reality a prairie State, has immense lumbering resources. The principal timbers made into lumber are the firs and cedars. These grow along the streams and on the mountain ranges, affording fine facilities for milling, and for exporting lumber. A large amount of lumbering is done along the coast, at Coos Bay and Port Orford. All along the Columbia River, from its mouth to the Dalles, a distance of nearly two hundred miles, are dense forests of the most magnificent sized trees, which make superior lumber.

The exports from the Columbia River are about 4,000,-000 feet annually, which find a market at San Francisco, and the Sandwich Islands, chiefly. The lumber trade of Oregon is but in its infancy, being capable of almost unlimited development.

Turpentine, Tar, and Rosin.—Not only do the forests of Oregon furnish exhaustless supplies of lumber, but they offer also an immense source of wealth to the enterprising manufacturer of turpentine, tar, and rosin. T. A. Wood & Co., of Portland, who are engaged in manufacturing these articles, give the following statement on this subject:

" Every day more fully demonstrates the fact that the supply of crude turpentine is inexhaustible, and the probabilities are that this supply will never grow less, from two facts :

1st. The forests best suited for and richest in balsam, are those rough mountain sides that the farmer can never reduce to tillage.

2d. The trees when robbed of their accumulated supply will, like the " busy bee," commence the work of replenishing their stores, or refilling the cavities or " shakes," to be annually or semi-annually robbed.

From the crude article we manufacture turpentine, pitch, bright varnish, rosin, and axle-grease. In the limited time we have been in operation we have consumed 21,000 gallons of crude balsam. From this our manufacture will approximate : turpentine, 5,000 gallons; pitch, 400 barrels; bright varnish, 70 barrels; axle-grease, 25 cases.

We claim that the above articles are equal in quality to any manufactured in the United States, and not without proof. The turpentine being made from balsam of fir, is as far superior to pine turpentine, for medical use, as fir balsam is superior to pine pitch for medical purposes. The Portland physicians who have tried it speak loudly in praise of its medical virtues.

Under date of July 16th, 1864, Mr. P. C. Dart, of San Francisco, says : " Your turpentine is now preferred over California make, and I obtained twenty-five cents on the gallon, in advance of the California article. This fact is certainly encouraging."

The boat pitch is superior to any ever shipped to this coast. Capt. Kellogg said he ' used on the steamer Senator one barrel of States pitch and one of Oregon pitch, and would rather by one hundred dollars have used all Oregon pitch. The calkers said the barrel of Oregon pitch was worth three of the States pitch.'

Though our business has not been very extensive, we have opened a trade with China, Sandwich Islands, Vancouver's Island, California, and are now making a shipment to New York. It is our intention to enlarge our works, and if we do, as now designed, we shall export, from July 1865 to July 1866, over 1,200 tons of manufactured articles. In fact, the crude turpentine is in such abundance as to supply the world, if brought into use."

Fish and Fisheries.—Oregon furnishes some of the finest fisheries in the world. From the roaring mountain torrent, filled with the beautiful speckled trout, to the largest rivers, and the ocean bays, all its waters are alive with fish. In the latter are found cod, sturgeon, carp, flounders, perch, herring, crabs, and oysters. Tillamook, and Yaquina Bays are the principal oyster beds.

All the rivers along the coast furnish salmon, the largest being taken in the Columbia. They run up the rivers twice during the year, commencing in May, and again in October. Notwithstanding their great numbers, but few are taken for commercial purposes, although 100,000 barrels might be secured annually, and sold for ten dollars per barrel.

The following interesting extract is from Father P. J. De Smet's book on the Oregon Missions:

"My presence among the Indians did not interrupt their fine and abundant fishery. An enormous basket was fastened to a projecting rock, and the finest fish of the Columbia, as if by fascination, cast themselves by dozens into the snare. Seven or eight times during the day, these baskets were examined, and each time were found to contain about two hundred and fifty salmon. The Indians, meanwhile, were seen on every projecting rock, piercing the fish with the greatest dexterity.

They who do not know this territory may accuse me of exaggeration, when I affirm, that it would be as easy to count the pebbles so profusely scattered on the shores, as to sum up the number of different kinds of fish which this western river furnishes for man's support; as the buffalo of the north, and the deer from north to east of the mountains furnish daily food for the inhabitants of those regions, so do these fish supply the wants of the western tribes. One may form some idea of the quantity of salmon and other fish, by remarking, that at the time they ascend the rivers, all the tribes inhabiting the shores, choose favorable locations, and not only do they find abundant nutriment during the season, but, if diligent, they dry, and also pulverize and mix with oil a sufficient quantity for the rest of the year. Incalculable shoals of salmon ascend to the river's source, and there die in shallow water. Great quantities of trout and carp follow them and regale themselves on the spawn deposited by the salmon in holes and still water. The following year the young salmon descend to the sea, and I have been told, (I cannot vouch for the authenticity,) that they never return until the fourth year. Six different species are found in the Columbia."

Game. The game of Oregon is principally Bear, Panther, Elk, Deer, Antelope, Squirrel, Geese, Swan, Ducks, Pheasants, Grouse, and Quail. In the Wallamet Valley are found some Bear and Elk, and an abundance of black and white-tailed Deer, and Geese and Ducks.

In the Umpqua, Rogues and Clamet valleys are found an abundance of Elk, Deer, Antelope, Geese, and Ducks. The Deer of this country have been represented by some as small and inferior. Such is not the fact. The meat of the Deer of Oregon is as tender and delicious as the Deer of any other portion of the United States. The meat of the black-tailed Deer of this country is much superior to the meat of the white-tailed Deer of New York, Pennsylvania, or the Western States.

Salt. The salt of Oregon is obtained from springs, and is of very superior quality. The springs are numerous in the western part of Multnomah County, in the valley of the Lower Wallamet, in Columbia County, adjoining, and also in Douglas County, or the Umpqua Valley. Those in Douglas County have been worked for some time, manufacturing about 1,000 pounds per day, which being consumed in the neighborhood of the works, does not offer itself in the Portland market; neither would the distance and difficulties of transportation admit of its seeking a market in this place. There may be other springs in different counties worked in a small way. The salt works lately erected in the Lower Wallamet Valley are situated half way between Portland and St. Helen, at the foot of the hills which skirt the river, and about half a mile distant from it. There are a number of springs in this locality, and extending along near the base of this range of hills from 12 to 20 miles. Only one spring is used at present at the Wallamet Salt Works, and the present works are only experimental. From this one spring, or well (for it has been deepened 27 feet) with all the surface water in it, and with only one furnace, the company have been making from 500 to 700 pounds of salt per day that probably has no superior in any part of the world. It crystalizes with a handsome, fine grain; is bright, sparkling and as white as snow. It is entirely free from lime, or any deleterious substance, so that as a dairy salt, or for curing of meats, fish, etc., it is of the very best quality. So strong are its preservative qualities that dairymen say they need use only two-thirds as much of it as of Liverpool salt; and the Portland butchers who have used it declare it worth $10 more per ton than any salt in the market,— that they use the brine over and over. Its quality, then, is perfectly satisfactory, and the company are about erecting new and extensive works for boiling, beside improving the saline properties of the water in the springs by boring and piping, to exclude surface or any other fresh water.

Coal. That there will be found to be a large supply of coal in Oregon is beyond a doubt. The Coos Bay coal is not unknown in San Francisco, though its quality has never gained for it much of a reputation. Other deposits have been discovered on the coast further to the north. A mine is now being worked on the Cowlitz river, six or eight miles from its junction with the Columbia, which bids fair to supersede in merit any yet discovered on the Pacific Coast. The structure and appearance of the Oregon coal are peculiar, and at first liable to mislead the judgment as to its quality. It has a glossy surface, is rather light in weight, is perfectly clean to handle and makes no soot in burning, all of which makes it a pleasant fuel for grates and culinary purposes. It also lights very readily, burns freely in the open air, and is free from sulphur. It shows, or appears to show, a woody structure, yet is a hard coal, making an intense heat and holding fire for many hours. When burnt it emits a clear white flame, and leaves a white ash, without depositing strong substances, or *clinkers*. It is not anthracite, nor bituminous, though nearly as hard as the first, and quite as inflam able as the latter. Some miners call it cannel; some say it resembles Scotch splinth; but altogether it is easier to say what it is not than what it is. The fossils found in connection with it have created some doubt as to its age, many of them seeming to belong to the tertiary period, while others evidently are palm leaves.

Iron. Extensive beds of iron ore of a very pure quality are known to exist both on the Wallamet and on the Columbia rivers. Those on the Wallamet are situated about six miles south of Portland, and about eighteen above the mouth of the river. Furnaces were erected two years since by a Portland Company, who after sending some iron to San Francisco pronounced equal to the Swedish iron, have stopped manufacturing on account of some difficulty about the land on which the beds are situated, or the water-power used in connection with it. It is to be hoped that the entanglement, from whatever cause it arises, will soon be removed. Very extensive beds of the same kind of ore are found on the Columbia in the county of that name, but so far have not been worked.

Lead. This metal is found in abundance in southern Oregon, and in the Cascade Mountains, but only in conjunction with other metals. No attempt has yet been made to work it on account of the difficulty of separating the ores, and its low price in the market. In the future, however, it will be brought into notice along with other mineral productions.

Copper. The copper mines of Oregon have never yet been worked, yet for richness and favorable location they surpass those on the lower coast. This metal is found on the Rogue, Umpqua, Coquille, and Santiam rivers. Those on the Coquille are the most favorably situated for the shipment of ores. Very rich mines are located in Josephine county, but await the era of railroads for their development.

Gold and Silver. Gold is found in paying quantities on the Umpqua, Rogue, and Illinois rivers, and their tributaries; on the sea-beach at the mouth of the Umpqua and Coquille rivers, and at various places along the coast. But the richest mines have been discovered in a district called the Santiam from the river of that name, about seventy miles east of Salem, in the center of the State. The ore from these mines assays from $20 to $10,000 per ton. Silver is also found in connection with it.

Oregon has never, until within the last five years, been known as a mineral region. The character of the early settlers predisposing them to agricultural pursuits caused them to overlook the possible mineral wealth of the territory, even after the breaking out of the gold excitement in California had made known to the world the existence of rich mineral deposits on the Pacific coast. Those who were taken with the gold fever went to California, leaving unexplored the country nearer home. Gradually, however, and little by little, it became known that there were deposits of the precious metals in Oregon. Placer diggings in Southern Oregon and along the coast began to be worked as early as 1851–2. Copper, iron, and coal were discovered, but with the exception of the coal mines near the sea-coast, remained unworked.

Meanwhile gold continued to be discovered on every side, in British Columbia, Washington Territory, and Idaho, while Oregon, ever slow and deliberate amidst the hurry of events, made no effort to unveil the mysteries of her bosom. In 1861, the mines of Idaho were discovered at the mouth of Oro Fino Creek by E. D. Pierce, an Indian trader, at the head of a prospecting party of ten men. The excitement which followed the published accounts of these mines, caused a rush of explorers in that region of country now known as Idaho, which resulted in the discovery of gold on the head-waters and tributaries of the Clearwater.

Among these adventurers were numbers from the Wallamet valley, who in crossing the country east of the Cascade range, made the discovery of placer diggings on the John Day, Powder, and Burnt rivers, in Eastern Oregon. In 1864, quartz leads were also discovered on Eagle creek between Powder, and Burnt rivers; and towns are already built on each of these rivers. Thus was Oregon at last revealed to the world as a mineral district, unsurpassed in richness by very few districts in the world.

Building Materials. The mountains, in which are probably deposited quarries of different kinds of building stone, have been but little prospected with a view to the discovery of these materials for substantial structures. Lumber has been so abundant, cheap, and excellent in quality, that it has been unnecessary to search out the treasures contained in the bosom of the earth. There is no lack, however, of stone suitable for masonry ; nor of clay to make excellent brick. Limestone deposits exist in the Umpqua valley, in the hills back of the Clatsop Plains, in the highlands back of the Tualatin Plains, and in other parts of the Wallamet valley, and along the Columbia river, especially near its mouth. Southern Oregon furnishes numerous fine ledges of the best crystalline marble, susceptible of the highest polish. Sandstone occurs in the Coast range of mountains.

Bark for Tanning Leather. The forests and plains of Oregon furnish an unlimited supply of oak, fir, and hemlock bark, suitable for tanning purposes, while the extensive pastures of the State can keep supplied, unlimited quantities of hides for manufacturing leather.

Grain Raising and Flour Making. The production of wheat must ever remain one of the greatest resources of the State. Surrounded on every side by pasture lands, Oregon has " the largest compact body of good wheat land on the Pacific slope, which surrounded and intermingled with never-failing water-power, makes the Wallamet valley adapted by nature for the cheap manufacture of breadstuffs."

Wheat yields an average of thirty bushels to the acre, and in cases of good cultivation nearly double that amount. Oats, fifty to seventy-five bushels to the acre. Other grains in proportion ; and all kinds of pulse equally well.

Flax and Hemp. Flax and hemp grow to a great size, and produce a better fibre than in any other country. Flax yields a large amount of seed, and an oil-mill would do well in this State. There is no reason why linen goods may not be profitably manufactured in Oregon.

Tobacco. Tobacco has been grown in Oregon, equal to the best Virginia leaf. Eastern Oregon is peculiarly fitted for the cultivation of this plant ; and only experienced hands to cure it are wanted, to make the Oregon tobacco as celebrated as any in the United States.

Hops. The rainless summers of this country, together with the absence of heavy dews, make it very favorable for hop-raising. The crop is always certain, and may be cured in the open air. Hops will become one of the regular exports of the State.

Fruits—Preserving. The great and steady fruit-crops of Oregon, together with the abundance of berries growing wild in all parts of the State, offer superior inducements for the establishment of preserving houses in the

Wallamet valley. No such establishment exists, though the miners away up in Idaho buy fruits preserved in the Atlantic States and California.

Honey. It is but about five years since bees were introduced into Oregon. They thrive well, and produce a large amount of honey.

Potatoes and Vegetables. Potatoes are excellent in this State, and yield abundantly; from three hundred to four, or even six hundred bushels being grown on an acre of ground. The very best cabbages in the world are grown in Oregon, and in great numbers. The same may be said of Cauliflower. Melons and squashes do well, growing to a great size. Onions, like cabbage are very superior in this soil and climate, being mild and sweet to a degree unknown in the Eastern States. All other vegetables and roots thrive well, and are of good quality.

In short, if an Oregon farmer does not enjoy the comforts of life, he has no one to blame except himself for the lack of these things.

EASTERN OREGON was long regarded as a desert country, unblessed by God and undesired by man. That was when the emigration to Oregon, coming overland all the way from Indiana, Illinois, Missouri, and more southern States, arrived at the South Pass of the Rocky Mountains, with stock and provisions more than half exhausted, to enter upon a country not only more rugged in appearance than that already passed over, but presenting new features and new characteristics, against which, from ignorance of the facts, they had failed to prepare themselves. They found, west of the Rocky Mountains, a totally different climate from any they had ever experienced: delightful enough in summer, on the mountains, but hot and dry on the plains. Their road led them over bare rocks, reflecting strongly the heat of a cloudless sky; over sands

35

burning hot, and terribly heavy for their teams; over
alkali deserts, which they knew not how to avoid, and
past boiling springs whose disagreeable fumes filled the
air. They were too weary to bring much energy to the
overcoming of such difficulties as fell in their way, and
too discouraged with these difficulties to be fairly thankful
for the occasional oases which beautified their desert; so
that, when once they had set foot within the ever-verdant
valleys west of the Cascade range, the tawny colored hills
and plains of Idaho and Eastern Oregon—then all Oregon
Territory—were remembered only as " that God-forsaken
country." A few emigrants and travelers were intelligent
enough to observe the evidences of extensive mineral deposits, but most of these never looked forward to seeing
this country occupied, and its minerals made the source
of wealth. And least of all did they foresee that much,
very much, of this " God-forsaken country " would prove
to be of wonderful fertility, so that, in the year 1869,
many portions of it have " blossomed like the rose."
Such, at all events, is the history of Eastern Oregon.

There is, undoubtedly, a large proportion of waste
lands in this part of the State. There are alkali plains
and sage deserts, and in some parts, bare rocks coming to
the surface. The alkali plains may never be made fit for
cultivation. The sage deserts are not quite so hopeless,
as some portions of them have been found susceptible of
cultivation in California, and they may not prove to be so
worthless as has been believed; but the rocks are a fore-
gone conclusion.

In Eastern Oregon, Eastern Washington, and Idaho,
the same general aspect of country prevails, except in
the most northern portions of the two latter Territories,
which are more heavily timbered, and rather better
watered. But south of parallel 47, and between the Cas-

cade Mountains and the westernmost divide of the Rocky
Mountains, the country consists entirely of high rolling
plains destitute of timber, and mountain ridges covered
with timber; with the exception, however, of depressions
between the mountains and high table-lands, where lakes
and marshes may sometimes be found. The soil, both of
the plains and the mountains, is excellent. But a small
portion of the plains will ever be cultivated, for want of
the means of irrigation, but they will prove very valuable
for stock-raising purposes, as they are covered with a
natural growth of excellent bunch-grass. The mountain-
sides, when cleared, will produce fruit of the best quality;
but it is upon the valley lands that the farmer will chiefly
depend for his grain-fields. There is no reason evident
why grapes should not do well east of the Cascades in
Oregon. The soil and climate are quite similar to those
of California, where the grape flourishes best. Corn
grows well in the valleys, and other grains and vegetables
produce remarkably well. It is worthy of mention here,
that, at the late agricultural fair in Eastern Oregon, the
premium for some kinds of vegetables was awarded to an
Indian farmer of the Umatilla tribe.

Eastern Oregon is crossed obliquely by the chain of the
Blue Mountains, which commence about at the eastern
boundary of Washington Territory, where the Snake
River bends to the south, and take a course southwest
to near the centre of Eastern Oregon, where they bend
more to the west, until they connect with the range of
highlands along the Des Chutes River, which runs between these hills and the Cascade range. Where the
Blue Mountains cross the State, they form, with the spurs
which they send out to the east and south, the divide,
or water-shed between the waters which flow into the
Columbia and those which flow into the numerous lakes

of the Oregon portion of the Great Basin, or sink into thirsty sands.

The scenery, the geology, and topography of this portion of Oregon (the Klamath Basin) are alike remarkable. The irregular hills, covered with burnt rock and scoriæ; the fearful chasms, and sharp, needle-shaped rocks of its basaltic mountains; its mysterious reservoirs of water; its salt lakes and alkaline plains, seem to mark it for a country uninhabitable by man, and the resort only of myriads of wild-fowl, which here hatch their young in safety, and the refuge of marauding Indians who retire here after a successful raid into the settlements. Yet it will not be left to these, for the explorer and surveyor are already traversing it everywhere, and roads are being opened in various directions, connecting with the mines of Idaho, and with the towns and mines near the Columbia River. Nor will it be found unfit for settlement. In many parts are very desirable places for farms or stock-raising; while the excellence of the routes which lead across the southern portion of Oregon, for the use of the emigration and traders to the mines, over those which cross near the Columbia River, will make every available section of land desirable for settlement.

The Great Basin consists of an elevated plateau, raised five thousand feet above the level of the ocean, and varying in surface between low hills, arid plains, marshes, salt and fresh lakes, and occasional fertile valleys. It is bounded by the Cascade Mountains on the west, whose foot-hills, covered with a beautiful growth of pine, extend away nearly to the eastern border of Klamath Lake; on the north by the divide of the Blue Mountains; and on the east by another low range of mountains. To the south it extends into California, Nevada, and Utah.

The following extracts from the report of Col. C. S.

Drew, 1st Oregon Cavalry, who made a reconnoisance through Southern Oregon to Fort Boise, in the summer of 1864, will furnish an idea of the cultivable country between Fort Klamath and Fort Boise :

Williamson's River takes its rise in Klamath marsh,—or, as the Indians claim, in Klamath Lake proper,—and running in a southerly course about thirty miles, empties into the east side of Big Klamath Lake, sixteen miles south of Fort Klamath. It is a considerable river—at the ford probably one hundred yards wide. It is somewhat alkaline, and rendered more unpalatable from having its source in swamps and tule marshes. The crossing is over a ledge of volcanic sandstone extending entirely across the river and into the banks on either side. The greatest depth of water is about three feet, and this only for about ten yards. From this ledge the water falls about two feet into a deep eddy below.

The soil immediately along the river, is a dark, sandy loam, but changes to a light granite, or volcanic ash, as we approach the uplands and mountains on either side.

The country between Fort Klamath and the ford of Williamson's River is covered with a fine forest of yellow and sugar pine, with now and then a white or red fir, and occasionally a good sized cedar, cotton-wood, or rather aspen, is frequent around the glades and along the smaller streams. There are also small forests and thickets of a species of pine having as yet no popular name, and seemingly peculiar to the Cascade Mountains. Fort Klamath is built in a beautiful grove of them, and they cover the summit of the Cascade Mountains along the northern base of Mount M'Laughlin, where the road crosses between Fort Klamath and Jacksonville.

*   *   *   *   *   *   *   *   *   *

Sprague's River Valley is about forty miles long, and from two to fifteen miles wide. Its general direction is from southeast to northwest. The banks of the river, and of the numerous streams putting into it on either side, are fringed with willows and cotton-wood, and the entire valley is skirted with a continuous forest of yellow pine, extending back to the summit of the mountains by which it is bounded. It possesses all the natural requisites for a good stock range, its low lands being covered with a fair growth of marsh grasses, while its uplands afford a bountiful supply of the more nutritious bunch-grass, with an occasional spot of wild timothy.

The soil here is a dark, sandy loam, growing lighter and somewhat gravelly towards the mountains. Outcroppings of lava and other volcanic products are general, but there are many tracts of land that offer eligible farm sites, and could be easily cultivated.

The climate is similar to that of Fort Klamath, but the soil is quick and vegetation matures early.

Wild flax grows here so abundantly that in many places it presents the appearance of tolerably fair cultivation, and produces a fine strong fibre. The stalk seems to spring from its root and continues to grow until checked by the frosts of autumn. In this way it seems probable that the old root retains substance enough during the winter to send out new shoots in the spring. * * *

"Passing out of Sprague's river valley in a southeasterly direction, we crossed the Goose Lake Mountains through a wide and smooth gap, and by an easy grade, and entered a small fine valley situated to the westward of the northern extremity of the valley around the upper portion of Goose Lake, but having an outlet into it some distance down its western border.

"This little valley is about fifteen miles long, having a general direction from north to south, and has an extreme width of about eight miles. It has a southern exposure and a fertile soil. Its surroundings on the north, east, and west, are timber-covered mountains, while a low range of grass-covered hills bound it on the southward, separating it from the basin of Goose Lake. It is well watered by several mountain streams, and by springs, fringed with willow, and in some places with the cotton-wood, and is covered with a luxuriant growth of grass. Its soil excels that of Sprague's river valley in its general adaptation to agricultural purposes. * * * *

"From a point on the east side of the little valley into which we had entered, and about twelve miles from its head, we diverged to the eastward, and passing over some low grassy hills and along the bank of a small mountain stream running in a southeasterly direction, we descended into Goose Lake basin by a very easy grade, through a remarkably smooth depression in its western rim.

"From this pass to the head of Goose Lake, the first four miles was across a sage desert that extends southward down the western border of the lake as far as the eye can see.

"From this desert to the head of Goose Lake the surface of the country is undulating, though from any considerable distance it has the appearance of being entirely level.

"The uplands are generally covered with a luxuriant growth of bunch-grass, but in many places the outcropping of lava renders them unfit for other than grazing purposes. For these, however, they excel any portion of the country yet passed over.

"The lowlands along the numerous little streams, all putting in from the northward and converging towards the head of the lake, but generally sinking before they reach it, are extremely fertile, and well adapted for cultivation. A small portion of them, bordering immediately on the lake, are somewhat alkaline, but produce in many places an excellent growth of rye-grass, and other vegetation incident to a moderate alkali region.

"The valley is beautifully studded with large willows and some cotton-wood that fringe its streams, and timber of good quality is abundant and easy of access around its northern extremity and down along its eastern border.

"The main portion of the valley, from its northern extremity down to the lake, is about twenty miles in length, and from the Sierra Nevada Mountains which bound it on the east to its western rim, the distance is nearly the same.

In this area is contained the most valuable agricultural land of the Goose Lake basin.

"Along the eastern shore of the lake, however, there is considerable good grazing country, with an occasional tract of good farming land, covered with luxuriant wild clover in addition to all the wild grasses common to the fertile portions of the country.

"Numerous creeks and springs of good water put into the east side of the lake from the Sierra Nevada Mountains.

"Timber is also abundant along the base of the Sierras, up their ravines, and in many places up their sides to the summit.

"In the way of game, antelope and deer are quite plenty, and 'old bruin' is met occasionally. Sand-hill cranes, ducks of every variety, curlew, and all other fowls incident to California, are abundant throughout this region, and along the streams in the upper portion of the valley we saw numerous 'signs' of otter.

"The lake is emphatically alkaline, but abounding with fish near its main inlets. Its surface is beautifully dotted everywhere with flocks of swan, resembling, through mirage, so many fleets under sail.

"Mirage exists here to about the same extent that it does in and around San Jose valley, California. * * * *

"Surprise Valley is a long, narrow strip of land, stretched along the eastern foot-hills of the Sierra Nevada mountains, and sloping down into alkaline lakes, and the sand and sage desert that forms its eastern boundary. These foot-hills and the lower portions of the spurs are generally covered with a bountiful growth of bunch-grass, while between many of them, and sometimes extending out around them toward the dreary waste to the eastward, are small tracts of excellent tillage land, covered with grass, rushes, and spots of clover and wild pea-vine. It is well watered by springs and streams putting down from the Sierras, but these usually sink on reaching the level of the lakes, and the sage fields into which they flow.

"Timber pine is abundant along the Sierras, and of fair quality. Game of all kinds common to California, seems to be plenty.

The Red Bluff *Independent* has the following of Surprise Valley.

"The prospects of the settlers are of the most flattering description. There are about one hundred families now settled down as industrious farmers, besides a large floating population from the Owyhee and Puebla. The recent opening of communication with Red Bluff as a place at which they can obtain supplies has stimulated them to further enterprise, as they have been heretofore almost shut out from the rest of the world; but now they are sending in their teams for their winter supplies and purchasing more advantageously in Red Bluff than at Susanville, and they say the road is about as near to Red Bluff as it is to Susanville. A party of fifteen teams are expected in here this week. Fort

Bidwell, which is established at the north end of the valley, is named after Gen. John Bidwell, our representative in Congress, and is located in one of the finest natural locations. Near the new post are two springs of water, the one hot and the other cold. The hospital is located between these two springs, and so situated that hot and cold baths can be had at all hours. In fact, the water (hot and cold) will be conducted throughout the whole garrison. The health of the valley is excellent, and settlers say they prefer it to the Sacramento valley. The last year's crop of barley has been disposed of to the soldiers at 3c. per pound. Already parties have been talking of machinery for a grist mill to be put up next spring.

"Warner's Valley is similar to Surprise Valley in point of location, form, and general character. Its direction is from south to north. The Sierras form its western boundary for a distance of about fifteen miles from its southern extremity, thence receding to the westward, and leaving a volcanic table to continue its border northward.

"Springs and streams are found at convenient distances along the base of the Sierras, and two or more streams find their way from the same source, through deep chasms in the table that continues its western rim."

Such are some of the oases in the most desert part of Eastern Oregon. The explorations already made have demonstrated the fact that there is much mineral in the mountains in this portion of Oregon, a circumstance which must lead to its further exploration by experienced miners. A military road is being built from a point in the neighborhood of Diamond Peak to a point in the Owyhee country, which will probably become the popular emigrant road from the east into the Wallamet valley. The Red Bluff route to Idaho City crosses this country, entering it at Goose Lake Valley. Also a road from Yreka, California, to Canyon City on the John Day River, comes in between the Klamath Lakes, and strikes across the country in a general direction northeast to the head-waters of the John Day. Other projected routes will soon be opened, leading from points on the Columbia River to the Owyhee mines.

The northern portion of Eastern Oregon which is drained by the Des Chutes, John Day, Umatilla, and Grande Ronde Rivers; and the extreme eastern portion which is drained by the Powder, Burnt, and Malheur Rivers, consist entirely of rolling grassy plains, wooded mountains, and fertile valleys, the principal ones being those on the rivers already mentioned. These valleys constitute the only inhabited portions at the present time, but the plains are certainly destined to be taken up by stock-raisers.

The *Des Chutes* is a rapid and rocky stream which will never probably be made navigable, rising in the Cascade Mountains near the borders of the Great Basin, and flowing almost directly north into the Columbia. The valley of the Des Chutes has some considerable settlement, but is yet chiefly unoccupied, though capable of supporting a large population. The settlers for the most part are stock-raisers; but the demand for farm products in the neighboring mines is stimulating agricultural improvements. The Des Chutes river abounds with salmon, and has numerous tributaries whose banks are thinly wooded. The Des Chutes, and nearly all the rivers of Eastern Oregon, have high and steep banks which make the crossing difficult except at certain points.

The JOHN DAY RIVER, like the Des Chutes, is unnavigable, being one of those swift rivers, full of rocks and rapids, which the salmon love to inhabit. It waters a large valley running in nearly the same direction as the Des Chutes, and only about thirty miles distant to the east. It has only been settled since the gold discoveries in 1862. It is very fertile, and has a good market in its mines. Owing to the mildness of the climate in this region, mining operations can be carried on through the greater portion of the year—the want of water being the only hindrance to mining at any season.

The UMATILLA RIVER is a small stream emptying into the Columbia, whose head-waters and southern tributaries flow through a delightful country, fit either for cultivation or grazing. It waters in part the famous pastures of the Nez Perce and Cayuse Indians, where formerly the chiefs sometimes had fifteen hundred or two thousand head of horses in one band.

GRANDE RONDE RIVER rises in the eastern spurs of the Blue Mountains, and has its course a little north of east until it falls into the Snake river. Its valley is of a beautiful round shape, and about twenty-five miles in diameter, having the river running almost directly through the center. It is enclosed between mountain ridges which send down numerous streams of limpid water, keeping the valley ever verdant. These streams are fringed with trees which mark their meanderings, and add a grace and picturesqueness to the landscape, which has gladdened the eyes of thousands of overland emigrants, scorched with travel over sun-burnt plains. In Grande Ronde valley the land is probably all claimed, owing to its nearness to the mines. Considerable grain is raised in this valley, and made into flour in its own mills. The climate of the Grande Ronde is agreeable, though sometimes subject to deep snows in winter.

POWDER RIVER is a small river, not navigable, but affording good water-power. Its valley contains about 200,000 acres of farming land, of which 10,000 acres are under cultivation. The climate is rather warmer and drier than that of Grande Ronde, and the valley is rapidly being settled up. Rich mines both of gold and copper have been discovered, and the gold mines are being extensively worked.

South of Powder River valley the country is rough and broken, not suited to agriculture, but very well adapted to grazing. Burnt river, and Malheur river, flow through this mountain country into the river Snake. Gold has been found in paying quantities on both these rivers, and

will doubtless be found on the tributaries of the Owyhee
in the less explored region of southeastern Oregon.

The mountains of Eastern Oregon are generally well
wooded with forests of fir and birch, spruce and cedar,
and some groves of pine. Cotton-wood and willow fringe
the smaller streams, and the forests generally extend from
the mountains down the foot-hills nearly to the valleys,
but never grow along the main rivers.

The climate of this part of the State of Oregon differs
entirely from that of the western portion. It is decidedly
a dry climate; rather warm in summer, and also somewhat
bleak in winter. The snow never falls to any depth on
the plains, but does occasionally fall heavily in the valleys.
The winters, however, are short, and farmers commence
putting in seed in March.

From what has been said of the resources of Eastern
Oregon, it will be seen that a great portion of the
wealth and importance of the State is in the future to be
derived from that portion lying east of the Cascade range,
and until recently considered of but little value. As a
beef-raising and wool-growing country it will become of
very great value, as auxiliary to its mines, which are rapidly becoming known, and already rival those of Idaho
and Montana. Although this portion of the State will
never, perhaps, become the seat of so dense a population
as the western portion, it will be found to contain the
means of great wealth and commercial prosperity in its
stock-ranches, its fields of corn and sorghum, its fruit
orchards, vineyards, flax and wool, as well as in its mines
of gold, silver, copper, lead, cinnabar, and plumbago.

The whole State of Oregon, East and West, comprises
an area of 102,600 square miles. Its population cannot
exceed 110,000.

CHAPTER XLVI.[1]

WASHINGTON TERRITORY is the northern half of the old Oregon Territory, from the southern half of which its people prayed to be separated in 1852. It has an area of 69,994 square miles; being considerably less than Oregon in extent. Its population is probably under 20,000.

In general terms Washington and Oregon resemble each other both in the principal features of the country and in climate. The chief difference consists in the more open appearance of the country, it not being so entirely made up of valleys as Oregon. The principal river is the Cowelitz, which is navigable a distance of only thirty miles; its valley being narrow and rich, but of very limited extent. Like Oregon, it is divided by the Cascade range of mountains, with the same relative differences of soil and climate on the east and west sides. Unlike Oregon, however, it is not so entirely separated from the sea by the Coast range of mountains, which in Washington are very much broken. The terminating point of the Coast Mountains is Mount Olympus, which rises to a height of nine thousand feet, standing forth as a glorious land-mark, visible from the sea; and being closely in view either from the Straits of Fuca, or Puget's Sound.

The richest agricultural portions of Washington are the small valleys of its numerous streams, all of which are well wooded with cotton-wood, maple, oak, ash, fir, cedar, willow, and alder. The best grain fields of Washington are contained in a tract of land called the Cowelitz Prairie, commencing about thirty miles north of the Columbia River, and extending only a few miles toward the Sound. Strictly speaking, Washington is not an agricultural country; its peculiar geography pointing it out rather as a commercial than a farming State. A glance at any good map will show the reader at once what is the evident future of Washington Territory. Considering the importance of the inland waters of this Territory, it will be quite apropos of the subject of a Northern Railroad to give a somewhat detailed description of them, taken from the reports of both English and American explorers. From the Pacific Railroad Report of the late Governor I. I. Stevens, we take the following account of *the Strait of San Juan De Fuca:*

" The STRAIT OF JUAN DE FUCA is the most remarkable inlet of the whole Pacific coast of the American continent. It is bounded on the north by the southern shore of Vancouver's Island and other smaller islands, and on the south by the northern shore of the Mount Olympus peninsula. On the east it is terminated to a certain extent by the western shore of Whidby's Island. Its general direction is from east to west, and its length is about eighty nautical miles. The north and south shores of this Strait are parallel as far as the southern end of Vancouver's Island, or to about the middle of its length. Up to this point the Strait has a general width of about eleven nautical miles. From Race Rocks on the north and Freshwater Bay on the south, exactly the middle point of the whole extent, the Strait widens about twenty nautical miles, and afterwards presents more the aspect of a broad interior basin. It is no longer bounded by straight parallel shores, but branches into several broad passages, bays, and channels. De Fuca Strait is very deep throughout its whole extent. In mid-channel its average depth is one hundred fathoms, and this depth is carried near the shore on both sides. It commences shoaling at a distance of two miles from shore; and in all the channels and branches of this Strait the depth is equally great. There are no impediments to navigation throughout the whole extent of this Strait. A deep sea bank is found at the entrance, which is a favorite fishing bank for the Indians in this vicinity." " The southern shores of De Fuca Strait are hills, in the immediate neighborhood of the water, of a moderate height. Many low sandy cliffs fall perpendicularly on beaches of sand and stone. From the top of the cliffy eminences the land takes a further gentle and moderate ascent, and is entirely covered with trees,

chiefly of the pine genus, until the forest reaches a range of high craggy mountains, which seem to rise from the woodland country in a very abrupt manner,
with their summits covered with snow.   The northern shore is not quite so
high.   It rises more gradually from the sea-side to the tops of the monntains of
Vancouver's Island, which gives to them the appearance of a compact range,
more uniform and much less covered with snow than those on the southern
side."*   The eminences with which the whole coast is lined have nearly all,
more or less, the same form.   They form little peninsulas, which all point to
the northwest.   The northeastern sides of these peninsulas are long, the north-
western short, and between the two neighboring points usually lies a little bay,
the shores of which are low and sandy."

Passing over the careful accounts of the several ports
along the strait, intended for the benefit of sea-going readers, we come to Port Discovery, at the entrance to Admiralty Inlet, the northern portion of what is now called
in a general way THE SOUND.

"This bay is about six miles long from north to south, and throughout two to
two and a half miles wide from east to west.   It is very deep, and has regular
soundings from thirty to thirty-five fathoms in mid-channel, to ten fathoms close
to shore.   In some places it is almost too deep for an anchoring place.   The
entrance of this port is formed by two low projecting points, Challam Point, to
the west, and Cape George to the east.   Wooded cliffs of a middling height
bound the coast of the interior basin.   It is protected from all winds, and
especially those of the north, by a little Island, called Protection Island, which
is two miles from its entrance and covers it.   "Had this insular production of
nature," says Vancouver, "been designed by the most able engineers, it could
not have been placed more happily for the protection of the port."

From all this it is evident that this bay forms one of
the safest and best harbors in the world.   It is also very
easy to fortify it against the attempts of an enemy.

"ADMIRALTY INLET is a most curious, irregular, and complicated compound
of inlets, channels, and bays, which lead to a narrow entrance from the southeastern corner of De Fuca Strait.   The principal body of these waters, taking
the whole as one mass, runs in a directly north and south line through more
than a whole degree of latitude; but branches run out from it in all points of
the compass, and fill a region seventy nautical miles in length from north to
south and thirty miles in breadth from east to west.   It may be compared to a

---

* Vancouver.

tree, of which the body is recognizable, which is called Admiralty Inlet proper, and the side branches have their particular names. All the water channels of which Admiralty Inlet is composed are comparatively narrow and long. They have all, more or less bold shores, and are throughout deep and abrupt, so much so that in many places a ship's side will strike the shore before the keel will touch the ground."*

Even in the interior and most hidden parts, depths of fifty and a hundred fathoms occur, as broad as De Fuca Strait itself. Vancouver found sixty fathoms near the Vashon Island within a cable's length of the shore, and in Possession Sound he found no soundings with a line of one hundred and ten fathoms. Our modern more extensive soundings prove that this depth diminishes towards the extremities of the inlets and basins. A high tide goes up from De Fuca Strait into all these sounds. Even at Nisqually, the most southern part of the Admiralty Inlet, the spring tides are eighteen feet high and the neaps twelve.

" Nothing can exceed the beauty and safety of these waters for navigation. Not a shoal exists within them; not a hidden rock, no sudden overfalls of the water or the air; no strong flows of the wind as in other narrow waters; for instance, as in those of Magellan's Strait. And there are in this region so many excellent and secure ports, that the commercial marine of the Pacific Ocean may be easily accommodated.

" The country into which these waters enter, and of which they fill the lowest and central parts, may be said to be a broad valley between the Mount Olympus range to the west and the Cascade range to the east; the high, snow-covered peaks of both ranges may be seen from the waters everywhere. They stand at a distance of about a hundred nautical miles from each other. The broad valley between them is, upon the whole, of a moderate elevation, and presents a pretty level depression. The higher spurs of the two mountain ranges do not come down to the water's edge. The shore lands in the immediate neighborhood of the channels may, therefore, be called only hills. They are partly handsomely wooded, partly covered with luxuriant grass."

Puget Sound proper, is that portion of this large inland body of water which extends south of Vashon Island, and

---

* Wilkes.

is a compound of many narrow inlets and sounds like **Admiralty Inlet**, and differs from it in no particular except in extent.

Hood's Canal is the westernmost arm of this great and complicated sound, the largest portion of which is called on the maps Admiralty Inlet, but which the people of the west coast have named without distinction of boundaries, PUGET SOUND.

When it is remembered that the many arms of the Sound are surrounded with the most valuable timber for ship-building, as well as with many beautiful shrubs and smaller growths of trees, the beauty and the wealth of this favored region may be faintly imagined. On a bright summer's day, when the grand snow-peaks of the Cascade range and of Mount Olympus stand distinctly out to view, a scene is furnished which probably is not surpassed by any in the world—certainly not by any on the American Continent.

The advantages of Puget Sound, as the great Naval Depot of the Pacific coast, cannot be over-rated. Here is the ample room and the safe anchorage; here the timber, the turpentine, tar, rosin, iron, copper, cordage, and a climate favorable to constant labor in the open air. It is impossible to doubt that the United States Government will avail itself of this magnificent gift of nature, or to believe that it will be blind to the necessity of Railroad communication between it and the great commercial marts of the east.

Lumbering Interests. We have already said that agriculture was not the great business of Washington Territory. Its greatest commercial interest at present is the lumber trade. The largest mills of the Pacific coast are located along the shores of Puget Sound. The plain lying north of the Cowelitz Valley and east of the Sound is mostly of a gravelly soil, dotted with scattering timber, and diversified with lakes and streams. It is a country very beautiful to the eye, and with proper care may be made to yield good returns to husbandry, though much less valuable than other portions. But in the immediate vicinity of the Sound the timber is very dense, and grows to a magnificent size, often reaching a height of 250 or 300 feet. This belt of timber which encircles the Sound, is from two to six miles in width, and consists chiefly of fir and cedar—the most valuable timber on the coast. Even the saw-dust of the cedar is valued, on account of its odor, and is carried to San Francisco to be used in saloons, market-places, etc.

The lumbering interests of Washington are controlled by companies who own large tracts of timbered land along the Sound, and at favorable points on the coast. Their market is in San Francisco, the Sandwich Islands, Sitka, and nearly all points on the Pacific coast south of Oregon.

Coal. Another great source of wealth in Washington Territory is the coal which it furnishes. Bellingham Bay coal has long been used in San Francisco as the principal fuel. Later, other mines have been discovered and opened on the Cowelitz River, only four or six miles from its junction with the Columbia. From their extent and thickness the Cowelitz beds are likely to rank high as an opening for the investment of capital.

Fish. Of the rivers which empty into the Sound, are the Skagit, Snohomish, Dwamish, Puyallup, Nisqually, and Skokomish, with their tributaries. Many of these streams are navigable at high tide by vessels drawing eight to ten feet of water, making access to commercial waters easy for the occupants of the land along their course. There are mud-flats of some extent at the mouths of the rivers, and some patches of salt-meadows. The river mouths are choice places for obtaining salmon, cod, and halibut;

salmon and herring are taken in the Sound, and trout in the streams.

The Coast Counties. Of the counties along the coast not much is known except that they have a rich soil, generally covered with a dense growth of timber. Many small streams flow from the Coast Mountains into the Pacific Ocean.

Gray's Harbor, in Chehalis county, together with the fine valley of the Chehalis River, make this portion of the coast a very desirable point for settlement.

Shoalwater Bay, in Pacific county, is an extensive body of water, receiving the waters of numerous small streams, among which the Willopah is the most considerable, having a fine valley like the Chehalis. Both these bays have extensive meadows and natural prairies contiguous, which furnish excellent grass through the whole year. A fine sand beach extends along the coast the whole distance between these bays, making the pleasantest summer drives imaginable. The entrance to Shoalwater Bay is five miles wide, with two channels, each half a mile wide, leading into it. The bay is filled with shoals, mud-flats, and sand pits, all of which are bare at low water; while at high water the tide sets up the rivers from eight to fifteen miles. This bay is the great oyster-bed of the Pacific Coast, and vessels are regularly engaged in the oyster trade between this point and San Francisco. Around the bay the country is heavily covered with fir, spruce, hemlock, and arbor vitae.

From Shoalwater Bay down to Cape Hancock, called on the maps Cape Disappointment, there extends another smooth beach for a distance of twenty miles. This beach is about one hundred yards wide, very even and hard, backed by a range of low, sandy, and wooded hills; and the whole constitutes a narrow peninsula extending to the

mouth of the Columbia River. The extreme southern
point of this peninsula is Cape Hancock, where the United States has a fortification.

Resume. Western Washington, so far as developed,
has been proven to depend chiefly upon its lumber, fish,
coal and other minerals, for its commercial position. This
is not really on account of the sterility of the country, as

MOUNT RANIER FROM PUGET SOUND.

has been shown, but is owing rather to the habits of the
people, and because until lately there existed no market
for farm produce in the Territory. Now, however, it is
different. Vancouver's Island right at their doors, depends
entirely upon Washington and Oregon for grain and vegetables, nor is the opportunity any longer lacking of send-

ing farm products to foreign markets, while the mines of Eastern Washington, like those of Oregon, make a constant demand on the labor of the farmer.

Western Washington possesses at once the finest inland harbors in the world, immense forests of valuable lumber, mines of coal, and precious metals, extensive fisheries, a healthful and mild climate, and is nearer by seven hundred miles to the great East Indian marts of trade than any other harbor of importance on the Pacific Coast.

The Puget Sound country must ultimately become a rich and thickly inhabited region, and there will undoubtedly grow up upon the Sound a great maritime city, where ships from China and Japan will disembark their freight upon the wharves of a Northern Pacific Railroad, to be conveyed by the shortest land carriage to the great chain of inland seas stretching from Lake Superior, by the aid of a ship-canal, to the Atlantic Ocean; or scattered broadcast over the land along the hundreds of branch roads that vein the eastern half of the continent in every direction.

Southern and Eastern Washington. That portion of Washington Territory bordering upon the Columbia River is not much settled. Farmers are, however, taking up the land in the valleys of the rivers flowing into the Columbia on the north side, quite rapidly of late. It is generally observed that the land seems warmer on that side of the river than on the Southern or Oregon side. The Cowelitz Valley and the Lewis River and Lake River Valleys are now pretty well filled up, and prove to be excellent fruit, grain, and dairy regions. Farther up the Columbia, and just west of the foot-hills of the Cascades, is another well-settled section of the Territory, where some handsome prairies lie toward the Columbia River, bordered with rich bottom lands.

East of the Cascades the country is unsettled for a long distance, except here and there a farm near the Columbia.

Walla-Walla. Not until we reach the Walla-Walla Valley, do we find any active life and signs of cultivation. But here, in the southeasternmost corner of the Territory, is a valley of great beauty and fertility, rapidly becoming populated. The productions of this valley are wheat, oats, barley, corn, fruits, and vegetables. Wheat yields thirty to sixty bushels to the acre, oats seventy-five, potatoes four to six hundred bushels, and other garden stuff in proportion. As a grazing country it cannot be excelled, for the quality of either the grass or water. Besides the streams, wells yield excellent cold water at a depth of from twelve to fifteen feet. There is no valley in the whole upper country superior to this in advantages offered for settlement. The climate is dry and healthful, with short winters, and long, warm summers. The chief objection to the climate is the high wind which prevails in summer, in common with all high, open countries.

CHAPTER XLVII.

The Columbia River has no valley proper—that is, continuous levels of agricultural land, commonly known as bottoms. From the junction of its two great forks to its outlet, it flows between high bluffs, which rise into mountains where the river breaks through the Cascade Range.

The mouth of the Columbia forms a large bay, twenty-five miles long by six to eight wide, with numerous smaller bays indenting its shores, and numerous points and promontories, the most conspicuous of which are Tongue Point, four miles above Astoria, Point Adams, which borders on the ocean on the southern entrance, and Cape Disappointment, (or Cape Hancock, as it is known to the Government,) which borders on the northern entrance. These two last named points are fortified. The following mention of these fortifications is from the Astoria "Marine Gazette:"

"Fort Stevens is situated on Point Adams, on the Oregon side, in full view of the ocean, and about one mile from the main channel of the river, and two and a-half or three miles from the ocean. The guns of Fort Stevens will command the channel for several miles above and below the Fort. Next summer a fort is to be built on Chinook Point immediately opposite Fort Stevens and nearly due north of it. The river at this point is about three and a-half miles wide, and is the narrowest point on the river within forty miles of the mouth. Fort Hancock, on Cape Disappointment, is about seven miles northwest of Fort Stevens, and about five and a-half west by north of Chinook Point. Thus the three forts will form a triangle, all commanding the entrance and the channels of the river. When all of these forts are completed, mounted and manned, an enemy would meet with a warm reception, in case he would attempt to pay us a hostile visit.

Fort Stevens is a nonagon, surrounded by a deep ditch thirty feet wide and nineteen hundred feet in length. Beyond the ditch is an outer earth-work, sloping gently back to the surface of the ground, to protect the perpendicular wall of the main work inside of the ditch. From the top of this wall, the earth-works of the main fort slope up to the top where the guns are mounted. An exterior view of the fort exhibits nothing but an inclined plane of earth-works, of so gentle a slope that shot or shell can do it no damage. The magazine in the centre of the fort is a substantial structure, covered deeply with earth, and is bomb-proof. The shell-houses are also bomb-proof, and are interspersed along the line of guns at convenient distances. The entire earth-works, including magazine and shell-houses, except the nice gravel walks through the fort, are covered with sod of sparkling green, and are beautifully pictured upon the broad surface of the deep ditch, as it stretches around the fort, between its parallel walls and numerous angles. Fort Stevens will mount forty-three guns, and some of them are the largest size. The great fifteen-inch pivot gun guards the prominent front facing the approach from sea. Here the grim monster stands sentry, bidding defiance to any foe that dares invade. This is said to be the most substantial and efficient fort on the Pacific Coast, and for beauty and symmetry we doubt if it is surpassed by any similar work in the United States."

There are two channels or entrances to the Columbia, over the celebrated "bar."

The north channel conducts past the light-house on Cape Disappointment, and follows the shore-line of Baker's Bay until abreast of Pacific City, then bears off to the right some distance, where it intersects the south channel which comes in by Point Adams. On the "middle sands" between the north and south channels are lying the bones of many a worthy vessel, and many a gallant sailor also, whom deceitful winds lured on to the bar and suddenly failing, left stranded by the ebbing tide, to go to destruction in the breakers. After the two channels unite in one, that one bears to the south, coming right up to the town of Astoria, where the Custom House is located, and where the first cargo of goods delivered in Oregon was discharged from the ship *Tonquin*, Capt. Thorn, from New York, in the service of John Jacob Astor, in the year 1811. The genius of a great and successful merchant touched by a wonderful foresight upon the very spot where a mighty People's commerce shall yet be disembarked.

The dangers which once beset the entrance to the Columbia have been overcome by steam. No steamer was ever lost on the bar, and since a proper pilot system has been established, but one or two vessels. The difficulty should be effectually removed by the employment of a steam-tug for sailing vessels.

The vessels which ply on the lower Columbia are the tri-monthly line of ocean steamers from San Francisco, a number of sailing vessels carrying lumber and produce to the same port, a line of vessels to the Sandwich Islands, a steamer connecting with the San Francisco line, taking passengers and freight to Vancouver's Island, and a semi-weekly steamer from Portland to Astoria. All vessels entering the river stop at Astoria to receive their clearances, and proceed to Portland, twelve miles up the mouth of the Wallamet, and one hundred and ten from the ocean, to discharge their cargoes.

Proceeding up the Columbia, the traveler sees little of interest except the great river itself. Like the Hudson, its banks are high and mountainous, but unlike that river, they are not yet dotted with towns, villages, and hamlets, at every accessible point. A few beginnings have been made, where a flouring mill or saw-mill have been established, and where a vessel comes to load with lumber or flour. Oak Point, Cathlamet, and Monticello at the mouth of the Cowelitz, are such examples. A few farms also have been begun where the small valleys of tributary streams come down to the Columbia. St. Helen is the first town which seems to promise a considerable future growth, and that chiefly on account of its fine and favorable situation. It has, however, ample resources, though undeveloped, and has been talked of as the terminus of the Oregon Central Railroad, where it should cross the river toward Puget Sound by way of the Cowelitz Valley. There is a sufficient depth of water at St. Helen to accommodate the largest vessels.

Just above this point the Lower Wallamet falls into the Columbia, the two rivers embracing a fertile island, called Sauvies, about twenty miles in length, where some of the Hudson's Bay Company's people formerly had farms, some of which are still held by them. The Lower Wallamet has a depth of water sufficient for the ocean steamers which sometimes pass this way in going up. At the upper mouth of the Wallamet are a number of small and beautiful islands, and the scene upon a fine summer afternoon is scarcely exceeded anywhere. The wide, blue, majestic Columbia receives the tributary waters of the clear and sparkling Wallamet, which join its nobler flood by several devious outlets among the islands, as if coy and teazing, and reluctant to betray itself all at once for the important adjunct that it is to its grander neighbor with whom it is silently being united, to be recognized no more in its individual character. With a fine sunset sky reflected in these waters, the lovely embowered islands, dotting them over, with the distant bluffs of the Wallamet in view on one hand, and the snowy peaks of Hood and St. Helen standing out grandly on the other, it makes a view scarcely to be surpassed in mingled beauty and sublimity: and must charm the eyes of a sea-weary emigrant with a double charm. It is a very pleasant sail from this point up to Portland on the Wallamet.

The Columbia above the mouth of the Wallamet grows more interesting, and sustains its interest for over a hundred miles. Vancouver on the Washington side, is the old post of the Hudson's Bay Company, and the present headquarters of the Military Department of Oregon. The situation of Vancouver is charming, as is also the view of the river and the mountains at this place. The Oregon side of the Columbia for some distance is low and well wooded, representing by its depression the valley of the Wallamet. Soon, however, the rise of the foot-hills commences, then the very mountains themselves, until when you have arrived at the Cascades, you are in their very heart—you actually stand in a gap where mighty mountains have been parted. Before arriving at this point, the Lower Cascades village, you have been almost sated with magnificence, but when you leave the steamer and find yourself standing pigmy-like in the midst of the giant cliffs and peaks, nothing is left you but silent awe and delight.

SHERIDAN'S FISRT BATTLE-GROUND, COLUMBIA RIVER.

The "Cascades" are five miles of continuous rapids, where the river forces itself over a rocky inclined bed, through the heart of the Cascade Range. These rapids are passed by six miles of railway portage; and this ride affords such opportunities of wonderful sight-seeing as occur but seldom to the traveler. There is not the wild force to these rapids that you see when the Niagara rushes to its fall; but the variety of play of the water is infinitely greater, and the accessories far more magnificent. At the upper end of the Cascades is another little village, in a most picturesque situation. The river sets back here before rushing through the narrow gorge of the rapids, and forms a beautiful bay with an island or two in it, and beautifully wooded shores. Just above this bay is a sunken forest comprising a belt of timber a mile or two

CASTLE ROCK.

long and half a mile wide, nearly submerged by the waters of the river. Beyond, the first thing that strikes the eye is an immensely high and bald perpendicular cliff of red rock, pointed as a pyramid at the top, which looks as if freshly split off or parted from some other mass of rock, which other mass is nowhere visible.   Here comes in the Indian tradition of a bridge that once existed across the Columbia at this place, and which subsequently fell in, blocking up the river below and forming the rapids.   It looks probable enough to have suggested such an idea, even to an Indian; though the savage must attach a legend of offended spirits to his more natural conclusion in order to account for it. The height and grandeur of the mountains above the Cascades is so great and overpowering that we feel no disposition to attempt anything like a description.   It cannot be described—it can only be felt; and that newspaper correspondent who lately pronounced the scenery of the Columbia River as insignificant, takes rank in our estimation beneath contempt.   The Hudson, which so long has been the pride of America, is but the younger brother of the majestic Columbia.   Place a hundred

HORSE-TAIL FALL.

Dunderbergs side by side, and you have some conception of these stupendous bluffs.   Treble the height of the Palisades, and you can form an idea of these precipitous cliffs. Elevate the dwarfed evergreens of the Hudson Highlands into firs and pines like these, and then you may compare. We confess that we never enjoyed a journey more from the completeness of its impressions. There seemed nothing to desire— we only could gaze and dream; for even these wild Western waters are not without their historical and romantic interest. Down this strong, rapid, high-walled river, fifty years ago, floated the annual "brigade" of the Hudson's Bay Company, bringing the year's accumulation of peltries and the annual express from the Red River settlements and Canada. Ten years earlier, Lewis and Clarke had descended this great river in the service of the Gov-

VIEW ON THE COLUMBIA.

ernment; and a few years later a part of the Astor Expedition suffered all but death passing these rugged mountains in the winter. Only twenty years ago the yearly immigration to Oregon, arriving at the Dalles destitute and sick, late in the season, were dependent on the Hudson's Bay Company's boats to bring them down to the settlements. It was a terrible passage, and many, both of boatmen and immigrants, lost their lives in the fearful rapids. These were the incidents of pioneer life, now passed away; while we, tourists at leisure, dream and gaze from the deck of a first class steamer, with all our wants anticipated. Twenty years more will work marvels, but it is with feelings of satisfaction that we reflect it is not possible to man to intermeddle with the eternal majesty of these mountains. As God made them so they shall remain to be the wonder of all.

"Here," says our captain, "is Wind Mountain. The Indian name answers to our word *enchanted:* probably because the Indians found it so difficult to pass here when the wind was foul." On the opposite, or Oregon side, just where the foot-hills commence, is a fine fruit-farm, in a delightful situation, with Mt. Hood showing just back of it. About thirteen miles above the Cascades is one of the finest, if not quite the finest point on the river. While the steamer lies at a wood-yard taking on fuel, we have time to observe that the view is closed on either side of us by wooded promontories jutting past each other, and that the mountains seem to have attained their highest on either side of the river, thus enclosing us in a little sea, girt round with lofty cliffs of rugged rocks, or forest-crowned mountain ridges. Not far from here Hood river comes in, cold from the snows of the mighty mountain; and the very best view of that mountain is to be obtained. So near does it seem that we can see the glistening of the snow where its cliffs reflect the sun. Nearly opposite, the White Salmon enters the Columbia, and between the cleft heights you catch a passing glimpse of Mount Adams.

On leaving the summit line of the mountains at the

Cascades, the fir begins to disappear and soon the only timber seen on the bluffs, is pine and spruce. Even this becomes scattering, and on coming near the Dalles, the hills are almost bare. The worn basaltic rock which has

MOUNT HOOD FROM THE DALLES.

cropped out all along the river, from its mouth upward, is here everywhere apparent, protruding from the hills and walling in the river on both sides. But the hills are less abrupt, and slope back in long swells and ridges, covered with grass and dotted with scattering pines.

The Dalles (town) is a thriving business place, and a point of importance on the Columbia; the possible terminus of a branch Pacific Railroad. The scenery about the Dalles has a most remarkable wildness and singularity. You stand surrounded with evidences of the time when the region of the Columbia river was one vast field of molten rock and liquid fire. Once burnt by fire, long since worn by the elements into horizontal terraces, or perpendicular columns, and needle-pointed peaks, scored and seamed in every direction, cracked and toppling to their fall, the rocks which characterize the whole region of the Dalles make a very marked impression on the mind and memory of the beholder. The word *Dales* signifies troughs, and was first used by the French voyageurs to describe the narrow passage through which the river is forced at this place. It was easily corrupted into its present agreeable pronunciation, and remains the cognomen, not only of the trough of the Columbia, but has been conferred upon the town which lies just below the *Dale.*

The river narrows on approaching Dalles City, the beginning of a second portage, of sixteen miles, and flows through a sunken channel in solid rock for the whole of that distance. The depth of the fissure which forms its bed may be guessed at, when it is remembered that just above these Dalles the river is over a mile wide, and that in one part of its passage between Celilo and Dalles City, it is not over one hundred and sixty feet! The water has a dark green color, and boils and bubbles like the witches' cauldron in *Macbeth.* A glance at the map will suggest what the tumult must be when a river, whose branches stretch over so vast an extent of country, is compressed within a channel fifty yards wide. Yet the writer has conversed with a lady who passed through this terrible strait in a Hudson's Bay barge, when the oarsmen were thrown from their seats by the violent dashing of the waves made by the fearful eddies—passed in safety, too, though it was a feat seldom attempted, the voyageurs preferring to make the portage at this place.

The geography of the country, and the rapid development of the mining regions above, seem to point to Dalles City as the second great commercial point on the Columbia river. The town stands right on the rocky margin of the river, and extends back over the gradual rise by terraces of the outcropping trap-rock. There is a thin soil of black mold over the hills, picturesque groves of pines, and a coating of fine grass. Mt. Hood and Mt. Adams are in full view, and in the cloudless atmosphere of Eastern Oregon, nearly always visible. A late slight eruption of Mt. Hood, lasting for several hours, must have been distinctly visible from this point. Some historical interest attaches to the spot where Dalles City stands, from the fact of its having been one of the early Missions, and one of the earliest military posts in Oregon.

A railroad portage conveys the passenger sixteen miles to Celilo; the greater portion of the distance being close along the river, in sight of its rapids and eddies. There are enormous drifts of sand, which the high winds keep constantly shifting, and which cause much annoyance both to the company who are obliged to employ men to clear the track, and to travelers who wish to see the country. These drifts extend the whole length of the road. In fact everywhere above the Dalles, sand and wind are the enemies of comfort during the summer months.

Celilo is a little new town, with no pretensions to business except such as the O. S. N. Company's transactions there furnish. Its distinguishing feature is an immense warehouse, nearly a thousand feet in length, built upon an incline of forty feet, to accommodate boats in all stages of water. This great warehouse is one of several that will be built at points along the river, if the business of the upper country increases as there is every reason to believe it must increase.

The river at Celilo and for a long distance above is one continuous expanse of foaming rapids. It hurries over broken torturing rocks, lashing itself into the wildest excitement, which the incline of its bed renders more impetuous. Such is the rapidity of its flow that the water is apparently, and no doubt actually, piled up higher in the middle of the channel, so that it seems to slope off on either side.

Just above Celilo comes in the Des Chutes River, very rapid and wide at its mouth; and a little further up on the other side is the town of Columbus, which at present is little more than a wood-yard. Twenty miles above Celilo, on the Oregon side again, John Day River comes by a narrow high-walled mouth which scarcely betrays its locality. A few wood-yards and the Grande Ronde Landing are the only improvements along the river, until we arrive at Umatilla, ninety-six miles above the Dalles. Along this whole distance not a single tree is visible, except such willows and shrubs as grow on the borders of sand-bars and islands. Umatilla, or Utilla, as the Indian name is spelled, is a new and still very small town at the mouth of the Umatilla river, and derives its business from the fact of its being a starting point for the mines of Boise and Owyhee. The banks of the Columbia here are low and smooth, and nothing is in sight from the steamer's deck but extensive rolling plains, covered with bunch-grass. Back ten or twelve miles from the river, however, some timber is found for fuel, and further back in the mountains is timber in abundance for lumbering purposes.

There is the same general aspect all along the Columbia to its forks, and also for the whole length of its southern branch, the Snake or Lewis river. Wallulu, situated a few miles below the forks, is the last town of any importance on the Columbia. It is beautifully located at the mouth of the Walla-Walla river, and is a point of considerable importance, where mining outfits are procured, and freight trains started out for the mines. It is a sort of port to Walla-Walla, thirty miles further on the road to

Idaho. Wallulu is old Fort Walla-Walla, while Walla-Walla City is near the old Presbyterian mission of Waiilatpu, and the modern Fort Walla-Walla.

" White Bluffs is situated about forty miles above the mouth of Snake river. From Wallula to White Bluffs the river is smooth and deep, offering no obstructions whatever to navigation. From this last named point the river cannot be navigated further until we reach Colville. Between these two places it makes a long detour, so that, following its course, the distance from one point to the other is about 350 miles. The stream is so broken by rapids the whole way that boats cannot run upon it. The bars along the river have long been worked, yielding small pay ; but they are now almost abandoned by the whites, who are looking for richer mines, and in their stead are come great numbers of Chinese ; some from Oregon, but the greater number from British Columbia. It is believed that there are now above one thousand of these persons working on the river between Priest's Rapids and Colville. They are said to be making from two to five or six dollars per day.

From White Bluffs to Colville by land, the distance is one hundred and fifty miles. The road is excellent, there being no mountains or hills, and but one considerable stream—the Spokane—on the way. White Bluffs is the nearest point to Colville which steamboats can reach, and is now a post of some importance. It seems to be favorably situated to receive a large share of the trade of the upper Columbia river.

Above Colville, for several hundred miles, the river flows through a succession of lakes, rendering navigation easy. A steamer is now running between Colville and Boat Encampment. Rich mines are said to have been discovered, near this latter place, which is about three hundred miles beyond Colville. About fifty miles above Colville the Hudson's Bay Company have established a new trading post which they call Fort Shepherd, by means of which they expect to command the trade of that region. There has been much activity in the search for gold throughout this whole region, and its trade steadily increases.

There has also been strong effort to make a road over from the waters of Fraser river to the Columbia, but the attempt has resulted in nothing. Between these two streams there is an exceedingly high chain of mountains over which it will be forever impossible to carry goods. Hence everything that is consumed east of these high mountains must go by way of the Columbia."

On all the other northern branches of the Columbia, the Kootenai, and head-waters of the Clark especially, gold has been discovered in paying quantities, causing a rush of miners to those districts, and the consequent accompaniment of trade. Already there is competition between the merchants of the Missouri and those of the Columbia as to the profits of trade in the Blackfoot country. Captain Mullan, in his "Miner's and Traveler's Guide," has given so favorable an account of the climate and agricultural resources of this northern region that there is good reason to believe it must soon be settled up by a permanent farming community. The numerous Catholic Missions established through this region confirm the account of its adaptability to settlement, while it is a well established fact that the Hudson's Bay Company's servants have had farms for twenty-five years in this latitude, and have raised the same crops raised in our north-western States. The yield of wheat was especially good, averaging forty bushels to the acre.

From these facts it will be seen that the Columbia does not rise in a barren, desolate region of country; and that instead, the mighty river flows from first to last through a country rich in mineral and agricultural wealth, only waiting for development.

The Snake, or Southern branch of the Columbia, offers no obstacle to continuous navigation by the Oregon Steam Navigation Company's boats, which line of steamers run regularly, except in low water, from Portland to Lewiston, Idaho, a distance of about four hundred miles. Beyond this point navigation is interrupted for the next one hundred and forty miles, by falls and rapids. Beyond this, however, it is believed there exists no obstacle to navigation for another two hundred miles; and the Oregon Steam Navigation Company have already made roads to, and built steamers on this portion of the Snake river, with the intention of carrying passengers and freight on this route as far as the crossing of the Boise and Owyhee wagon-road. It is expected to bring the boats of the Missouri and Columbia within five hundred miles of each other. Under these circumstances there must be a lively competition for the trade of the great interior mining territories—a competition which will do much, with that of California and the Colorado river projects, to open up and develop the country, and to hasten on the advent in these mountain regions of the iron horse and the great Pacific Railways.

Very much of the development of Eastern Oregon and Idaho is owing to the well conducted enterprises of the Oregon Steam Navigation Company; and it is only proper in speaking of the resources of the Columbia to make the following extract from the letter of an Oregon gentleman and pioneer:

" Some dozen or more years ago different steamboat projects commenced upon the Columbia. Then there were no mines found, and the inducement was to carry the freight of the United States Government to military posts and Indian Agencies in the interior; transport the overland emigrations, and have a natural increase of travel with the expected growth of the upper country. Gradually steamboats of primitive make and small dimensions were built on the navigable stretches of the river to connect with the portages, of which there are two—the first at the Cascades, seventy miles from Portland, of five miles; and another, at the Dalles, forty-five miles above, of fifteen miles. The discovery of gold far north, at Fraser river and Powderway, gave some of these steamboat and railroad men a confidence that the mountains east were all gold-bearing. On the strength of which rude tramways or railroads were made at great expense around the Cascades on either side of the Columbia river, and indebtedness and expense incurred that would inevitably have ruined the men who undertook them, only that time justified their belief, and the result made them rich, for which they have to thank no one but themselves. Some eight or ten years ago, all these steamboat interests were consolidated under the present company. As the business increased, the improvements of the company kept pace with it, and to-day elegant boats are running on each stretch of the river, connected by twenty miles of excellent railroads, one of six miles at the Cascades, and one of fourteen miles at the Dalles. The Oregon Steam Navigation Company, whose original capital was some $300,000 (or at least the different steamboat lines which were consolidated were assessed at that figure,) now own, by purchase, the railroad lines on each side of the Cascades, which gives them an effective monopoly, and have property valued at not less than $2,000,000. They have made but few dividends, never more than twelve per cent. per annum, but have constantly kept adding their earnings to their capital in the way of improvements, until their enterprise has made the difficult channel of the Columbia one of the most varied and agreeable lines of travel upon this continent. Their wharves, warehouses, railroads, and steamers are magnificent proofs of generous enterprise, and their honorable pride is to extend and improve them constantly in the future.

Thirteen years ago this spring I ascended the Columbia to the Dalles in row-boats against the current. It took us seventeen days of hard labor to make the up trip. Now it takes us ten to twelve hours to accomplish the same distance in comfort and safety."

The scenery of the Snake River resembles that of the main Columbia above the Dalles, except that it is upon a smaller scale. Like the Upper Columbia, it is distinguished for its falls and rapids. The American Falls furnishes one of the finest views of the wonderful forms of columnar basalt to be found anywhere. The river here flows between high picturesque bluffs of weather-worn trap rock, and falls over a ledge of the same; the fall being divided by a rocky island in the middle, around which the water sweeps in wild haste and is dashed to foam as it descends upon other rocks below, rising again in clouds of spray from the bosom of the tortured river.

The Owyhee, the Boise, the Payette, the Salmon, and the Clearwater, are all more or less important tributaries of the southern branch of the Columbia; flowing as they do through the richest mineral districts, watering fertile valleys, or affording water and water power to the miner. High divides generally separate the several water-courses, which mountains are covered with excellent timber. The early emigrant to Oregon who traversed the weary road from the Mississippi to the Lower Columbia, thought all a desert that laid between the Rocky and Cascade ranges of mountains. The aspect of this intermediate territory will henceforth rapidly be changed. No more weary marches over alkali deserts, sage or sand plains; no more toiling over the Blue and Cascade Mountains. No more

starvation and misery on the last end of the journey.
Boats will meet the emigration somewhere about the Big
Camas Prairie at all events before it enters upon the rough-
est portion of the route, and thence the transit to the
Wallamet Valley, or to any other point of settlement will
be made easy.

CHAPTER XLVIII.

GOLD was first discovered on the eastern side of the Rocky Mountains, in the month of August, 1862, by a party of miners who wintered on the head-waters of Jefferson's Fork: since which time new discoveries have been constantly made, and Montana seems in a fair way to grow rapidly into a State. Towns are starting up in every part of the Territory, whose growth will not be permanently checked even by a failure of the mining interests of the country.

All writers from Montana agree in pronouncing it to be the most delightful mountain country they have ever visited; but as successful gold-hunters are not always to be believed by those who have no interests in their favorite region, we have thought best to ignore their opinions entirely, and quote from authorities whose only business in that country has been to explore it. In the Report of Gov. Stevens, on the Pacific Railroad, we find the following:—

"If the voyageur traveling over this country, whatever route he takes, be asked what sort of a country it is, he will tell you, an excellent country for traveling—wood, water, and grass everywhere. But the pine of the Spokane extends nearly to its mouth, and for some miles south of the river. The Spokane is the name of the main stream to its junction with the Coeur d' Alene river, when its name is given to a smaller tributary coming from the north, the Coeur d' Alene being the main stream. One of the most beautiful features of the Coeur d' Alene river and country is the Coeur d' Alene lake, which is embosomed in the midst of gently sloping hills, covered with a dense forest growth; the irregularity of its form, and the changing aspect of the scenery about it, makes it one of the most picturesque objects in the interior. The Coeur d'

Alene river itself has tributaries flowing from near the main divide of the Bitter Root, the most considerable of which is the St. Joseph's river, which has a general parallel direction with the Coeur d' Alene, and is about twenty miles south of it.

"The whole valley of the Coeur d' Alene and Spokane is well adapted to settlement, abounding in timber for building and for fires, exceedingly well watered, and the greater portion of the land arable.—North of the Great Plain, that is from the Spokane to the 49th parallel east of the main Columbia, the country for the most part is densely wooded, although many valleys and open places occur, some of them now occupied by settlers, and all presenting advantages for settlement. Down Clarke's Fork itself there are open patches of considerable size, and so on the Kootenai River. North of the Spokane is a large prairie, known as the Coeur d' Alene prairie, through which the trail passes from Walla-Walla to Lake Pend d' Oreille. This prairie contains some six hundred square miles. * * * * * *

"It is the country, therefore, between these two great backbones of the Rocky Mountains which I now wish to describe, and especially will I first call attention to that beautiful region whose streams, flowing from the great semicircle of the Rocky Mountains before referred to, pass through a delightful grazing and arable country, and find their confluence in the Bitter Boot River, opposite Hell-Gate.

"From Big Hole Prairie, on the south, flows the Bitter Root River, which has also a branch from the southwest, up which a trail is much used by Indians and voyageurs passing to the Nez Perce country and Walla-Walla. The Bitter Root valley, above Hell-Gate river, is about eighty miles long, and from three to ten in width, having a direction north and south from the sources of the Bitter Root river to its junction with the Hell-Gate. Besides the outlet above mentioned,* towards the Kooskooskia, which is the most difficult, it has an excellent wagon-road communication at its head by the Big Hole Pass to Jefferson's Fork, Fort Hall, and other points southward, as well as by the Hell-Gate routes to the eastward. From its lower end, at the junction of the Hell-Gate, it is believed the Bitter Root river is, or can be made, navigable for small steamers for long distances, at least, thus affording an easy outlet to its products in the natural direction. Hell-Gate (Pass) is the debauche of all the considerable streams which flow into the Bitter Root, eighty-five miles below its source at the Big Hole divide. The distance from Hell-Gate to its junction with the Bitter Root is fifteen miles. It must not be understood from the term Hell-Gate that here is a narrow passage with perpendicular bluffs; on the contrary it is a wide, open, and easy pass, in no case being less than half a mile wide, and the banks not subject to overflow. At Hell-Gate is the junction of two streams, the one being the Hell-Gate river, and the other the Big Blackfoot river. The Hell-Gate itself drains the semicircle of the Rocky Mountains from parallel 45° 45' to parallel 46° 30', a distance on the divide of eighty miles. The upper waters

---

* Omitted here.

of this river connect with Wisdom River, over a low and easy divide, across which Lieut. Mullan with his party moved on Dec. 31, 1853.

"Moving down this valley fifteen miles, we come to a most beautiful prairie known as the Deer Lodge, a great resort for game, and a favorite resting place for Indians—mild through the winter, and affording inexhaustible grass the year round. There is a remarkable curiosity in this valley—the Boiling Springs, which have been described by Lieut. Mullan. This Deer Lodge Prairie is watered by many streams, those coming from the east, having their sources also in the Rocky Mountain divide, and these coming from the west in the low, rolling, and open country intervening between the Hell-Gate and Bitter Root rivers.

"The Little Blackfoot, which has been referred to, is one of the most important streams on the line of communication through this whole mountain region. It has an open, well-grassed, and arable valley, with sweet cotton-wood on the streams, and pine generally on the slopes of the hills; but the forests are quite open, and both on its northern and southern slopes there is much prairie country. The Little Blackfoot river furnishes two outlets to the country to the east. It was the southern one of these passes, connecting with the southern tributary of the Prickly Pear creek, that Mr. Tinkham passed over in 1853, and determined a profile of the route. It was also passed over by Lieut. Mullan on his trip from the Muscle Shell, in 1853, but the northern pass was first discovered by Lieut. Mullan when he passed over it with a wagon from Fort Benton, in March, 1854. There is another tributary of the Little Blackfoot flowing into it below the point where Lieut. Mullan struck it with his wagon, which may furnish a good pass to the plains of the Missouri. Its advantages and character were described to him by the Indians.

"Passing down the Hell-Gate river, from the mouth of the Little Blackfoot, we come to several tributaries flowing from the south. Flint Creek, one of them, is a large stream, up the valley of which there is a short route to the Bitter Root valley, in a direction west-southwest from its junction with Hell-Gate. On these rivers are prairies as large as the Deer Lodge prairie, and the whole country between the Deer Lodge Prairie due west to the Bitter Root valley consists much more of prairie than of forest land.

"The Hell-Gate river is thus seen to be one hundred and thirty miles long, flowing for sixty miles through the broad and fertile Deer Lodge Prairie, which is estimated to contain eight hundred square miles of arable land. Then taking a direction more transverse to the mountain, opens its valley, continues from two to five miles wide, until its junction with the Big Blackfoot, at Hell-Gate, after which it widens out to unite with the valley of the Bitter Root. On this part of it there are least one hundred and fifty square miles of fine arable land, and as much grazing prairie on the adjoining hills. * * * * * *

Passing from the Hell-Gate to the Flathead River, we cross over this spur by a low divide, going through the Coriacan defile, and coming upon the waters of the Jocko river. The height of this divide above the Hell-Gate is 560 feet, and above the Flathead river, at the mouth of the Jocko, is 650 feet. From this divide a view of surpassing beauty, looking northward, is presented to the beholder. He sees before him an extraordinarily well-grassed, well-watered, and inviting country. On the East are the divides, clothed with pine, separating the Jocko and its tributaries from the streams running into the Big Blackfoot, and into Flathead Lake. To the North the Flathead Lake, twenty-five miles long and six miles wide, is spread open before you with extensive prairies beyond, and on the West, sloping back from the banks of the Flathead River, a mingled prairie and forest country is seen. Here in a compact body, is one of the most promising countries in this whole region, having at least 2,000 square miles of arable land.

Below the lake the Flathead River flows, following its windings some fifty miles, to its junction with the Bitter Root, where the united streams assume the name of Clarke's Fork. In this distance it is 100 to 200 yards wide, and so deep as to be fordable with difficulty at low water, its depth being three feet in the shallowest places. Its current is rapid, and there is a fall of fifteen feet, five miles below the lake. About eighteen miles below the lake it receives a considerable stream from the northwest called Hot Spring Creek. In its valley, and around it, is also a large extent of fine land. Nearly opposite, a small stream runs in from the East, and another from the same side ten miles below, by which there are routes to the upper part of Big Blackfoot Valley. None of the branches of Clarke's Fork above the junction can be considered navigable, but the river itself, (Flathead,) with the exception of the rapids and falls below the lake, which may be passed by a short canal, gives a navigation of at least seventy-five miles to the head of Flathead Lake. * * * *

About one hundred and thirty miles above the mouth of Clarke's Fork is the Pend d'Oreille or Kalispelum Lake, which is a beautiful sheet of water about forty-five miles in length, formed by the dilation of the river. The river is sluggish and wide for some twenty-six miles below the lake, where rapids occur during low water. Steamboats could ascend from this point to a point nine miles above the lake, or eighty miles in all. At high water they could ascend much farther. Between the Cabinet (twenty-five miles above the lake) and a point seventy-five miles below the lake, (a total distance of one hundred and forty miles,) the only obstacle which occurs is where the river is divided by rocky islands, with a fall of six and a-half feet on one side. The valley of Clarke's Fork is generally wide, arable, and inviting settlement, though much of it is wooded. * * * * * * * * *

From the divide of the Rocky Mountains to the divide of the Bitter Root Mountains there is an intermediate region, over one-third of which is a cultivable area, and a large portion of it is prairie country, instead of a wooded or mountain country. The following estimate gives in detail the areas of arable land, so far as existing information enables it to be computed: In the region watered by the Bitter Root River and its tributaries, not including Hell-Gate, the prairie region may be estimated at three thousand square miles; in that watered by the Hell-Gate and its tributaries, including the whole country south and west to the Bitter Root, but not including the Big Blackfoot, there is a prairie region of two thousand five hundred square miles; in that watered by the Big Blackfoot and its tributaries, the prairie region is one thousand three hundred square miles. The country watered by the Flathead River, down to its junction with the Bitter Root, and thence down Clarke's Fork to the Cabinet has a prairie region of two thousand five hundred square miles. The country watered by the Kootenai has two thousand square miles of prairie. Thus we have, in round numbers, eleven thousand three hundred square miles of prairie land. The whole area of the mountain region, (from the divide of the Rocky Mountains to the divide of the Bitter Root, and from 45° 30′ to 49°) is about thirty thousand square miles, and it will be a small estimate to put the arable land of the prairie and the forest at twelve thousand square miles. Thus the country in the Forks of the Flathead and Bitter Root, stretching away east above the Blackfoot Canon is mostly table-land, well watered and arable, and on all these tributaries—the Bitter Root, the Hell-Gate, the Big Blackfoot, the Jocko, the Maple River, the Hot Spring River, and the Lou-Lou Fork itself—the timber-land will be found unquestionably better than the prairie-land. It will not be in the immediate bottom or valley of the river where farmers will find their best locations, but on the smaller tributaries some few miles above their junction with the main streams. The traveler passing up these rivers, and seeing a little tributary breaking out in the valley, will on going up it, invariably come to an open and beautiful country. The observer who has passed through this country often, who has had with him intelligent men who have lived in it long, who understands intercourse with the Indians, and knows how to verify information which they give him, will be astonished at the conclusions which he will reach in regard to the agricultural advantages of this country, and it will not be many years before the progress of settlements will establish its superiority as an agricultural region."

The prediction of the late distinguished explorer is about to be realized, more rapidly perhaps than he had ever contemplated. Though owing its rapid settlement to the discovery of mines of gold and silver, Montana Territory is destined to retain a large proportion of its adventurous population, and to invite permanent settlers by the greatness of her varied resources, for besides the precious metals, her valleys abound in the more common and useful materials of marble, limestone, cinnabar, copper, sandstone, lead, plumbago, iron, coal, and the best of timber for lumbering purposes. Add to these a most healthful and delightful climate, and the most agreeable scenery, and there is nothing left to desire which should constitute a happy home for thousands of hardy emigrants.

Remarks on the Climate of Montana. The first invol-
untary remark of those who have never considered the
subject, is, that a railroad carried as far north as Montana
would be almost certain to be annually obstructed by
snows. A brief review of the facts, however, will speedily
convince the intelligent reader that of the two roads the
Northern and the Central, the former will not be in as
much danger from a snow blockade as the latter. In the
first place, the actual altitude of the Rocky Mountains is
not so great in the latitude of Montana as it is on the line
of the Central road by about two thousand feet. Secondly,
Montana has a climate modified both by the warm winds
that blow from the hot plains of the southwest, and over
the boiling springs of a large tract of volcanic country to
the south of it, or rather in its southern part. And besides
all these modifying local circumstances the isothermal line
which crosses it, and has its course westwardly to Puget's
Sound, has a mean annual temperature of 50°, thus deter-
mining the question of climate.

Experience, however, is the one authority to which men
safely and confidently refer, and this is in favor of Montana.
If the reader has noted the fact so often mentioned in the
narrative portion of this book, that the hunters and trappers of the Rocky Mountains seldom or never wintered
near the South Pass, but had their favorite wintering
grounds in the bend of the Yellowstone, or upon the borders of one of the affluents of the Missouri nearly directly
east of the Pass talked of for the Northern Railroad, he
must at once have come to the conclusion that the climate
of this region is superior in mildness to that farther south.
It was here that the fur-hunters found grass and sweet cotton-wood for their animals, and it was here that game
resorted for food during the snows of winter in such
numbers as to fairly invade the camps of the companies.

Resources of Montana. Besides the precious metals, which have yielded since 1864 a sum of $80,000,000, Montana contains also an abundance of copper, iron, coal, salt, and other metals and minerals. Its lumbering resources are about equal to those of Washington Territory, and its farming resources probably are superior. Nowhere in the new Territories is there a better opening for regular and legitimate labor, notwithstanding the reputation of Montana is based principally upon its mines.

CHAPTER XLIX.

Climate of the Pacific Coast.   The Western coasts of all large bodies of land have a warmer temperature than the Eastern.   Latitude on the Pacific coast seems to have but little influence on climate, compared to its effect on the coast of the Atlantic.   Astoria, at the mouth of the Columbia river, has a mean temperature of 54°, while Nisqually, on Puget Sound, being a degree further north, but also a considerable distance inland from the ocean, has a mean temperature of 58.5°.   Frost seldom penetrates the ground anywhere near the coast, and it never snows at Astoria, though snow sometimes falls in the northern portion of the Olympic peninsula in Washington Territory. The places named, be it remembered, are in the same latitude with the Lake Superior region and the Sault St. Marie of the Western States, and of the frozen coast of New·Brunswick.

As we proceed inland, greater extremes of heat and cold are experienced.   At Portland, which is in latitude 45° 30′, the mean summer temperature is 66.33°, although there are occasional days, two or three together, when the thermometer stands at 110° in the shade during three or four hours of the afternoon, suddenly falling at the approach of evening.   The winters in the interior vary greatly in degrees of cold.   It is very rarely that the ground is frozen, or that snow lies upon the ground; yet the "oldest inhabitants" remember one winter when the thermometer fell to 15° below zero in the Wallamet valley, and to 26° below zero in the Umpqua valley, which is rather more elevated.   It is to elevation in fact that the great differences of climate are due in this region.   Sixty miles away from Portland, in the Cascade Mountains, it is cold and snowing heavily, when there is a warm rain at this point.   Snow also falls in the Coast Mountains, while on either side of them there is perpetual verdure.

At the Dalles, very nearly east of Portland, but on the other side of the Cascade Mountains, there is an entirely different climate.   From the superior elevation of the country we might look for much more severe cold in winter, and a cooler temperature in summer.   But here another modifying influence comes in—that of the warm air from the great burning plains of California and the south.   The Cascade Mountains intercept the moisture from the ocean, which is discharged in rain on the valleys of Western Oregon, while Eastern Oregon lies under a cloudless sky, and is warmed by the heated air from the rainless country farther to the south.   This rarefied air rising, causes the setting in of the strong current of air from the ocean which gives to Western Oregon its steady prevailing winds; these winds blowing from the northwest in summer, and from the southwest in winter.   Under these influences while Western Oregon and Washington have a moist climate, Eastern Oregon and Idaho have a very dry climate. The summers are hot and dry, frosts commence in October, but the winter does not begin until quite late, and lasts but a short time, with little rain and snow.   Ten degrees below zero is reckoned exceedingly cold on these plains. Nearer to the mountain ranges to the east, there is more rain, and greater variability of climate, though it still continues mild.   On the Clearwater, in Northern Idaho, three years observations place the mean temperature at 53°;

and at Ft. Colville the mercury sometimes rises to 100°
in summer, and falls to 12° in winter. This portion of the
country is subject to heavy frosts in Spring, which makes
the season of planting and harvesting shorter.

Captain Mullan accounts for the mild climate of the
Rocky Mountains in Montana by supposing that the infi-
nite number of hot-springs and geysers which exist at the
head-waters of the Columbia, Missouri, and Yellowstone
Rivers, must modify the climate of this elevated region.
He also says further:

"The meteorological statistics collected during a great number of years have
enabled us to trace an isochimenal line across the continent, from St. Joseph's,
Missouri, to the Pacific, and the direction taken by this line is wonderful and
worthy the most important attention in all future legislation that looks towards
the travel and settlement of this country. This line which leaves St. Joseph's
in latitude 40°, follows the general line of the Platte to Fort Laramie, where,
from newly introduced causes, it tends northwestwardly between the Wind
River chain and the Black Hills, crossing the summit of the Rocky Mountains in
latitude 47°; showing that in the interval from St. Joseph's it had gained six
degrees of latitude. Tracing it still further westward it goes as high as 48°,
and developes itself in a fan-like shape in the plains of the Columbia. From
Fort Laramie to the Clarke's Fork, I call this an atmospheric river of heat, varying in width from one to one hundred miles. On its either side, north and south,
are walls of cold air, and which are so clearly perceptible, that you always
detect when you are upon its shores.

It would seem natural that the large volume of air in motion between the
Wind River chain and the Black Hills must receive a certain amount of heat as
it passes over the line of hot boiling springs here found, which, added to the
great heat evolved from the large volumes of water here existing, which is constantly cumulative, must all tend to modify its temperature to the extent that
the thermometer detects. The prevalent direction of the winds, the physical
face of the country, its altitude, and the large volume of water, all, doubtless,
enter to create this modification; but from whatsoever cause it arises, it exists
as a fact that must for all time enter as an element worthy of every attention
in lines of travel and communication from the eastern plains to the north Pacific. A comparison of the altitude of the South Pass, with the country on its
every side, with Mullan's Pass, further to the north, may be useful in this connection. The South Pass has an altitude of seven thousand four hundred and
eighty-nine feet above the level of the sea. The Wind River chain, to its
north, rises till it attains, at Frémont's Peak, an elevation of thirteen thousand
five hundred and seventy feet, while to the north the mountains increase in al-

38

titude till they attain, at Long's Peak, an elevation of fifteen thousand feet; while the plains to the east have an elevation of six thousand feet, and the mountains to the west, forming the east rim of the great basin, have an elevation of eight thousand two hundred and thirty-four feet, and the country between it and the South Pass an elevation of six thousand two hundred and thirty-four feet above the level of the sea. The highest point on the road in the summit line at Mullan's Pass has an elevation of six thousand feet, which is lower by fourteen hundred and eighty-nine feet than the South Pass, and allowing what we find to be here the case, viz: two hundred and eighty feet of altitude for each degree of temperature, we see that Mullan's Pass enjoys six degrees of milder temperature, due to this difference of altitude alone. At the South Pass are many high snow peaks, as Frémont's Peak, Three Tetons, Laramie Peak, Long's Peak, and others, all of which must tend to modify the temperature; whereas, to the north we have no high snow peaks, but the mountains have a general elevation of from seven to eight thousand feet above the level of the sea, and of most marked uniformity in point of altitude.

The high range of the Wind River chain stands as a curvilinear wall to deflect and direct the currents of the atmosphere as they sweep across the continent. All their slopes are well located to reflect back the direct rays of the heat of the sun to the valleys that lay at their bases. These valleys, already warm by virtue of the hot springs existing among them, receive this accumulative heat, which, driven by the new currents of cold air from the plains, rises and moves onward in the form of a river towards the valleys of the Rocky Mountains, where it joins the milder current from the Pacific and diffuses over the whole region a mild, healthy, invigorating, and useful climate."

While the climate of the Valleys, Plains, and Mountains is such as we have described, it is possible to find almost every modification of heat and cold, and moisture and dryness, within these general limits, by seeking certain altitudes or depressions more or less remote from the sea, and having the aid of certain other influences. The vales of Italy, or the glaciers of Switzerland are alike accessible.

Reclamation of Dry Lands by Irrigation. In a recent letter of Hon. John Bidwell, of California, is the following sensible proposition :

"There are millions of acres of dry and apparently sterile land to be found all over the Pacific slope. Is it always to remain in the present condition? There exists no necessity that it should do so. The land possesses in abundance all the elements of fertility. There is one and but one remedy—irrigation. Some have prejudices against irrigation, that must be overcome, because it will require the united effort of all who have a property interest in the State, to begin and carry on such an enterprise upon a scale worthy of the object in view.   Once accomplished, lands that are now absolutely worthless would become most valuable.   The same encouragement should, in my judgment, be given to bringing water on land that is worthless without it, as to take water from land that is useless with it.   The dry, as well as the swamp, lands require reclamation—one will cost relatively as much as the other.   Why, then, should not the Government be willing to donate the dry lands to the State as well as the swamp lands?"

to which the *Alta California* adds:

"It is strictly true that there are millions of acres in California now lying unclaimed, unproductive, unoccupied, and worthless, simply because of lack of irrigation, which might be supplied.   If our State were as well provided with ditches as was ancient Judea, Spain under the Arabs, or India at the present day, we should have thrice as much land fit for gardens as we actually have. More dry land than swamp needs reclamation in California.   The waters of winter and the snows of the Sierras, by careful management, might be made to yield as much treasure as the auriferous sands of the Sacramento basin.   Other nations have reclaimed tracts as large and as dry as the San Joaquin and Tulare valleys, and why should we not do as much?"

The same necessity will exist for irrigation in Eastern Oregon and Idaho that exists in California at present, and the means for irrigation are much more abundant, inasmuch as there are thousands of mountain streams of the very best water which might be conveyed and converted to purposes of irrigation.   The climate of the West Coast is in all respects very similar to that of ancient Judea, Spain, and other countries where by irrigation the barren plains were made gardens of beauty.   The great aqueducts of the Romans, and even those of the Spaniards in Mexico, still remain to testify to the importance and value of irrigation in warm and dry countries.   There will yet be some wonderful engineering performed west of the Rocky Mountains, proving that Moderns are nowise inferior in energy or expedients to the Ancients.

Productiveness of the soil.   There is no country which will better repay the expense of irrigation than this.   Almost every square mile, not entirely naked rock, is rich and productive to a wonderful degree. You have only to cast seed and water upon the loose sand-hills about San Francisco in California, to have them become beds of bloom. Wherever water is given to the soil anywhere, vegetation springs up.

In Western Oregon, where there is plenty of moisture, there is a perfectly wonderful amount of vegetation, from gigantic trees to gigantic ferns; and never has the farmer failed of his harvest since the settlement of the country.

There is no doubt whatever but some method will be found of neutralizing the effect of the too great proportion of alkali in some parts of Eastern Oregon, by which process great results in the way of grain and vegetables may be expected. Those foot-hills of the mountains where the light volcanic ash is found, ought to be put into grape culture, as there is no better soil for the production of that delicious fruit. There are marsh lands for meadows and uplands for sheep-grazing; in short, every reasonable want of humanity may be supplied in this truly wonderful region, which will become in time the glory and pride of the great Republic of the United States.

Scenery of the North-West Coast. Hardly can there be in any one country in the world more of the elements of the grand and wonderful than are to be found among the mountains, and along the rivers of Oregon and the adjacent Territories. The massive size and extent of the Rocky Mountains rather lessens the idea of their superior height, but the steeper slopes of the Cascade Mountains, rising as they do, on one side, from a valley, and made more striking by the numbers of snowy peaks, covered too with magnificent forests far up their rugged sides, all enhances their appearance of grandeur.

But it is when they are explored and their solitary wonders brought to view that their real magnificence is understood. Notwithstanding their narrow base, the Cascade Mountains are not to be crossed by one dividing ridge, but are formed of many ridges running in all directions, and thrown together in extraordinary confusion, making awful chasms which impede the progress of the explorer, and presenting acclivities up which it is in vain to attempt to proceed. Once upon their summits, however, and the traveler's toil is repaid. " In one view he may embrace the rugged steeps of the Green Mountains, the blue, wooded slopes of the Alleghanies, and the ice-crowned peaks of the Alps; the volcanic piles of the Andes, the broad plateaux of Brazil, the fertile prairies of the upper Mississippi, and the lawns, groves and copses of the sunny South. To the eastward he beholds an immense plateau, or elevated plain, relieved at distant intervals by spurs from the mountain chains, and sloping gently in different directions, toward the various streams, which, wending their way through mountain gorges to the ocean; or to some silent lake, drain the eastern portion of the State. To the west he surveys a country diversified by great rivers, and small streamlets; by tall mountains, and deeply embosomed vale; by gentle undulations, and precipitous, high-walled canons; by dark, frowning forests of pine and fir, spruce and cedar, which the eye fails to penetrate, and natural gardens all carpeted over with luxuriant grasses, redolent with the odors of wild flowers, and full of the music of winged choristers."

Down the precipitous cliffs rush mountain torrents, leaping from rock to rock, by their number giving to this chain of mountains their characteristic name. And when these mountain torrents have reached the level of the plain below they scarcely lose their mountain peculiarities, but go dashing and foaming over rocky beds, almost to their very mouths; so much disturbed by rocks, and so rapid that very few rivers having their source in the Cascade Mountains can ever be made navigable.

Very many curious things are found on the summits of the Rocky and Cascade Mountains; wonderful lakes, mountains of cinders, fresh as if just from the volcanic forge; sea-shells and corals. One of these wonderful mountain lakes is thus described by a gentleman who visited it:

"Upon rising the slope bounding the lake, the first impression made upon your mind is one of disappointment; it does not come up to your expectations; but this is only momentary. A second look and you begin to comprehend the majestic beauties of the scenery spread out before you, and you sit down on the brink of the precipice, and feast your eyes on the awful grandeur; your thoughts wander back thousands of years to the time when, where now is a placid sheet of water, there was a lake of fire, throwing its cinders and ashes to a vast distance in every direction. The whole surroundings prove this lake to be the crater of an extinct volcano. The appearance of the water in the basin, as seen from the top of the mountain, is that of a vast circular sheet of canvass, upon which some painter had been exercising his art. The color of the water is blue, but in very many different shades, and like the colors in variegated silk, continually changing. Now a spot will be dark blue, almost approaching black, in the next moment it will change to a very pale blue; and it is thus continually changing from one shade to another. I cannot account for this changeableness, as the sky was perfectly clear, and it could not have been caused by any shadows; there was, however, a gentle breeze which caused a ripple of the waters; this may account for it.

At first sight a person would not estimate the surface of the water to be more than two or three hundred feet below the summit of the surrounding bluffs; and it is only after a steady look, almost perpendicularly down into the water, that you begin to comprehend the distance. In looking down into the lake the vision seems to stop before reaching the bottom, and, to use a common expression, you have to look twice before you see the bottom.

Heretofore it has been thought by those who have visited the lake, that it was impossible to get to the water, and this was also my impression at first sight, and I should have been contented to remain on the summit, and view its beauties from that point, without attempting to get to the water, but for Sergeant Stearns and Mr. Ford, who, after gazing awhile from the top, disappeared over the precipice, and in a few minutes were at the bottom, near the water's edge, where no human being ever stood before. Their shouts induced Mr. Coats and myself to attempt the feat, which is in fact only perilous in imagination. A spring of water bursts out of the mountain near the top, on the side where we were, and by following down the channel which the water has made, a good footing may be established all the way down. In all probability, this is the only place in the whole circumference of the lake where the water is accessible, although Sergeant Stearns clambered around the edge of the lake for a short distance, and ascended to the summit by a different route from the one we descended; yet he does not think he could go down where he came up. The water in the lake is clear as crystal, and about the same temperature with the well water in Rogue River valley. We saw no fish of any kind, nor even insects in the water; the only thing we saw that indicated that there are fish in the lake was a kingfisher. In ascending, I measured the distance as well as I could, from point to point, by the eye, and conclude that it is from seven to eight hundred feet perpendicular from the water to the summit of the bluff. The lake seems to be very nearly circular, and is from seven to eight miles in diameter; and except at two or three points, the bluff is about the same altitude. Near the western shore of the lake is an island, about one-half mile in diameter, upon which there is considerable timber growing. The island is not more than one-quarter of a mile from the western shore of the lake, and its shape is a frustrum of a cone : the top seems to be depressed, and I think there is a small crater in the summit of the island. I think a path could be made from the summit to the water's edge, at the western edge of the lake ; for the formation seems to be entirely pomice stone at that point, and to slope to the water's edge at a less angle than any place else around the lake ; at this point also, a boat could be let safely down to the water by a rope.

I do not know who first saw this lake, nor do I think it should be named after the discoverer. Sergeant Stearns and Peyton Ford are the first white men who ever reached its waters, and if named after any person, should be named for them ; but as I do not believe a more majestic sheet of water is to be found upon the face of the globe, I propose the name of " Majesty." It will be visited by thousands hereafter, and some person would do well to build upon its banks a house where visitors could be entertained, and to keep a boat or boats upon its waters, that its beauties might be seen to a better advantage."

The grandeur of the Columbia River, which has elsewhere been partially described, the wonders of Puget Sound, the splendor of the snow-peaks bathed in sunrise or sunset colors, the noble Mt. Hood blushing like a rose from summit to base—the beautiful blue and purple of the distant ranges, either east or west, all these united, make Oregon and Washington more remarkable for scenery than any other States in the Union, not excepting renowned California, and mountainous Nevada.

Advantages for Commerce.   We make use of the following extract copied from a *Report on the Wealth and Re-sources of Oregon*, and which applies equally well to Wash-ington, only adding to the sections enumerated, the names of other sections north of the Columbia :

" The internal trade of Oregon will always be confined to the trade between the agricultural counties in the Wallamet, Umpqua, and Rogue River valleys, and the mining counties of Eastern Oregon and Idaho Territory, and will consist simply in the transportation of the produce and manufacture of one section to the other, to be exchanged for the bullion or coin of the mines, and will be carried on by means of a railroad to be constructed through the Wallamet valley, terminating at some point on the Columbia, from which river steamers will ply as far up as the centre of Idaho.   To satisfy the most incredulous that this trade will be rapidly and greatly enlarged, we have only to look at its present rapid growth, the territory to be accommodated, and its resources.

The extent of country which is tributary to the agricultural resources of Oregon is embraced in all that country from the summit of the Rocky Mountains westward to the Cascade Range, and between the head-waters of the northern and southern branches of the great Columbia, and reaching from the head of the Owyhee on the south, away to the Kootenai River and its lately discovered rich mines on the border of British America, being an extent of country about eight hundred miles wide, and nine hundred miles long, or seven hundred and twenty thousand square miles.   This vast, and as yet almost unexplored region, is by no means barren or inhospitable.   The Catholic Missionaries have maintained their Missions among the Indians at the farthest point north for many years, raising all the vegetables and grain necessary for their use.   Throughout the whole extent there are now mining settlements spreading in every direction.   What was two years ago a vast, unbroken wilderness, inhabited only by wild beasts and Indians, now contains not less than thirty thousand American citizens, with cities and towns, saw-mills, quartz mills, flouring mills, with all the busy hum of peaceful industry.   And from this great internal, mountain-locked basin, is now being shipped down the Columbia one million dollars of gold-dust per month, in exchange for flour, bacon, beans, and merchandise sent up.   This handsome yield of gold will, according to the present rate of progress, be increased to two and a half or three millions per month in the course of another year.

Oregon possesses peculiar facilities for the creation and maintenance of a large foreign commerce.   She possesses unlimited means for building ships— timber, copper, iron, coal, water-power, agricultural productions, a harbor equal to that of New York, and a maritime situation on the direct line of that immense trade carried on by the nations of the West with the nations of the East.   The harbor of the Columbia River looks out upon the ports of Russian America, British Columbia, and Vancouver Island, the west coast of Mexico, Central America, New Granada, Equador, Peru, Chili, and Patagonia on the

American Continent, and on the Eastern ports of the Russian Empire, India, China, Japan, Australia, the Islands of Oceanica, the Sandwich Islands, and the whale fisheries. The ports of all these countries are much nearer to the Columbia River than they are to any of the ports of the Atlantic States. They are all of easy access, and there is no reason why Oregon should not commence competing for their trade. In the year 1860 the United States exported to the above named ports domestic produce amounting to the sum of $19,645,998, and imported from the same places, in exchange, the produce of said countries amounting to $19,551,186. The imports from China alone amounted to $13,566,587. But we are told that the Pacific Coast cannot compete with the Atlantic States for this trade. The custom-house exhibit shows that the Pacific Coast can and does compete for this trade already, and not only this, but also the trade to Liverpool."

Then follow quotations from the "Market Review" of the *San Francisco Bulletin* which show that the export trade from the port of San Francisco for 1864, amounted to $6,337,090.38; an increase of two millions over the year 1862.

" How much of this produce exported from San Francisco should be credited to Oregon, we are unable to say, but that a large portion of it is Oregon produce, we know from the fact that the steamers and sailing vessels plying between San Francisco and the Columbia River, always return to California freighted with Oregon produce. We simply give this report to show what has already been done in foreign exportation from San Francisco, and even admitting that it is all California produce, we know very well that what will pay a California farmer to ship abroad, will also pay an Oregon farmer, with equal advantages.

The only matter which should now prevent the merchants of the Pacific Coast from becoming importers to the United States of the teas, coffee, spices, barks, dye-woods, cotton, sugar, rice, Japanese ware, matting, gold and silver of the above named countries, is, that we have not yet got the ships, or money to do this business. For the year ending June 1st, 1864, Shanghae, China, exported more than $25,000,000 worth of cotton, and now we should endeavor to exchange our produce for this cotton of China, and manufacture it here in Oregon, and build up a Lowell on the Pacific.

This golden harvest of trade is not yet ours, but when the Northern Pacific Railroad shall have been completed, it will become ours from the necessity of the case. What we want most now is a line of ships running direct from New York to the Columbia River, bringing out our merchandise, and carrying back *via* China and the East Indies, our produce, lumber, spars, &c. We are now paying an immense annual tax to California capitalists by receiving and shipping everything through the San Francisco warehouses. All our wheat, wool,

&c., that reaches a foreign market, except what little direct trade we have with the Sandwich Islands, is shipped first to San Francisco, where it has to pay wharfage, drayage, storage and commission, before it can be reshipped. Our merchandise coming to this State has to pass through the same taxing process at San Francisco, in addition to the profits of the importer before it. It is no wonder that Oregon is in the shade of California, and it ought to remain so as long as we will not make some effort to remedy this state of affairs."

The above quotation throws some light upon the commercial condition of the Northwest Coast, and explains pretty clearly the feeling of its people regarding that position. So far the Manufactures of this country have been confined to lumber, flour, woolen goods, some coarse leather, a little turpentine, an inferior article of pottery, a limited quantity of matches, and as much machinery as three or four small foundries and machine shops could turn out. Everything that is used on the farm, in the garden, household, or in the mines, is imported at a great expense. Iron has begun to be manufactured in Oregon, and so has salt, but the complete development of these things must wait, first for capital; secondly, for railroads.

Probable Railroad Routes. The only railroad under construction on the whole Northwest Coast, is the one now building down the Wallamet Valley, and called the Oregon Central. It is intended to connect the Columbia River with San Francisco Bay, and will form a portion of that great line of railway by which Lake Superior, Puget Sound, and San Francisco Bay will eventually be united. Owing to the influence exerted by Portland capital, the Oregon Central has been commenced at that point, but that Portland will long remain the northern terminus is incredible, when its position, and its distance from the Columbia River are considered. A point for the northern terminus of the Oregon Central will undoubtedly be fixed where it will connect by ferriage over the Columbia, with a road down the Cowelitz Valley from Puget Sound, thus making one continuous road through the whole length of Washington, Oregon, and California, as far as San Francisco, if not as far as San Diego.

The question undecided at present by the Oregon Central is, whether to carry the road over the Calapooya, Umpqua, and Siskiyou Mountains, directly south, and open up the Umpqua and Rogue River Valleys to commerce, or to take it by a single easy pass through the Cascade Mountains, at or near Diamond Peak, and thence southward along the almost level country to the headwaters of the Sacramento. The latter would be the cheapest of construction, and might be made to form a branch of the Central Pacific, while the former would take in its course some of the most desirable country in Oregon.

Strong efforts are being made to get a branch road from the Union Pacific to some point on the upper Columbia, either at the Dalles, Umatilla, or Wallulu. It is said that in case the road comes to the Dalles it will cross the river there, and pass on down the Columbia to some point below the mouth of the Wallamet, either there to build up a commercial town, or to connect with the road up the Cowelitz Valley going north, and the Oregon Central, going south.

Idaho and Montana are waiting on the action of these railroad projectors, glad to see communication with the coast made easy on any terms, and willing to lend their aid to the first company in the field.

A strong sentiment, however, prevails throughout the Northwest in favor of the Northern Pacific Railroad. To this favorite enterprise, Montana and Idaho, Washington and Oregon, all and each, lend their preference, and so far as it is available, are willing to lend their material aid. All understand that the Columbia River, taken in conjunction with Puget Sound, offers to the commerce of the whole

Pacific the most complete resources which the trade of the world could require.   And every intelligent citizen of the Northwest looks forward in fancy to a day when busy millions shall occupy this territory we have so inefficiently described, and when it shall be the most favored portion of the greatest earthly Republic.

When Thomas H. Benton, in a speech delivered at St. Louis, in 1845, prophecied that the men then listening to him should see with living eyes a railroad to the Pacific Ocean, and the trade of China and Japan flowing over it, he was believed to be an enthusiast, if no worse.   In twenty-four years his prophecy has been accomplished, and doubtless some of his hearers of that day have enjoyed, or will yet enjoy, a trip by railway across the continent.

But Benton's pet scheme was a railroad which was to connect with the mouth of the Columbia River.   It was Oregon, then undivided, that he looked to as the greatest country on the American continent.   Perhaps some listener to his speech of 1845, may live to see his judgment vindicated.   That is our hope at least.

THE END.

NOTES

To identify people and places by their full and correct names, check the index. Books referred to here by the author's name only are cited fully in the bibliography.

CHAPTER XXI

P. 26: The Wallamet/Willamette river-spelling controversy was getting well underway when this book was written. Obviously Mrs. Victor took her stand with Judge Matthew P. Deady, chief proponent and publicist for what he considered the more English, more historic, and more phonetic option, "Wallamet." Given Deady's reputation as socio-cultural arbiter of Portland, if not Oregon, and his influence with popular writers like Victor, it is remarkable that his choice lost out. For an entertaining rundown of this little orthographical tempest, see Clark (ed.), *Pharisee Among Philistines*, Volume I, pp. 171-172, 177-178; and McArthur, p. 797.

P. 28: The Louisiana Purchase, bounded on the west by the continental divide, did not constitute an Amerian claim to the Oregon country, as Mrs. Victor states. In her chronological account of such claims, too, she omits the Lewis and Clark Expedition, which as one of its objectives intended formally to claim the region. And she fails to mention the British capture of Fort Astoria during the War of 1812, and their surrender of that post to the United States as a result of the Treaty of Ghent, which sequence lent an official character to a private fur-trade venture, and strengthened American claims.

P. 38: It was just before Christmas, 1836 (not 1837) when the brig *Loriot*, captained by William A. Slacum (not Slocum), entered the Columbia River. The great majority of such minor errors of detail in this book are corrected later by Mrs. Victor in her Bancroft histories. On the above, see Bancroft, *History of Oregon*, Volume I, pp. 100-101.

P. 39: The tribe that attacked Jedediah Smith's party in 1829 was not the Rogue River Indians, but the Kalawatset tribe, whose territory was on the Umpqua River, over 100 miles north of the Rogue. (Morgan, p. 267.)

CHAPTER XXII

P. 43: Victor's charge that there were no genuine Indian conversions, only pretended ones, is countered by convincing primary sources. Methodist H. K. Hines ministered in Oregon for several decades after his arrival in 1853, and tells of more than twenty Indian Christians who were converted at The Dalles in the 1839-40 revivals, who were his personal acquaintances after 1870, and who were still consistently practicing their faith. (Hines, pp. 167-170.) Victor's judgment was indeed supported by the fact that many "conversions" were undoubtedly superficial and temporary, and so reported by the missionaries themselves. (Lee and Frost, pp. 241-242.) Her conclusions, too, obviously owed much to the prevailing racism of her era, and to her personal style of playful or cynical skepticism in matters of religion.

CHAPTER XXIII

P. 51: In declaring that Jason Lee and his mission "deceived" the Board of Managers of the Missionary Society of the Methodist Episcopal Church, Victor adds her faggot to a fiery historical controversy that has smoldered for 140 years. The most thorough and thoughtful analysis, and the most recent one, is convincing in its conclusion that Lee's policies were not deceptive nor intended to deceive, that changed conditions account for his revised policies. The problems lay in his lack of administrative skills, his careless financial records, his inadequate communication with the Board, and biased reports submitted by unsympathetic co-workers. When he personally appeared before the Board, he was always appreciated, understood, and vindicated. (Loewenberg, pp. 106-139, *passim*.) See also Hines, pp. 282-295; and Brosnan, pp. 228-270.

P. 54: Consider merely as extravagant rhetoric Victor's statement that the Protestant missionaries feared an extermination plot from McLoughlin and his Catholic allies. Such fears are undocumented. Victor abandons the point in her more mature historical work for Bancroft. Was some of Joe Meek's joyful talent for tall tales rubbing off on his interviewer?

P. 55: Pressure on Young to discontinue his distillery project came from the Hudson's Bay Company as well as from the missionaries. See Lt. William Slacum's report in Holmes, pp. 117-119.

P. 56: Ewing Young died in February, 1841, not that summer as stated here. And the implication of missionary chicanery in stealing the estate is gratuitous and unsubstantiated. The careful inventories and recorded transactions of the estate—the first business of Oregon's informal pre-territorial government—are still preserved in the Oregon State Archives, and appear very much in order. Estate proceeds were used for state purposes (jail construction in Oregon City), and the balance was claimed by Young's son when he showed up in 1854. (Holmes, p. 148.)

CHAPTER XXIV

P. 59: Meek's subtle "Peacock" joke will be lost on all but the most avid naval history buffs, though it was well understood by those present. During the War of 1812 the American sloop *Hornet* sank the British brig *Peacock*. In official celebration of the victory, the U.S. launched a new sloop-of-war, christening it the *Peacock*. This was the same ship that foundered on the Columbia bar in 1841. So the mountain man had heard some history, and was willing to taunt British subjects a bit at a time when tensions were building again between the two nations. See Tobie, 99-100.

Pp. 61-62: Victor is said to have acknowledged later that this prayer-and-cow incident did not really happen. Was it too good a story to exclude, illustrating as it did the missionaries at their overbearing, insensitive worst? (Tobie, pp. 100, 292.)

P. 65: Mrs. Victor fails to specify that when Joe and Virginia Meek were married under church auspices in 1841, the ceremony was performed by a Methodist minister and missionary, the Rev. John S. Griffin. (Tobie, pp. 100-101, 293.) Historians select and omit incidents and details according to their philosophical commitments, the prevailing pattern of reality and significance that they accept. Having concluded that the Methodists were particularly arrogant and obnoxious, and guilty further of that most reprehensible of sins, hypocrisy, she omits indications of their cordiality and services, such as the wedding, and includes stories of dubious authenticity, such as the cow-and-prayer incident. There was no shortage of authentic evidence for missionary obtuseness, of course, and the horrors of hypocrisy always make good stories. It is simply worth pointing out that thus early in her career as historian Victor adheres to the "devil theory of history," seeing the past in terms of the villains and the virtuous. And she was delighted, as were and are many of her readers, to find the center of devilish activity to be among the pious. In this interesting process, however, she slants and distorts the story somewhat.

CHAPTER XXV

Pp. 70-71: Victor participates in the early promotion of some elements of the "Whitman myth," in stating that the Presbyterian missionary's 1842-43 trip east was taken specifically to advise Secretary of State Daniel Webster on the boundary question, and that this advice saved the Secretary from giving up U.S. claims to Oregon in return for a codfishery off Newfoundland. Mrs. Victor abandoned these views in her later *History of Oregon* in the Bancroft series, and in fact wrote a book on the Whitman myth in her later years, but could find no publisher for it. For a full treatment of the Whitman myth, its supporters, its promotion, and the later rebuttals, see Drury's *Marcus and Narcissa Whitman*, Volume Two, appendices three and four, "The Evolution of the Whitman-Saved-Oregon Story," and "The Literature of the Whitman Controversy," pp. 375-389.

Jesse Applegate strongly rejected Victor's implication in this passage that Whitman's encouragements for Missourians to emigrate had any effect whatever on the 1843 migration. Applegate could recall no one in that group who had been influenced by Whitman. Whitman joined the migration after it had reached the Platte, which was the first time Applegate knew he was in the area. (Applegate to H. H. Bancroft, summer 1878, Bancroft Library, University of California, Berkeley.)

CHAPTER XXVI

Pp. 78-94: Mrs. Victor's later views (in Bancroft, *History of Oregon*, Volume I, p. 305) that Lee and the mission party conspired to set up the Provisional Government, do not appear in this earlier account. No evidence for such a conspiracy has been discovered. See Loewenberg, pp. 141, 157-158.

Pp. 82-83: Victor here presents the most prominent early source of the popular legendary version of the famed Champoeg meeting on May 2, 1843. This dramatic telling worked its way into scores of speeches, articles, and books, and since 1982 into the impressive annual on-site outdoor drama, the Champoeg Pageant. Tiresome revisionist historians have gone to the official minutes, however, to find that the margin was five instead of two, that at least seven Canadians voted for organization, and that Joe Meek was unmentioned. (Clark, *Eden-Seekers*, p. 158.) See, however, the plausible reconstruction in Tobie, p. 106.

Pp. 83-86: Jesuit missionary Father Francis Norbert Blanchet wrote this "Address of the Canadian citizens of Oregon to the Meeting at Champoeg." Robert Shortess was the author of the first "organic law," or provisional government constitution. (Applegate to Bancroft, 1878.)

368

CHAPTER XXVII

P. 95: All the 1843 immigrants did not make it to The Dalles in wagons, as Mrs. Victor implies. Seventy or more travelers, including the Applegates and Burnetts, left their wagons at Walla Walla and went to The Dalles by boat. (Applegate to Bancroft, 1878.)

Pp. 100-102: The unnamed young lawyer was Peter H. Burnett, of the migration of 1843. He went to California for gold in 1848, and was elected first governor of that state in 1850.

CHAPTER XXIX

Pp. 117-123: This chapter contributes to the considerable, contradictory, emotional literature on the Oregon City land-claim dispute between McLoughlin and mission representatives, especially Alvin Waller. McLoughlin's heroic status grew in the decades after his death, in significant part because of Victor's admiring analysis of his career and character in her Bancroft volumes. Correspondingly, Methodist writers like James W. Bashford and H. K. Hines attempted increasingly to make Waller the villain and to protect the reputation of their own hero, Jason Lee, by insisting that he had nothing to do with Waller's duplicity. (Bashford, pp. 216-224; and Hines, pp. 353-355.)

But it seems clear that even as McLoughlin entered his original claim in 1829 as an agent of the Hudson's Bay Company, so Waller entered his claim in 1841 as an agent of the Mission, and thus evidently under Lee's direction. Without doubt Lee cooperated with attorney Ricord's maneuvering, as well as in the March, 1843, settler's petition to deny McLoughlin rights to the Oregon City site, though he did not sign the petition. And further contradicting the impressions of hands-off neutrality that he consistently gave McLoughlin, Lee delivered Waller's letter and claim documents to the Commissioner General of the Land Office in Washington, D.C., in 1844 on his last trip east. See documents in Brosnan, pp. 291-315.

That all along Waller was a Methodist minister under appointment (though his religious career is unmentioned in the letter to the government) seems clear from the fact that he gave up any personal land claims readily and obediently accepted his new appointment in 1844 to the Wascopum station, at the direction of Lee's successor, George Gary. In other words, Victor is factually accurate in her account of the controversy. What her understandable partisanship does not consider is that indeed Waller did have much the stronger claim to the land under American law, emphasizing as it did the importance of occupancy and the privileges of preemption. Realizing that the site was all but certain to go to the United States when the boundary was determined, McLoughlin neglected to protect his interests with the only action that would be legally meaningful, namely residency. He was beaten out by astute, claim-wise American frontiersmen, acting as a front for mission interests. The fact that those men were ministers and that their methods, though legal, violated their Wesleyan ethics, naturally released Victor's romantic moral indignation. See Loewenberg, pp. 18-19, 117-192; Clark, *Eden-Seekers*, 155-168; and Montgomery, pp. 263-265, 282-283, 287-288, 302-303.

CHAPTER XXXII

Pp. 149-151: Jesse Applegate was the "prominent member of society and the legislature" who in partnership with Levi Scott and with the help of thirteen others, plotted this alternate route with care, hoping to attract immigrants to southern Oregon. Applegate took strong exception to the author's brief treatment of the southern route, "about which," he said, "Mrs. Victor is more at fault than in any other part of her historical sketch, and must have derived her information from *one of the sufferers.*" The real problem that year, said Applegate, was the extra-dry summer and the very early severe rains, which combined with the imprudent delays of the travelers to betray them. Had the migrants been five days earlier, or had the rains delayed five days, there would have been no problem.

It was not the early travelers to arrive safely in the valley (p. 151) who sent back aid to their fellows. Rather, those who explored the route assisted by other older residents took food, horses, and oxen, and stayed with the travelers until all were safe.

Applegate pronounced one Victor phrase ("this unfortunate termination of their hopes for a southern road had a dispiriting influence on the colony";), short as it was, to contain *two* serious errors: "It *did not* terminate the southern road for it continued to be the favorite route for immigrants to southern Oregon and northern California until interrupted by Indian hostilities seven years later. . . . It *did not* dispirit the colony, for in the winter of 1846 its Legislature passed a law by a large majority . . . entitled 'An Act for the Further Improvement of the Southern Route to Oregon.' " (Applegate to Bancroft, 1878.)

Applegate was there, and while he had personal interests to defend, the facts bear him out. J. Quinn Thornton's presence and disappointments in that first ill-fated attempt at the southern route helped perpetuate the "feuds" to which Victor refers, by his influence and eloquence and published reminiscence. Yet it seems doubtful that Thornton was her primary source, in view of her obvious lack of sympathy with that Methodist attorney later in her book.

Victor errs in implying that the tragic Donner party of that year (p. 150) had also taken Applegate's new route. The Donners had no contact with the Applegate group.

Having given some detail to this 1846 immigrant difficulty with a new route, Victor is open to the natural question as to why she omitted all mention of Stephen Meek's much more irresponsible and devastating experimental route of 1845, the unhappy Meek Cutoff, which involved around 1,000 immigrants, and cost 75 deaths and untold property losses and hardship. The answer is, of course, as natural as the question. She did not wish to embarrass the villain guide's brother, her informant, Joe Meek. See Unruh, pp. 340-341, 345-350.

CHAPTER XXXIV

Pp. 162-166: Victor's early analysis of the causes of the Whitman massacre compares well with the best modern treatments, by Drury and Jones, with their greater access to the full range of sources.

CHAPTER XXXV

Pp. 172-184: For the correction at several points of details of the massacre as given by Victor, see the authoritative distillation of nineteen eye-witness accounts and other contemporary evidence, in Drury, *Marcus and Narcissa Whitman*, Volume II, pp. 205-265, 387-389. A few of these discrepancies deserve mention here. Victor's blanket statement (pp. 176-177) that none of the Cayuse Indians showed compassion to the victims, that all participated in an orgy of celebration, is countered by numerous reminiscences of survivors. They spoke of Cayuse women and others who were openly grief-stricken at what had been done, and who comforted and assisted the surviving women and children in several ways. (Drury, Volume II, p. 239.) Further, the "Miss Bulee" mentioned on pp. 174, 183, and 184 is often not readily identified by readers of this book by her real name, Lorinda Bewley. Also, with regard to Victor's account of Protestant suspicions of Catholic complicity in the massacre (pp. 168, 181-184), Presbyterian minister and historian Drury has a carefully researched and reassuring conclusion, that all such allegations are to be "rejected in toto." (Drury, Volume II, p. 219.) Finally, Victor's statement (pp. 164-165) that Whitman would never leave his station to the Catholics is found to be contradicted in specific plans Whitman had discussed with Spalding. Whitman was planning to learn the preferences of the Indians, and if they approved, to turn over the mission to the neighboring priests. (Drury, Volume II, p. 221.)

CHAPTERS XXXVIII through XLI

Pp. 196-243: This is the richest available source of Meek's heady 1848-49 trip to Washington, D.C., and return, without doubt the climactic adventures of his public life. That Meek is the primary authority for the detail and color of this section in no way diminishes its importance, nor certainly its entertainment value. It is remarkable, as Meek's best biographer Harvey Elmer Tobie has found, how Meek's versions of these months—as well as the rest of his reminiscences—agree in all significant matters with other contemporary reports.

CHAPTER XLIII

Pp. 259-261: In this trial with its humorous fining incident, Oregon City hotel proprietor Sidney W. Moss was accused of selling liquor to Indians. The official record shows this case to have been tried *before* the Cayuse trial, not *after*, as Mrs. Victor states. (Tobie, pp. 205-206, 303.)

CHAPTERS XLV through XLIX

Pp. 275-364: These last five chapters give a descriptive overview of the Pacific Northwest, including Idaho and Montana, a thorough summary of scenery, climate, terrain, crops, minerals, population, towns, and transportation. It is the sort of instructive regional service that Mrs. Victor was to render at much greater depth in *All Over Oregon and Washington* (1872), and in *Atlantis Arisen* (1891). This addendum injures the informal unity given the rest of the work by the broad frame of Joe Meek's life. The book has a nice natural ending, obviously intended as such, on page 273 (511 of the original Bliss edition). So why did the author "deem it expedient" (p. 275—513 of original edition) to go beyond her original intentions?

I am indebted to Victor biographer Hazel Mills for the answer to this question. In negotiating with R. W. Bliss & Co., Victor learned that they adhered to a strict minimum length of 600 pages for subscription sales books. *River of the West* needed 87 more pages to meet that standard. She did two pages better than that. (Hill, pp. 13-14.)

Further Reading on Joe Meek and Early Oregon

This volume covers the years 1840 to 1856, the latter part of that period sketchily. Maximum detail on those years, and attractively presented, rests in the 900 relevant pages in H. H. Bancroft's *History of Oregon*, Volumes I and II, written, of course, by Mrs. Victor. For additional particulars on Joe Meek's post-1840 years, see his standard biography, Harvey Elmer Tobie's *No Man Like Joe: The Life and Times of Joe Meek*.

On the missionaries, who figure so largely in the foregoing pages, the most interesting and revealing works are the diaries and letters of the Presbyterian and Congregational women, edited in three volumes by Clifford M. Drury as *First White Women Over the Rockies*. Novelist/historian Nard Jones has written the most readable account of any northwest missionaries in *The Great Command: The Story of Marcus and Narcissa Whitman and the Oregon Country Pioneers*. Clifford M. Drury's carefully-researched biographies of the Whitmans and of Henry Spalding add detail to Jones' treatment. Despite all efforts, some major, both Dr. John McLoughlin and his sometime adversaries the Methodist missionaries, yet await adequate historic/biographical treatment.

The most recent retelling of the 1840s and '50s—and of the two preceding decades—is Malcolm Clark's *Eden Seekers: The Settlement of Oregon, 1818-1862*. Dazzling in style, skillful in synthesis, bold in judgment, Clark's book is always good for vigorous discussion among regional historians. Even those who question his particularly polemic interpretations do so in a context of admiration for his industry and his gifts. His foot-notes are fewer than we historians would prefer, but *Eden Seekers* includes the best bibliography available on those years. And Clark gives evidence that he has mastered the sources.

Readers who like their history dramatized and evoked through quality fiction have exciting options. A. B. Guthrie's *The Big Sky* personifies the mountain man and relates to the first half of *River of the West*. *The Way West*, also by Guthrie, is the best by far of the fifty-plus Oregon Trail novels. It may be read as a backdrop for Ernest Haycox' *The Earthbreakers*, which recounts the last dangerous jag of the journey, and is highly instructive on the techniques and technology of running the Columbia and establishing farmsteads. See Don Berry's three quality novels, *(Trask, Moontrap, To Build a Ship)* about moun-tain men-turned-farmers and how they and their native wives fitted into frontier society in the 1840s and '50s, for direct parallels to Meek's and Newell's situation.

BIBLIOGRAPHY

Bancroft, Hubert Howe. *History of the Northwest Coast*. Two volumes. San Francisco, 1884-1886.

Bancroft, Hubert Howe. *History of Oregon*. Two volumes. San Francisco, 1886-1888.

Bancroft, Hubert Howe. *Washington, Idaho, and Montana*. San Francisco, 1890.

Bashford, James W. *The Oregon Missions: The Story of How the Line Was Run Between Canada and the United States*. New York, 1918.

Berry, Don. *Moontrap*. New York, 1962.

Berry. *To Build a Ship*. New York, 1963.

Berry. *Trask*. New York, 1960.

Brosnan, Cornelius J. *Jason Lee: Prophet of the New Oregon*. New York, 1932.

Caughey, John Walton. *Hubert Howe Bancroft: Historian of the West*, Berkeley, 1946.

Clark, Malcolm, Jr. *Eden Seekers: The Settlement of Oregon, 1818-1862*. Boston, 1981.

Clark, Malcolm, Jr., ed. *Pharisee Among Philistines: The Diary of Judge Matthew P. Deady, 1871-1892*. Two volumes. Portland, 1975.

Drury, Clifford M., ed. *First White Women Over the Rockies: Diaries, Letters and Biographical Sketches of the Six White Women Who Made the Overland Journey in 1836 and 1838*. Three volumes. Glendale, 1963-1966.

Drury. *Henry Harmon Spalding*. Two volumes. Caldwell, 1936.

Drury. *Marcus and Narcissa Whitman and the Opening of Old Oregon.* Two volumes. Glendale, California, 1973.

Gray, W. H. *A History of Oregon, 1792-1849, Drawn from Personal Observations and Authentic Information.* Portland, 1870.

Guthrie, A. B., Jr. *The Big Sky.* New York, 1947.

Guthrie. *The Way West.* New York, 1949.

Haycox, Ernest. *The Earthbreakers.* Boston, 1952.

Hill, Hamlin. *Mark Twain and Elisha Bliss.* Columbia, Missouri, 1964.

Hines, H. K. *Missionary History of the Pacific Northwest, Containing the Wonderful Story of Jason Lee, etc.* Portland, 1899.

Holmes, Kenneth L. *Ewing Young: Master Trapper.* Portland, 1967.

Johansen, Dorothy O. *Empire of the Columbia: A History of the Pacific Northwest.* New York, 1967.

Jones, Nard. *The Great Command: The Story of Marcus and Narcissa Whitman and the Oregon Country Pioneers.* Boston, 1959.

Lee, Daniel, and Frost, Joseph. *Ten Years in Oregon.* Fairfield, Washington, 1968.

Loewenberg, Robert J. *Equality on the Oregon Frontier: Jason Lee and the Methodist Mission, 1834-43.* Seattle, 1976.

McArthur, Lewis A. *Oregon Geographic Names.* Fifth Edition Revised and Enlarged by Lewis L. McArthur. Portland, 1982.

Montgomery, Richard G. *The White-Headed Eagle: John McLoughlin, Builder of an Empire.* New York, 1934.

Morgan, Dale L. *Jedediah Smith and the Opening of the West.* Lincoln, 1953.

Tobie, Harvey Elmer. *No Man Like Joe: The Life and Times of Joseph L. Meek.* Portland, 1949.

Unruh, John D., Jr. *The Plains Across: The Overland Emigrants and the Trans-Mississippi West, 1840-60.* Urbana, 1979.

Vestal, Stanley. *Joe Meek: The Merry Mountain Man.* Caldwell, 1952.

Victor, Frances Fuller. *All Over Oregon and Washington.* San Francisco, 1872.

Victor. *Atlantis Arisen; or Talks of a Tourist About Oregon and Washington.* Philadelphia, 1891.

Victor. *The Early Indian Wars of Oregon.* Salem, 1894.

INDEX

People and places are listed under their modern spellings. When the author has not given a complete name, it is supplied in parentheses. Where a name is left incomplete, the editor cannot discover the full name.

380

382